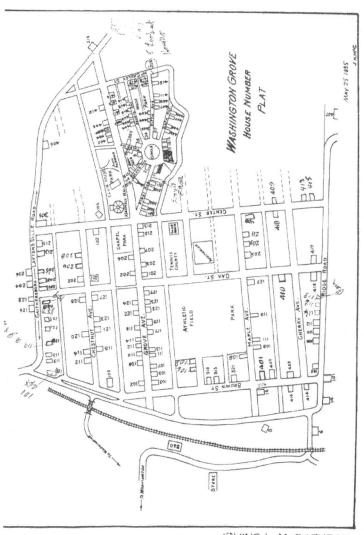

WASHINGTON GROVE
HOUSE NUMBER
PLAT

MAY 25 1935   J.M.MC

IRVING L. McCATHRAN

WASHINGTON GROVE

1873-1937

a history of the

WASHINGTON GROVE
CAMP MEETING ASSOCIATION

by Philip K. Edwards

December 1988

SECOND EDITION

Second Edition ISBN 9781097729333
Published 2019

The cover art for "Washington Grove Camp Meeting"
was taken from the Association's letterhead design in use
between 1895 and 1900.

The plat on the inside flyleaf was originally drawn by
James K. McCathran in 1927, and was updated in 1935.
It had not changed in May of 1937 when the Association
was succeeded by the Town.

The photograph on the rear cover was taken in the
vicinity of the Washington Grove United Methodist
Church, looking out toward the Cooke farm. It may
represent a 'building party' assembling in the early
1880's to construct cottages for the next season.

.

Table of Contents

THE ASSOCIATION

PREFACE

Washington Grove has survived a hundred years of changing values and shifting populations largely intact because it still has the essential qualities for which it was first chosen: beauty, serenity, isolation, and access.

The purpose of this book is to summarize the history of the Washington Grove Association and, hence, of the town of Washington Grove in its earlier incarnation. The scope of the narrative is primarily the years of the Association's existence, 1873-1937, but a great deal of background is provided to help make sense of how the Grove came to be started in this place and at that time. (It is amusing to think that, had things been just a little different, there may still have been a Washington Grove, by that name, but somewhere else in the Washington area. What, in that case, would be here?)

The history of the Washington Grove Association is not always exciting, and I have attempted to report it the way it was. I have not reached out for dullness—I have not reprinted each year's annual budget, for example—but neither have I shunned it, for sometimes it is in the mundane that we find the profound. There were several generational transitions in the history of the Grove that bridge the significant global events—wars, epidemics, and financial crises—between which most history is bracketed. I have tried to relate global events to the Grove, rather than the other way around.

Some of the material may seem over-researched. This could be the result of a heightened interest on the part of the author in a particular theme, or of the sheer volume of material available on a given subject, but it can also be because those who were acting on the subject at the time, in history, were themselves preoccupied with it. I want to share their preoccupation with sewers, if that be the subject, with you.

Some subjects may seem under-researched. Sometimes a name or an event will pop into the text without explanation. Most of the families I mention are under-researched, with the consequence that even those members who are directly important to the Grove's history remain rather pale figures. Family cross-connections are particularly difficult to trace, as the sons are seldom identified with their maternal antecedents, and the married daughters are almost always identified with their husbands' paternal antecedents.

Certain physical features of the Grove have been difficult to reconstruct, such as the exact physical condition of the grounds on the 4th of July, 1873 (could you see into Gaithersburg while standing on the rocks on political hill?), and the origin and development of Atchison Crossing, about which I have mostly had to speculate.

A number of issues in the Grove's history I have left virtually unexplored, begging either that they deserve a history of their own or that their impact on the

Grove was only peripheral. Among them is the story of Emory Grove: whether it was important to the founders that it existed nearby, to what degree its personalities and customs affected Washington Grove, and why its camp meeting went on for 40 years after ours had ended. Another is the history of the Oakmont School, now Washington Grove Elementary, whose first building may have been originally an Episcopal church. And Oakmont itself, a failed real estate development, like dozens in Montgomery County (including, some would say, Washington Grove), which nevertheless contributed many of the Grove's more memorable friends and neighbors. The Grove's earliest history suggests a study of the power and politics of the Washington Methodists in the period from 1800 to 1900. This, too, I have left to others.

As this was being written and re-written my helpers and I found many examples of erroneous statements I had made and misconclusions I had drawn, some taken from blatantly wrong earlier accounts (of whose authors, mistakes I take pains to inform you in the course of the text), but others the result of sloppy research or (most embarrassing of all) wishful thinking. Those which were found have been corrected, but one thing is certain: there remain others to be found.

Whether exciting or not, the existence of the Washington Grove Camp Meeting Association was historically important to the Methodist community of the city of Washington, and was a significant factor in the development of Montgomery County. It is tied up with the individual histories of the city of Gaithersburg, the B&O Railroad Company, and the thousands of people who have been spiritually enriched by merely being a part of it. It is also important for all of us to know how it came to be what it is today, to shun false views of a utopian design and recognize that in a dull, muddlesome way the Grove managed to capture and combine the best of what mankind has to offer: the strength of community and the spirit of peace.

THE ASSOCIATION

NOTES TO THE SECOND EDITION

The purpose of this edition is to provide the material online in eBook form as well as in print copy. This is intended to be a verbatim reissue of the original text, correcting only for typos, misspellings, and egregious misuse or omission of capital letters. I have not corrected for my own idiosyncrasies of writing. The index has been simplified as the eBook version will be a searchable document.

Many of the illustrations had to be reproduced from the first edition print copy with concomitant reduction in resolution.

ACKNOWLEDGEMENTS

There were many people who helped in the construction of this history, and I am grateful to them all:

Giving valuable aid in the regional history was the Columbia Historical Society of Washington, DC; in the history of the Methodist Church in the area, the Lovely Lane Museum, maintained by the Baltimore Conference of Methodists; in the history of Montgomery County, the fine collection of the Montgomery County Historical Society, in the expert hands of librarian Jane Sween.

Of tremendous help in collecting both the facts and the feelings of the times were the many people inside and outside the Grove who were willing to tell stories about themselves or their parents, or their parents' parents, and who were willing to open their family memorabilia to my perusal.

Many of the illustrations are from documents belonging to the present town government and photographs in the collection of the Heritage Committee of Washington Grove, but a large number are from the private collections of Philip Winter and Donald McCathran.

Finally, I am grateful to my editors: my wife, Suzanne Edwards, who advised me on tone and readability; Roland Blood, who sought out poor grammar and syntax; Donald McCathran, who looked for errors of fact; Fred Tippens, who advised me on word usage, continuity, and clarity, and my father,

Philip K. Edwards, Jr., who gave the manuscript a professional editor's review.

1
Three Ingredients

IN 1873, WASHINGTON, DC was a flourishing city, Methodism was a large and aggressive religious movement, and Montgomery County an inviting rural retreat. These elements combined to produce a community that would last.

THE CITY

The nation's roots and foundation were originally in Philadelphia, its first seat of government as well. The Continental Congress first met there, but later met in Baltimore, Lancaster, and York. It moved back to Philadelphia in 1773, but also met in Princeton, Annapolis, and Trenton before it settled in New York City. It was there that the legislation establishing a permanent capital was written.

Recognizing the potential conflicts in operating a national government from within a sovereign state, the authors of the Constitution of 1787, "the miracle of Philadelphia," stipulated that the central government would be relocated to a neutral area, to be ceded by one or more of the states. President Washington desired to locate the capital in his familiar Potomac valley, and in 1790 Congress authorized the creation of the new capital city. Maryland and Virginia each offered to donate a share of the land.

President Washington was empowered to select a site on the Potomac somewhere between the Eastern Branch of the Potomac, now called the Anacostia River, and the village of Williamsport, Maryland to the northeast. Williamsport, sarcastically referred to by some congressmen as "that Indian place," lost its chance to be our nation's capital when Washington chose the area just above the Eastern Branch and just below Three Sisters Island instead.

The District of Columbia was to be ten miles square, and was to take in the port cities of Alexandria in Virginia, and Georgetown in Montgomery County, Maryland. The area on the Maryland side included also the villages of Hamburg, later known as Foggy Bottom, and Carrollsburg, at Greenleaf s Point at the confluence of the Potomac and Anacostia Rivers. Three commissioners selected the name Washington and ordered a survey of the grounds. Pierre L'Enfant, a Frenchman and self-proclaimed architect who had served as a major in Washington's corps of engineers, was selected to lay out a plan for the city. He was to empowered to operate independently of the commissioners. His controversial grid-and-radials design, (of which Annapolis, Maryland is the earliest American example) is said to have been inspired by Rome.

The city of Washington was to be governed by Congress. Georgetown, incorporated into the District geographically but divided from the L'Enfant plan by Rock Creek, continued to operate a separate town government, as did Alexandria. The outlying areas of the District were considered to be outside the City of Washington but within the County of Washington, which had yet another government.

Georgetown had been a successful and growing tobacco port, and by 1781 it was exporting a third of

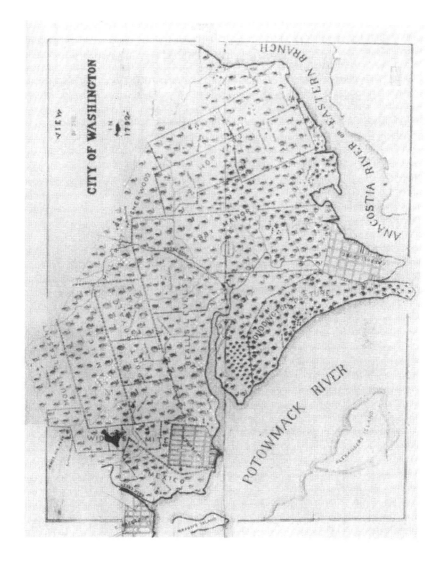

Washington at the time the L'Enfant plan was drawn. Georgetown is across Rock Creek on the west side.

Maryland's crop; by 1800 its share had grown to 50%.But tobacco was its only major export and the tobacco market was uncertain—prices varied wildly from one season to the next. In 1800, soil depletion was already biting into Maryland's marketable yield per acre, and tobacco was in decline. Alexandria, in the meantime, had a variety of export products, and was growing at a greater rate. By 1800 it had surpassed Georgetown's export volume by a factor of five.

Though L'Enfant never completed his task, his basic city plan had been approved and put into action by 1795, and clearing, grading, and building operations had begun. Georgetown became the innkeeper and shopkeeper for an army of timbermen, teamsters, and masons. When the government finally set up housekeeping in 1800, Georgetown again benefitted: civil servants had arrived to find the capitol and the president's house unfinished, with few roads, fewer shops, and no housing. The area around the Capitol was a swamp. Washington came to be known as "The City of Magnificent Distances," "Capital of Miserable Huts," and "A Mudhole almost Equal to the Great Serbonian Bog."

If the capital of the country were to grow from its population base of 3000 it would need capital investment. There were heavy expenditures for federal projects, but private development was slow. Two events had conspired to freeze local capital: a sudden sharp drop in the price of tobacco, and the collapse of an enormous land speculation scheme—several prominent families were bankrupt, and some formerly wealthy men went to debtor's prison.

Without growth the new city had only a tenuous hold on the government. Even before the first spade of earth had been turned for the new city there were proposals to move the capital back to New York, or to Richmond, Annapolis, or Boston instead. Even after the government moved in, the controversy continued. The real estate panic was only one of many reasons that some congressmen wanted to move the capital. Another argument was that the city was deemed indefensible. In fact, the British entered the city with little effort in August of 1814 and burned the Capitol, the White House, and the Navy Yard. When the estimate for rebuilding costs of a half million dollars was presented to Congress the "capital-movers" almost succeeded.

Although the invention and implementation of the telegraph in 1837 quieted most critics of Washington's isolated location, the subject of abandonment came up again in 1847. Virginia had petitioned for the recovery of Alexandria, which was then in a state of decline and neglect. Most of the District's Virginia portion (nearly a third of the city) was returned, and Virginia was reunited with its Potomac port, and the new county of Arlington was formed.

As the Civil War approached, relocation of the capital city was discussed on more practical grounds. If the southern states were to become a new country, as they were threatening, the U.S. would need a new capital further to the north. Virginia did secede, but Maryland, under virtual federal occupation, reluctantly stayed in the Union, and the capital stayed in Washington.

Lincoln's inauguration, the secession of the southern states, and the firing on Fort Sumter in the spring of 1861 quickly brought hundreds of new bureaucrats and thousands of fresh soldiers to the city. Washington became a garrison, protecting itself from the shadowy

Army of the Confederacy just across the Potomac, and from the hundreds of real and imagined secessionists, spies, conspirators, and assassins who lurked in its barrooms and skulked in its streets.

The city was never in serious danger from the lower Potomac—the main strength of the Union forces was kept close by, and Union troops occupied Alexandria for most of the war. But in July of 1864 an army of 12,000 veteran troops under Confederate General Jubal Early crossed the Potomac north of the city and advanced on the District through Maryland. It entered the District via the 7th Street corridor and got as far as Fort Stevens, which was defended at that time by only 6000 Union soldiers who were unseasoned by battle. A veteran contingent of General Grant's forces was sent from Virginia the next day and drove the gray army away.

From a population of 8000 in 1814, to 23,000 in 1846, to 100,000 in 1865, and close to 150,000 in 1873, the city grew north and east and established new neighborhoods along the 14th and 7th Street corridors and out North and East Capital Streets. As the tobacco trade continued its decline, Georgetown's waterfront areas were given over increasingly to manufacturing. The opening of the C&O canal in 1830, though it was never a success for its investors, brought a new prosperity to Georgetown as it became a hub in the transfer of agricultural and manufactured goods.

In the years before the Civil War the swamps south and east of the Mall were tamed by landfill and canal construction. A major canal connected the Central Market, a huge enclosed trading center on 7th Street at B Street, to the Potomac. The C&O canal crossed the Potomac on an elevated aqueduct to connect with Alexandria. Then came the war, and the Union Army joined a burgeoning bureaucracy to bring a flourishing, though temporary, prosperity to Washington. The soldiers went away when the war ended, but the bureaucracy stayed. The war's legacy was the establishment of a powerful new financial and commercial base, centered at 7th Street and Pennsylvania Avenue, one of the first paved crossroads in the city. It was the center of power for the city's upper middle class Methodists.

The year 1872 was eventful in the capital city. The Hero of Appomattox, General Grant, was elected to his second term as president. Postwar scandals had motivated Congress to rescind home rule and install a territorial form of government for Washington with more control, and more money, to come from Congress. A new branch of the B&O Railroad Company was under construction northwest of the city towards Rockville, Maryland. That fall, the ministers and lay leaders of most of the Methodist churches of Washington met at a special assembly at Foundry Church to plan a permanent ground for their summer camp meetings.

THE METHODIST CHURCHES

The Reformation of the sixteenth century was a religious revival, inspired generally by a desire to return to more fundamental forms of Christian worship, and specifically in protest of corruption in the Roman Catholic church. The Protestant movement began early in the century with Martin Luther in Germany, was taken up by Zwingli in German Switzerland and Calvin in French Switzerland, and led to the establishment of the Presbyterian Church in Scotland under John Knox in

1560.

Meanwhile, in England, there was increasing friction between the Roman Catholic church and Henry VIII; in November of 1534 he issued his Act of Supremacy, which established the Anglican Church, with himself as its supreme earthly head. Though retaining many of the traditions of Roman Catholicism, the Church of England incorporated some of the Protestant reforms as well. For the next century it was pulled in one direction by loyal Catholics and in the other by more fundamental Protestants: Congregationalists, Nonconformists, and Separatists. The English separatist movement led to the founding of the Baptist Church by John Smyth in 1609.

A century later John Wesley, a grandson of Nonconformist minister John Westley (sic), was born at Epworth, England. He entered the Anglican ministry not professing to be particularly holy, but he became impressed with the piety of the German fundamentalists called Methodists. He subsequently studied German and Spanish Protestantism and was led to a more fundamentalist view of religious life. In 1738, during a reading of Luther's works he had a sudden revelation—he described it as an inner warming—which convinced him that his vision of a new Protestantism was valid. He and his brother Charles, also a minister, developed these ideas into a movement; they held their first meeting with a small group of converts in an abandoned factory called the 'Foundery' in 1739. For the rest of his life he worked brilliantly and tirelessly to spread the new doctrine, riding as much as 5000 miles a year and preaching as many as fifteen times a day, often to threatening crowds. His movement came to be called Wesley Methodism.

While not antagonistic to Anglicanism, the Wesley

doctrine differed from it in emphasizing more fundamental Christian beliefs. He and his group trimmed the 39 Articles of Anglicanism to 24. They practised the saving of souls by redemption of sin through conversion, which they termed rebirth. They encouraged singing as a means of praise; they published hymnals. They were dynamic and out-reaching; they wanted to rid man of sin and the temptations of sin, and they counted their success in numbers of new converts.

Wesley Methodism was brought to the United States before the American Revolution, chiefly by the Irish. Its early centers were in the port cities of New York and Maryland, with congregations in Baltimore, Annapolis, and Georgetown. In 1771 Wesley sent two preachers, Francis Asbury and Dr. Thomas Coke, to strengthen the Methodist community through the same itinerant style which Wesley had used with such success in England and Ireland. The American Revolution temporarily cut off communication with Wesley's home church, and eventually separated Wesley and Coke politically.

After the war some of the preachers chose to return to England, including Dr. Coke, but Asbury decided that his duties were with the Americans. In 1784, to accommodate Asbury's decision, Wesley sent Coke back to America to ordain Asbury as bishop and head of the church in the United States. The following year in the Baltimore Conference the establishment of Methodism's American branch, the Methodist Episcopal Church, was announced.

Asbury became the Wesley of the American church: organizing, preaching, and traveling thousands of miles a year in Maryland, New Jersey, Pennsylvania, and Ohio. Due largely to his efforts, the movement grew from 300 converts and 4 preachers on his arrival in 1771 to 214,000 members and more than 2000 ministers at his death in 1816.

Asbury often traveled through Washington, and usually stopped overnight with his friend Henry Foxall. Foxall's parents had been direct converts of John Wesley and friends of Asbury when he was still in England. As a youth, Foxall had learned the trade of iron founder, and eventually became foreman of a large foundry in Ireland. After a dramatic nighttime escape with his family from a house under siege by disgruntled workers who, among others things, resented what they considered an excess of piety on his part, Foxall emigrated to Philadelphia in 1796. He entered into a partnership with Robert Morris, a signer of the Declaration of Independence and a financier of the American Revolution, to build and operate a foundry in Philadelphia. In time the U.S.Navy came to be dependent on his foundry, the Eagle Works, for its cannon, and Henry Foxall became a wealthy and socially prominent man.

When the capital city was relocated, Foxall was urged by Jefferson to come to Washington and set up a foundry to serve the new Navy yard there. Foxall moved from Philadelphia to a house on Bridge Street (now M Street) in Georgetown and constructed the Columbia Foundry just upriver. The new foundry bored cannon and cast grape shot and shells for the U.S.Navy and the armies of Maryland and Virginia. The war of 1812 brought an avalanche of new business, which added to Foxall's wealth and prestige.

In the height of his material success Foxall remained a deeply religious man and concerned himself with many social causes. He organized the financing of two new churches in the city of Washington (Ebenezer, a church whose congregation was white, and Mt. Zion, a church whose congregation was black), and was himself the major contributor to a new church for Georgetown's Methodist congregation. He was a trustee of the Georgetown Lancaster School. He was a sought-after lay preacher, an elected Elder in 1814, and ultimately became Mayor of Georgetown. His house was frequently visited by business, government, and church leaders, including President Jefferson himself. Though Foxall owned slaves, Calkin reports in his "Castings" that one of them once said, "If we had been his own children, he could have treated us no better."

As the British were advancing through the city in August of 1814, tradition has it that Foxall made a pact with the Lord: if Georgetown and the foundry were saved he would make a material offering of thanks. While burning the Navy Yard, the British accidently touched off a cache of explosives, causing many British casualties, and the explosion was followed almost immediately by a sudden and violent thunderstorm. The British advance stopped just short of Rock Creek. Foxall's prayers were answered!

When it came time to pay the debt, Foxall observed that the downtown area of Washington near the President's House was without a church; he decided to show his gratitude by building a new Methodist chapel to serve what would become the heart of the city. A year later Foundry Chapel was dedicated; it was named, according to Foxall, not for his foundry but for the Foundery in London, Wesley's first church. In 1817 Foxall sold his Washington foundry and gave his remaining eight years to preaching and furthering good works in America and England.

Originally located at 14th and G Streets, NW,

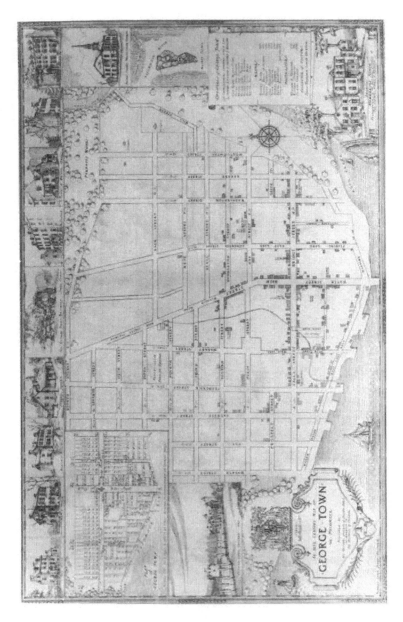

Georgetown in the time of Henry Foxall

Foundry Methodist Episcopal Church quickly took a vigorous leadership role in the advance of Methodism in the city, and spawned several other congregations. Wesley Chapel grew out of Foundry in 1829. In 1836 Asbury Church for blacks was dedicated out of Foundry; the same year the Hamline Church congregation shared a site and a building with Foundry. In the 1840's Ryland Church at 10th and D Streets, McKendree at 8th and K, and Union in the western outlying part of the city were organized by members of the Foundry congregation. In the 1870's a new Mt. Zion Church was organized out of Foundry at 15th and R Streets.

The political and religious institutions of the country were deeply enmeshed in the slavery issue in the 1840's; Washington was a center of intellectual discussion and the focus of political action. From 1844 onward, the Protestant religions began to split, one-by- one, along Northern-Southern lines, with congregations dividing into a "Baptist Convention" and a "Southern Baptist Convention", a "Methodist Episcopal Church" and a "Methodist Episcopal Church of the South". The Presbyterian division was so profound that the Northern and Southern branches remained apart into the 1980's.

There was only one Southern Methodist congregation in the city in 1860 (its building was razed and its congregation dispersed when war actually broke out), but even the Northern church's position on slavery was still hotly contested. It was not until after the Emancipation Proclamation of 1862 that the Baltimore Convention of the Methodist Church North was finally able to agree on a formal call to end the institution of slavery.

The war was hard on the churches in other ways.

Many Washingtonians left the city for the duration; congregations were drastically reduced and it was difficult to recruit new members from among the fast-changing population. Membership at Foundry dropped almost 50% to a low of just 203 persons; collections dwindled and the church building went into disrepair. Recovery finally began after the war when Bishop Matthew Simpson of Ohio relocated in the Baltimore-Washington area, and acted as a magnet for new talent.

One of the men drawn to Foundry in this period from Virginia was the Reverend Benjamin Peyton Brown of Virginia. Appointed pastor of Foundry in 1866, Brown was active in missionary work among the American Indians. In 1868 he accompanied a federal peace commission sent to negotiate a treaty with the Sioux over forts being built along the Bozeman Trail in Montana. The Treaty of Fort Laramie subsequently agreed to remove the forts and declared the territory north of the North Platte River and east of the Big Horn to be Indian territory. Brown served as pastor of Foundry from 1866 to 1869, and again from 1876 to 1879. He was elected Presiding Elder of the Conference in 1879.

From the beginning, Methodism renewed its strength and vitality by reaching out for converts, using a range of methods from itinerant preaching to extensive foreign missions. The Sunday School was an invention of the Methodists in the 1780's to reach out more effectively to young people. It reached out into its own neighborhoods, too, with holiday picnics, revivals, and camp meetings. Camp meetings of the Washington District were held as early as 1815; Foundry participated with other churches at camp meetings in 1829 and 1838. In 1848, there was a combined camp meeting for all the churches in the community. Foundry was the point of departure for an August, 1855 meeting that took place in Montgomery County. According to a Washington reporter, "wagons, carts, bales, boxes, and beds" were packed up the night before. Babies and "other light ware" would be packed the next morning. A similar meeting was held two years later near Warrenton, Virginia.

The site of a camp was always an important consideration. There had to be adequate space for hundreds or even thousands of campers. Clean water was required in abundance for drinking by both humans and horses and for cooking, washing, and sanitation. Shade from the summer sun was necessary, either from structures or trees. The site should be less than a day's journey from the city by train or wagon. Equally important was the ability of the site to be protected from those less pious of the local community who would sell liquor to the campers or, having consumed the product themselves, would ride through the camp during prayers, whooping and firing weapons into the air.

The hazards of the Civil War had brought a total halt to the camp meetings, as well as a general decline in the church population. But with the installation of Rev. Brown at Foundry and the post-war revival of the Methodist community in Washington came a renewed interest in the camp meeting as an effective local mission—and a way to escape Washington's August doldrums. At a quarterly meeting in April, 1868, a camp meeting committee made up of the Reverend Brown, Benjamin H. Stinemetz, and Robert Ricketts was appointed. In July the committee called in Methodists from all over Washington to Foundry Church to consider a proposal for a camp near Annapolis Junction (near Laurel, Maryland) on the B&O Railroad.

Reverend Halliday of Foundry presided, with E.F.Simpson, an active lay leader, acting as secretary. Fifty persons present indicated they would attend, and reported their congregations were also in favor. Rev. Brown was made chairman of the arrangements committee, while Stinemetz represented Foundry in the planning of details. Camp opened on August 21 with about 150 tents pitched.

Again in 1871 Foundry's pastor, now the Rev. Alexander E. Gibson, invited all the Washington churches to join Foundry at the Annapolis Junction site in August. According to Homer Calkin's history of Foundry Church, "The camp meeting proved to be the best in many a year. No booths were allowed on the grounds; nothing could be sold except necessary food supplies. Meetings were very orderly, and congregations were large. Conversation among those attending was confined almost entirely to religious subjects. The preaching was simple and pointed." Foundry held a revival at the close of the camp from which it netted twenty-eight immediate converts.

In a hundred years of Methodism, the camp meeting, like the Sunday School and the revival meeting, had developed a formula for success. The right time was mid- to late summer, to escape the heat and smell of the city. The right place was a spacious ground, with trees for shade and plenty of water, accessible from the city but isolated enough to discourage intruders. The Methodist community had shown it would support the camp meetings; now it was time to find a permanent camp meeting ground.

THE COUNTY

At the beginning of the seventeenth century, an explorer sailing into Maryland's Chesapeake Bay would first encounter miles of grassy marshland at its shores. If he chose to enter the mouth of the Potomac River for further exploration he would soon leave the tidewater area; the marshes would give way to gentle slopes and the grasses would give way to trees. Several miles up the river, when the rocks were too numerous and the channel too shallow for further safe progress, he would see steep rocky slopes on one side and dense timber on the other. If he dropped anchor and paddled over to the east shore he would be landing at an village inhabited by a settlement of Piscataway Indians—and once on shore he would be standing on the future site of Washington, D.C.

Captain John Smith made just such a trip in 1608; he left detailed notes on the flora and fauna and on the several Indian villages, representing many tribal affiliations. One variation of the story of Smith's journey says he landed at Piscataway and promptly burned it. Another early adventurer/explorer named Henry Fleet made the same trip in the 1620's. From their descriptions and those of later missionaries and settlers the Potomac area above Piscataway was a vast forest, abundant with streams and rivers and rich with game, but without permanent Indian settlements. A Piscataway group took Fleet prisoner on his first trip and held him for five years. He returned in 1632 for further exploration.

The eastern Maryland Indians were more peaceful by nature and custom. When the Ark and the Dove landed at St. Clements Island in 1634 the Indians welcomed Maryland's first settlers. The Indians traded them half their village, and then joined the settlers in farming the fields nearby. Joint hunting parties of Indians and whites also hunted turkey, deer, boar, and buffalo in the vast forests to the west.

Though friendship and mutual assistance with the Indians continued, in time the fellowship aspect waned as boatloads of new settlers began to make permanent changes in the landscape. Thousands of acres a year were cleared and planted in corn and tobacco. Wilderness stations were established by missionaries on the Patuxent near Tridelphia and on the Monocacy near the site of Frederick. In 1693 a small fort was established at the site of Georgetown from which a militia known as the Maryland Rangers patrolled the area north and west to control the unfriendly hunting parties of Susquehanna Indians from the north. In 1700 the administration of the region became more formal under the newly-established Prince George's County.

The areas under cultivation expanded rapidly as land grants from one hundred to 3000 acres were given to speculators, who would first survey the land then solicit settlers to farm it. The first farmers in what was to become Montgomery County were a small band of Quakers brought by Robert Brooke to the Patuxent River in 1650. It was not until 1715, though, that settlers began to move further into the county. In 1728 a descendant of Robert Brooke, James Brooke, was granted land in the Sandy Spring area which, with additions, eventually totalled 17,000 acres and included the villages of Sandy Spring, Laytonsville, and Brookeville.

Land taming and farm building in the early 1700's expanded along the traditional Indian trails. Trails turned into roads and crossroads became villages, linking farms with each other and with trading centers. The navigable Potomac River drew farm commerce to its headwaters at Georgetown along three routes through the county; one southeast from Poolesville parallel to the river, one south from the settlements near Frederick, and one southwest from the area of Sandy Spring, which served also as the overland route to Baltimore and Annapolis.

When Prince George's County was separated from Charles County in 1700, its western boundary was the Potomac River. In 1748, Prince George's itself was halved and a new county, Frederick, formed from its western half. The governors of Maryland, ambitious for growth, began planning the establishment of cities to stimulate development and trade in the rural areas.

Annapolis had been the Maryland's capital city almost from the beginning, but in 1708 it was officially so recognized and properly incorporated. By 1729 a first plan for the city of Baltimore had been approved. Frederick became the second planned city in 1745 and Georgetown the third in 1751.

Hamlets sprang up along the roads connecting these new cities. By 1750, villages were established in Darnestown and Poolesville to the west, Olney and Sandy Spring to the east, and in the center of the county, a convenient day's ride from Georgetown was the settlement that would become Rockville, then known only as (Charles) Hungerford's Tavern. General Braddock paused at Hungerford's in 1755 on his ill-starred march to defeat and death at Fort Cumberland during the French and Indian wars.

Settlement was so rapid in this area that by 1775 there was little unclaimed land left. The population of what was called Lower Frederick County had topped 10,000. There were simple churches and rude schools. Tobacco had become a highly profitable cash crop, in more ways than one: it was not only the source of cash to exchange for manufactured goods from Europe, but it was also the cash itself, for Maryland had declared tobacco legal tender in 1732, at one penny to the pound.

As the colonists sought greater independence in their legal and fiscal affairs, relations with mother England deteriorated. When the British blockaded Boston Harbor after the Boston Tea Party, angry county leaders met in June of 1774 at Hungerford's Tavern, in what would become Rockville, to discuss an appropriate response. They resolved that the colonies should break off all relations with England "until the blockade be withdrawn." Their action was one of the first volleys in the war of words that led to the war for freedom from England and, two years later, to the Declaration of Independence.

When war began, Maryland took up the cause with enthusiasm, sending several contingents to fight in Massachusetts, New York, and New Jersey. In September of 1776 Frederick County was divided into Washington, Frederick, and Montgomery Counties, the latter named for General Richard Montgomery. Montgomery was a former British soldier who had settled in New York after the close of the French and Indian wars. In 1775 he became the first General to die for the American cause.

During the war the new county prospered, but afterward faced a succession of economic problems. The war had left the state without a hard currency, and there were no precious metal reserves in the state treasury. Trade with Europe revived quickly after the

Treaty of Paris but, in the midst of a great surplus, the price of tobacco, Maryland's staple crop, collapsed in 1784, and never fully recovered. Large land holdings were sold at auction and broken up. At the same time, nitrogen- depleted soils were slowly reducing the annual yield of tobacco, Montgomery County's only trading commodity. The county badly needed to diversify, but did not know how.

In some cases individual farm families continued to increase their holdings and wealth, but the trend at this time was for young men and unlanded farm families to emigrate west to Ohio and Kentucky, or south to the Carolinas or Georgia. The population of the county actually dropped over the succeeding decades from over 18,000 at the 1790 census to a low of 15,456 in 1840, while the rest of the country was growing rapidly. Fields and fences fell into a neglected state as old farms slipped into poverty or ruin. It would take new technology to make the county a healthy and competitive agricultural producer again.

Two farming concepts, fertilization and crop rotation, were mid-nineteenth century revelations in the United States. Montgomery County farmers, first in the Quaker communities to the east, began experimenting with these alternate farming methods. Soon after, entrepreneurs began importing large quantities of bird droppings from South America, and annual fertilization of fields became standard practice. This greatly increased crop yields, though at an uncomfortable expense, and in time alternate fertilizers were developed. Other farm products and land usage were considered, too: beekeeping as a source of sugar and peach plantation farming were among the diversification efforts made by innovative county farmers.

A newly stabilized and growing population began to transform the county in the 1840's and 50's. With their new methods the farms began to pay again, the roads were increasingly well-traveled, and the existence of the nation's capital city nearby brought urban visitors to this once westernmost outland of Maryland. The county looked south to the city of Washington for cultural, political, and financial opportunity, while the city of Washington looked north at cheap rural land for its investment and recreational value. Church groups made excursions into the county for picnics, camp meetings, and revivals. Wealthy families would go to the country for relief from the city heat. The victims of tuberculosis and other debilitating diseases would take to the clear air and clean water of the county for rest and rehabilitation.

By 1860 the county was in a state of renaissance, but unfortunately the country was approaching a state of war. Maryland was a southern state, a slave-holding and slave-breeding state. In Montgomery County a third of the population was black, mostly slaves. Though many pro-slavery landowners were against secession (and some were even anti-slavery—the Quakers in the county had freed their slaves in 1779), most were pro-secession and then pro-Confederacy once the fighting began. Many county men quietly forded the Potomac in the night to join Virginia or rebel Maryland outfits.

The Civil War in the county was a war of nerves more than battles. With half the men away, and most of those with the rebels, the county was host mainly to encampments of Union soldiers guarding the strategic points along the Potomac. For the first year all was quiet, but in 1862 the entire Army of the Potomac was moved north on its way to the terrible encounter with

Lee at Antietam. More action came the following year when Jeb Stuart's cavalry crossed into the county and dipped south of General Hooker's forces at Poolesville, then being mobilized to move toward Gettysburg. Stuart's men captured a Union supply train, then moved down through Rockville and captured Bethesda, where they took prisoners. The prisoners were paroled a few at a time along the road as Stuart raced north toward Gettysburg only to arrive too late to be of help to Lee.

The only significant shooting in the heart of the county came in 1864 with the defeat of General Lew Wallace's 5000 men at the Battle of the Monocacy. This enabled Jubal Early's small army to ride south from the Monocacy through Gaithersburg and Rockville where he attacked Fort Stevens in the District of Columbia. The fresh Union troops that forced him to abandon that effort the next day pushed him back through Rockville and Darnestown. At times the armies were so close that they fired at each other as they rode.

With these troop movements was associated considerable damage to the farms in the County, especially as the Union Army was little known for its gentility in this hotbed of secessionists. When the farmers slipped back, as quietly as they had gone, at war's end, they also found themselves in a postwar economic recession. The small farms had damaged fences, missing horses, and depleted livestock; the bigger farms had lost what they considered a far greater asset—their slave laborers.

The enormous challenge to rebuild the county was met by the combined resources of a war-toughened group of farmers and an inter-county fraternity of farm and merchant interests that had developed over 150 years of county history. An emerging new capital base

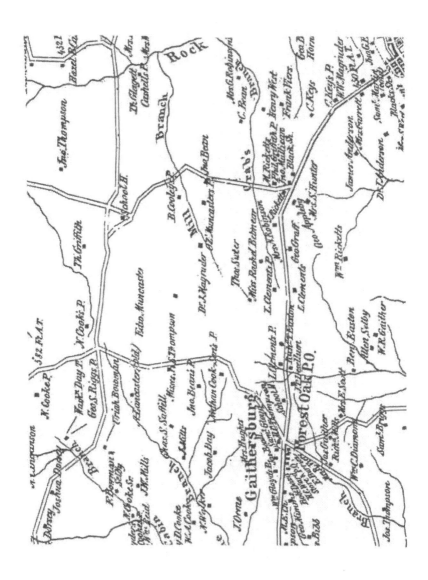

Extract from a map drawn in 1865 from surveys by Martinet and Bond. Nathan Cooke's farm is on the Gaithersburg-Laytonsville Road where it takes a turn to the north.

in Washington, D.C., which had doubled in population during the war, provided the money. Just six years later, pulling prosperity behind it, came the beginning of construction for the Baltimore and Ohio Rail Road's new Metropolitan Branch.

The B&O was the nation's first commercial railroad company. From 1827 it had operated trains along its main line out of Baltimore, through Frederick to Point of Rocks, and on to a Potomac River crossing at Harper's Ferry. A B&O branch line connected Washington to Baltimore, but by mid-century the nation's capital needed a more direct link to the west.

The Metropolitan Railroad, an independent railroad line through the county, was originally surveyed in 1855 but politics and the recession of 1857 deferred immediate construction. Under the threat of civil war the project was again delayed and then abandoned for the duration of hostilities.

Finally, with the restoration of peace in 1865, a State charter for the new line was awarded to the B&O and work began. Its right-of-way was laid across the county in nearly a straight line from the northwest corner of Washington to the mouth of the Monocacy River, bending a little to pick up Gaithersburg as a stop.

The great land grants had been buffeted, eroded, and broken up into smaller and smaller tracts by the tides of a developing county history. The railroad was one more wave washing through the heart of the county, breaking off wedges and re-forming farm and village boundaries. Three of the early grants—Deer Park on the Muddy Branch Creek, Fellowship on Whetstone Branch, and Valentine's Garden on Mill Branch of Rock Creek— converge just south of Gaithersburg. The railroad passed by a small piece of high ground, a watershed for all three of these streams, and said to be a virgin forest. It had, curiously, been left undeveloped in a sea of cleared farmland around it. It was owned by Nathan Cooke's widow and children, and it was for sale.

B&O Railroad stock was popular even during the depression of the 1870's.

THE ASSOCIATION

2
The Founding

CAMP MEETINGS were a successful means of making conversions, but their picnic atmosphere also made camp meetings a popular summer outing for already established Christians. Having held meetings at several rented camp grounds in both Maryland and Virginia over the previous twenty years, the united Methodist churches of Washington now desired to find a permanent camp ground—a common ground for the converted sinner and the enlightened parishioner—a ground that could be under their ownership and control. A group of clergy and church laymen—always a potent combination for it united the will of God with the means of Man—set out from Foundry Church to find a piece of ground on which to build a camp and summer community.

Records do not show who participated directly in the search, how far they traveled, or how many fields, woods, and farms they explored. But the men who were finally empowered to make the purchase, and in whose names the land was officially titled for years, were William R. Woodward and Flodoardo Howard.

The Reverend Page Milburn, in his 1927 Reminiscences, describes the search committee as having been composed of two laymen, the original trustees Woodward and Howard, and two ministers, Reverend B. Peyton Brown and Presiding Elder James A. McCauley. The enthusiastic Brown and the formal McCauley probably had help from at least two other ministers, Reverend William Burris, and Reverend John Lanahan, the man who had earlier induced Brown to join the ministry. Woodward, a Washington attorney, and Dr. Howard, a doctor and pharmacist, probably also had help from Edward F. Simpson, a man who was omnipresent in Methodist community affairs, usually as the recording secretary, and several other laymen, possibly including John T. Mitchell, Benjamin H. Stinemetz, Thomas Somerville, and John W. Wade.

The search was probably undertaken in the late winter and spring of 1873. Some of the locations examined were on or near the existing B&O line connecting Baltimore and Washington. The delegation could have started for those sites by train and switched to coach or wagon if required. Sites in Virginia would have begun with a train trip across the Long Bridge through Alexandria. Locations in Montgomery County could be reached only by coach or carriage (Laytonsville, then Cracklintown, had hosted several camp meetings during this period, and Clarksburg is listed by Milburn as a possible site) since the Metropolitan Branch of the B&O was then still under construction. The *Montgomery County Sentinel* listed several county farms from 40 to 400 acres for sale during this time.

The parcel eventually recommended for purchase was a corner of Nathan Cooke's farm near Gaithersburg. Made up of parts of the original Pottinger and Saffell farms from the days of the land grants, the Cooke farm began along Gaithersburg's eastern boundary, and ran West along the B&O right of way through the site of Washington Grove and beyond, nearly to the present alignment of Shady Grove Road. Cooke's house, barns, livestock and tilled fields were all in the area now bisected by Girard Street. The sources of Whetstone Branch (the Grove's Maple and Whetstone Springs) provided water for the farm and family.

East of the springs and up a grade was an old woods, reputed to be a virgin forest. The dominant species were oak and chestnut, with a mixture of other hardwoods. To the northwest of the woods was pine and scrub, probably second growth over an area which had been burnt over or once cleared. In this area the springs were among the headwaters of Mill Branch of Rock Creek which flowed south to Georgetown; the southeastern comer of the woods drained into Muddy Branch. Along the western edge of the woods was another small cleared area of fifty acres called the "old farm." Before the B&O branch line went through, a county road left Gaithersburg and headed east, roughly along the future railbed, toward Laytonsville. The Cooke farm was on the left. At the woods it made a right angle turn north towards Laytonsville cutting through the Cooke property across the high ground of the woods. At the turn a small farm lane probably continued on east to provide access to the old farm.

A trail led north from that lane along the future alignment of Grove Road out to the mineral springs just south of Emory Grove. The road that connected the old farm to the Laytonsville Road probably had a connection to the Suter farm on the southeast; Suter's farm had a long lane (now Oakmont Avenue) linking it to the Frederick Road which may have served as a

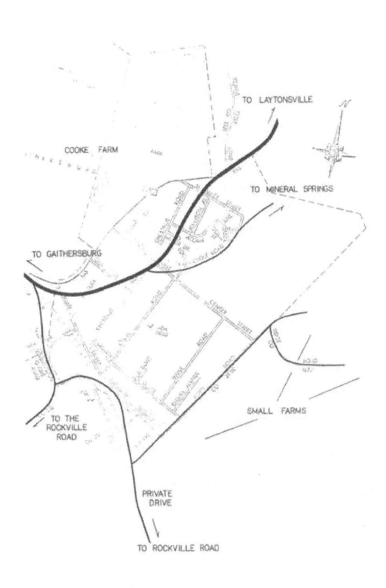

Possible alignment of trails through the Grove grounds before and after the railroad.

welcome shortcut to Rockville for some of the farms between Gaithersburg and Laytonsville. It is possible that by this time there was also another connection to the Frederick Road via Central Avenue—though none is shown on maps of the time, a small road may have connected Suter's with Clement's farm which lay to the west of Suter's.

When the railroad came through it cut the link between the Cooke and Suter farms, leaving a wedge of Cooke land south of the track and a smaller wedge of the Suter farm on the Grove (north) side of the track. A new connection between the farms was soon established in the vicinity of the current Atchison grade crossing, possibly by the railroad itself, to act as a supply road between Rockville and Gaithersburg.

Railroad construction is a series of cutting and filling operations—cutting into the earth where the land is high and pushing the earth and rock ahead to fill in where the land is low. This requires meticulous engineering so that maximum forward progress can be made with minimum movement of earth. After every cut there is a fill, and where the two meet the railbed is at ground level—on grade. Since a level crossing is the least expensive one, railroad crossing points all the way from Washington to Point of Rocks were determined more by where the cuts and fills came together than by previously existing roads or other topographic considerations.

The railroad may have brought another change, this one of greater significance to the Grove. There is evidence to suggest that, at about the coming of the railroad, the Gaithersburg-Laytonsville road was moved from its original position on the high ground of the woods, roughly along Grove Avenue, to its present location at the edge of the old woods, just above the springs. Two bits of data in support of this idea are (1) that a map of the first camp meeting shows the existence of a "County Road" approximately along upper Grove Avenue, and (2) that county highway maps of 1865 and 1879 show a distinct difference in the alignment of the Laytonsville Road.

The evidence that the change was made before mid-1873 is simply that the camp would not have been set up in a way that one would have to cross a thoroughfare to reach the dining tent, which is shown on the plat of the first camp as being on the opposite side of the County Road, especially as there were 267 and one-half acres on which to locate the facilities. Finally, it can be argued that the present location of the road would not have been the logical one: one does not make a path—which would evolve to a trail, then to a lane, then to a road—along the most difficult of routes (down a steep slope, across a gully, up a hill, down a hill, across a wide wash, and up another hill) when one could travel another 40 feet east and move unimpeded across high, dry, level ground.

The coming of the railroad promised greater prosperity for the Cooke family, distinguished as being among those County farm families which had held together during the bad years of the first half century and put together a successful farming formula for the second half. Nathan Cooke, Sr. did not live to see the branch completed; his wife had been three years widowed by the time the first trains came puffing up the hill from Rockville to bring fertilizer by the carload to Gaithersburg farmers. The widow Cooke, acting as trustee for herself and the other heirs, contracted to sell the woods and the old farm, 267 and one-half acres including the railroad right of way, to the Methodists of

Washington for $6636.25. They would be paid with a small down payment and three annual installments. It is not clear from the records whether the contract was binding on the Methodists immediately, or whether it was contingent on their being able to raise enough money, none having been pledged beforehand.

The organizers held a meeting at Foundry Church in Washington on June 16,1873 to describe the grounds and take initial stock subscriptions at $20 each. Reverend Brown was the first subscriber with a five share pledge, to be paid in three installments; a total of 249 shares were pledged that evening in all. Ninety-one families were represented in the initial subscriptions, many of whom would go on to be major contributors to the Grove over the next twenty-five years: John T. Mitchell, Richard H. Willet, William R. Woodward, Warren Choate, Dr. Flodoardo Howard, John W. Wade, Thomas Somerville, Reverend John Lanahan, Thomas P. Morgan, James L. Ewin, Sr., William J. Sibley, Benjamin H. Stinemetz, and Edward F. Simpson all of whom later made memorable contributions to Grove life. Among those at Foundry that evening was Ignatius G. Warfield, of Laytonsville, who became the first County stockholder.

Not all pledges were honored—some were declined outright, some reduced to fewer shares, others were forfeited in lieu of making the second or third installment, and others yet were transferred to other parties to complete the installments—but eighty percent or more were redeemed in full. The sums pledged were sufficient to assure that the initial commitment to Mrs. Cooke could be met (249 shares would bring in $4980, over two-thirds of the purchase price) and on July 3, 1873 the land was conveyed to the trustees of the

Washington Grove Camp Meeting Association of the District of Columbia and Maryland on the strength of a deposit of $200 made by Dr. Flodoardo Howard.

A promotional picnic for the Fourth of July had already been announced for the purposes of taking additional subscriptions and building up enthusiasm for the upcoming camp meeting. It was a "monster picnic" according to Page Milburn: "Excursion trains were run from Washington. It was a wonderful sight, the crowding of men, women, and children with their baskets. The old station at the comer of New Jersey Avenue and C Street was a noisy place that day, and the railroad men were excited over the unusual pressure. I was there with my little basket. When we got to the Grove we walked up a path which had been cut through what is now Grove Avenue, and then scattered in every direction. It was a great day, and a good advertisement for the Grove. The people were given an opportunity to see the beautiful woods of oak, cedar, pine, chestnut and hickory, and the wild flowers which grew in abundance thereabout."

The picnic was announced by the *Sentinel,* a Rockville newspaper, saying that there was "a grand picnic to be held on the grounds on the 4th of July." In the issue following the picnic, the *Sentinel* reported that the ground had been formally dedicated, that lunch was followed by several addresses, and that then "the directors selected a route for the railroad switch by which passengers are to be conveyed to the camp ground." It went on to say that additional subscriptions for stock were taken, and that the first ten-day camp meeting was scheduled to begin Wednesday, August 13. The excellent weather, the new train service, and the beauty of the grounds themselves must have been truly inspiring—an additional 149 shares were pledged at the picnic, and names from Bladensburg, Gaithersburg, Hunting Hill, Rockville, and Sunnyside were added, showing a widening of interest in the concept of a combined camp meeting ground and summer community.

The positive reception at the picnic by both the downtown Methodists and their county counterparts assured the trustees of a well-attended first camp meeting, and further persuaded them that enough stock would be sold that they should proceed with incorporation. Among other provisions the proposed charter would exclude liquor sales for a radius of one mile around, excepting only those establishments in the town of Gaithersburg.

The organizers published and distributed an announcement dated July 9,1873 entitled "

"Rooms of the Washington Grove Camp Meeting Association of the District of Columbia and Maryland." It is very clear in the text of the flyer that a permanent summer community was anticipated from the beginning: "The Association is formed for the promotion of a great public and personal good, for soul and body, without special privileges to any. The tract is located on the line of the Metropolitan Railroad, some twenty miles from the city, is elevated and healthy, and embraces near two hundred acres of beautiful woodland, with abundance of pure cold drinking water. For the purpose, it is said not to be surpassed by any land within one hundred miles of this. After the land has been plotted, it is the intention of the Trustees to issue renewable leases to sites suitable for summer residences, for which its nearness to the railroad, its elevated position—being over five hundred feet above tide-water, its salubrity, and numerous other

ROOMS OF THE

Washington Grove Camp-Meeting Association

OF THE DISTRICT OF COLUMBIA AND MARYLAND,

Washington, July 9, 1873.

For the information of stockholders and friends of our Association, the Executive Committee present the following information:

The Association is formed for the promotion of a great public and personal good, for soul and body, without special privileges to any. The tract is located on the line of the Metropolitan Railroad, some twenty miles from the city, is elevated and healthy, and embraces near two hundred acres of beautiful woodland, with abundance of pure cold drinking water. For the purpose, it is said not to be surpassed by any land within one hundred miles of this. After the land has been plotted, it is the intention of the Trustees to issue renewable leases to sites suitable for summer residences, for which its nearness to the railroad, its elevated position—being over five hundred feet above tide-water, its salubrity, and numerous other advantages, renders it more desirable to the public than any other place in the vicinity of Washington.

The capital stock has been fixed at $20,000, divided into 1,000 shares of $20.00 each, and is now offered to our friends. In time for the Camp to be held the 13th of next August, the railroad company will provide us with a side track, platform, and station house, and we will erect two dining courts, with a pump of cold water in each, a pump at the station, and others through the Camp.

The prices of all tents rented through the Association are as follows:

For a tent with a fly, 10 x 12		$9 00
" " 12 x 16		12 00
" " 14 x 20		15 00

Which price includes the tent put up and floored. The furniture of tents is left to the pleasure of the rentees. Private tents will be put up on the same terms; but persons not stockholders will be charged a rental not exceeding $4.00. Freight and personal property will be charged pro rata. Rent of lumber will be one cent per foot, and lumber cut, three and a quarter cents per foot.

Competent persons will have charge of the dining courts, and the prices for board will be—

Permanent Boarders	$1 00 per day.

Clergymen, Children, and Servants, Half Price.

Transient, under three days	1 25 "
Breakfast and Supper	50 each.
Dinner	75
Dinner on Sabbath	1 00

Liberal arrangements will be made for the sale, at the Camp Market, of fresh meats, fruits, and produce at suitable prices. It is intended to have present a proper police force for the preservation of order.

Round-trip tickets will be ninety-five cents. Any additional information will be cheerfully given by any of the officers or members of the Executive Committee.

Flyer distributed by the Association after the successful 4th of July picnic.

advantages, renders it more desirable to the public than any other place in the vicinity of Washington."

A central idea behind buying and operating their own campground was the ability of the Methodists to make and enforce their own rules. They believed that if the camp meeting ground were enclosed within a larger sympathetic community, it would be well protected both physically and spiritually. They did not rely entirely on that premise, however; the same flyer went on to say, "It is intended to have a proper police force for the preservation of order."
"

FIRST CAMP

The first camp was set to open on Wednesday, August 13, 1873, and scheduled to run ten days. A great deal of work had to be done at the site in preparation for the deluge of campers and visitors: roads for wagons needed to be put in shape, and paths for pedestrians; tent sites and meeting places had to be surveyed, marked, and cleared. More important, wells had to be dug and pumps installed —for in spite of the "abundant water" described in the promotional literature, the springs were too far from the center of camp, and across the new Laytonsville Road besides, to be practical sources of water for daily needs.

Outhouses had to be provided, and a yard for maintenance of the horses set aside. Meanwhile, in Washington, tents had to be rented, arrangements for two dining halls ("boarding saloons") made (since not all campers would want to provide their own meals), and services contracted for including a barber shop, a vegetable market, a confectioner's, and a shop for the sale and rental of furniture.

Some of the expenditures for preparatory work included $200 for cleaning the grounds, which involved cutting brush, hauling deadwood, and clearing paths; digging wells (there were three wells dug in the camp area, and one at the depot, $300.; pumps for the wells, $84; and labor on the grounds, which included construction of platforms and sheds associated with the boarding and sanitary facilities, and with the worship services and meetings, amounted to $450. Tents were rented from two Washington suppliers at a total cost of $1215. These were heavy expenditures for a new, nonprofit corporation whose stockholders were redeeming their pledges on the installment plan, but the new subscribers enlisted at the 4th of July picnic had added another $3000 to the anticipated capital base, and a significant amount of stock was expected to be sold at camp itself. The collection of pledges was running well, too; the first installment of $2200 for the land was presented to Mrs. Cooke on the 19th of July.

The original 1873 Association checkbook (which was turned upside down seven years later and used as a minute book for the Committee on Grounds and Supplies) recalls a simpler era of banking. The checks were printed folio style, with no perforations—one would have to cut them out with a pair of scissors. Of course there was no ABA number on the checks, and they showed only the name of the bank, not its address. Neither the account name nor number were printed on the checks, though on some unused checks the legend "J.A.Ruff, Treasurer, Washington Grove Association" was handwritten. In 1873 one would not casually take a check from a stranger.

On the late afternoon of the Tuesday before camp opened, the workers could look with pride on what they had accomplished: From the depot a wide path had been cut and cleared, leading up toward the highest ground in the woods. In a level area between the Mineral Springs trail and the abandoned county road they had cut out a great square called the Plaza, about two hundred feet on a side, and placed benches around it. They had built a great platform along the eastern side of the Plaza where a preacher could stand and look out over hundreds of potential converts at a time. They had established and marked rows of tent sites, 15'x20' for small tents and 15'x30' for large ones, on a gridwork of avenues that ran north-south past the Plaza, and which were named for the major churches participating—Foundry, Wesley, McKendree, Hamlin, and Metropolitan.

A major cross-street on the north side of the square was named for Dumbarton Church. Other unnamed cross streets were established to allow the campers free movement between the long avenues and give easy access to all the facilities. Two boarding tents were set up on the periphery—one across the old county road near a pump and storage building, the other on the mineral spring trail by another pump. East of the trail holes had been dug for waste and outhouses placed over them. Further up the trail on the right an area was cleared for a carriage park and horse corral, close to a well and pump. Back across camp was a market tent for supplies and services.

In all, two hundred fifty-eight tent sites had been laid out with plenty of room for more if they were needed. Spaces for campers were apparently not assigned ahead of time, but it is likely that the large groups from Washington churches were intended to be clustered each in the area that bore its church's name. A large site was set aside on Metropolitan Avenue near the square for the head preacher, a tent to be provided without charge to act as his residence and for holding preacher's meetings. A site on the south side of the Plaza was provided for B. Peyton Brown. Sites were established on the path from the depot (a path as yet unnamed, but to become Grove Avenue), for the sale and rental of furniture, tents, and straw. Some of the organizers and early stockholders who had planned and supervised the work were spending this night away from home to help get the camp off to an early start the next day. Among them were probably some of the following: Stinemetz, Somerville, or Willet, and Mitchell, Wade, or Morgan— and perhaps even Reverend Brown himself. As they met for evening prayer, they had every hope of the next day dawning on the beginning of a glorious camp meeting.

It rained. It rained buckets and didn't stop for a week. The camp ground which had been born under the sunny skies of the Fourth of July was baptized by immersion on the Thirteenth of August. The anticipated deluge of people turned into a deluge of water. Camp started out a little slowly that first year: camp meetings had been rained on before, and most campers and leaders knew how to cope with rain once camp was underway, but it more difficult to set up a camp in the rain.

That it was a new campground did not help either, for although the tent sites had been thoughtfully planned and carefully laid out, the practical art of stormwater management is best tested in the presence of the water itself. There must have much moving about of boundaries as tents were placed where they were practical instead of in neat rows. But camp did start that

Wednesday, and when the *Sentinel* reporter filed his first story on late Thursday he could report that

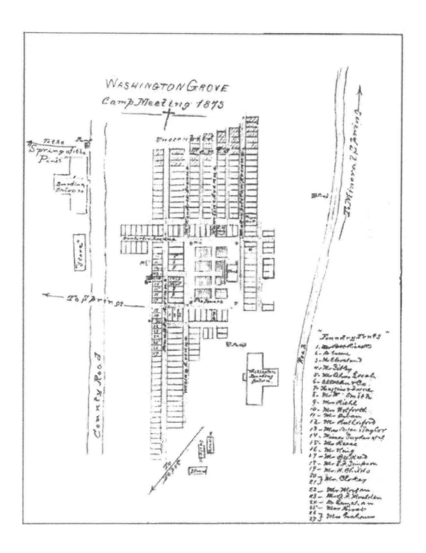

Sketch made during the first camp meeting by James L. Ewin, Sr., shows that the circle was originally a square. This plat also helps establish the location of the original trails and first wells. The sketch was preserved by the Ewin family and presented to the Town in 1986.

"notwithstanding the heavy rain that has fallen almost incessantly up to now," one hundred and fifty tents had been erected.

Though the current Presiding Elder, F. W. Speakes, was to occupy the Preacher's tent it was B.Peyton Brown—organizer, stockholder, evangelist—who preached the first day. The cessation of rain was surely one object of prayer, though in the first few days more camping than praying took place. The organizers looked forward to the coming weekend with increasing anticipation. Saturday would bring out the remainder of those who would be tenting for the balance of the Meeting, and Sunday would bring the first Sabbath of camp, which was always expected to bring multitudes from the city and the surrounding area as well. This year there was a double attraction for those coming from Washington—a ride on the brand new train line, and a look at the brand new camp ground. More campers did arrive Saturday in spite of the rain, but the rain continued in spite of the campers. The heavens were truly open to this gathering of souls.

Fires were kept burning at the comers of the plaza to help drive away the chill and damp, and mercifully the YMCA had set up a large meeting tent on the edge of camp; it was used to continue the sermons out of the rain. As Page Milburn noted in his "Reminiscences", "Camp Meeting was conducted with one object in view, to get people converted." So a vigorous schedule of meetings and prayer was kept up all weekend, with excellent results. The first convert of the new Washington Grove Camp was Pottinger Cooke, a son of the late Nathan Cooke from whose widow the land had been purchased! Two other conversions on the first Sunday were reported by the *Republican,* a Washington newspaper: "the first being a young man named William Spencer, a cigar maker from Washington, the other was a young lady." The young lady was Elizabeth D. Jackson, Mary Ellen Jackson, or Jennie Catheart from Boyds, Maryland: Milburn did not record her name but he wrote that her conversion so moved her father that as a result he and a merchant in Boyds built a church and Sunday school and offered it to any Christian church which would bring regular prayer service to the community. A Presbyterian minister accepted his offer, and soon a regular Presbyterian congregation was established there.

Beginning that Sunday at camp a regular daily schedule of sermons was begun; at 10:30 a.m., 3 p.m., and 7:30 p.m. The *Republican* reported Sunday evening's sermon almost verbatim. Reverend Richard Norris of Waugh Chapel spoke on John XV:28: "They hated me without a cause." Rev. Norris used the text to make the point that "It is base ingratitude to reject Christ," that the rejection "is a crime of the greatest enormity," and that "it is the millstone which will sink you to hell if continued." The talk moved a dozen people to the mourner's bench, which was a special seating at the front of the Square for those in special need of prayer, seven others requested the "prayers of God's people" by a show of hands.

The first Sabbath at camp had been a success sure enough, though bodies and souls alike were dampened by the continuous rain. The *Republican* reported: "The Sabbath passed off quietly enough, although most uncomfortably to our numerous visitors. The orderly conduct of all was especially noteworthy, the police having occasion to interfere but once, when they made an arrest on the outer edge of the camp, of a disorderly person under the influence of rum." And, "It continued to rain with great severity all the afternoon and night. The Sabbath visitors—nine crowded cars—left at 4 p.m. for Washington, instead of 6 o'clock as usual."

By Monday camp was down to a routine, in spite of the weather. The three sermons gave each day a structure; the time in between was filled with the chores of cooking and cleaning, the pleasures of eating and napping and the madness of children fighting and playing (though never on Sunday!). Three or four trains a day brought fresh visitors and a series of preachers to the camp; a steady flow of wagons and carriages brought supplies and curious country people to the camp, too, and vendors offering anything those who were voluntarily reduced to the most primitive of circumstances anything they might want to add a little luxury to life.

The same trains brought a few black people who would get off at the Grove and begin the long walk to Emory Grove; for this was before the advent of Jim Crow, when a black person could still ride the same train as a white person and sit in any seat he could pay for. By Monday the camp had some cause to rejoice for, as the *Sentinel* said, "on Monday, at noon, the sun shone out brightly for a time, but the sky is occasionally overcast with clouds which have a threatening aspect."

Though more rain did come that week, it was not as great a storm as before. On the strength of their success so far, and to make up for the wet start, the leadership voted to extend camp to two full weeks, breaking the old tradition of a ten day camp, and adding a second full weekend of activities.

The improved weather not only made the campers more comfortable, the vendors more prosperous, and the trains more crowded, but it also made the sermons more vigorous. As the crowds swelled so did the hearts of the preachers, a rotation of fervent laymen and ordained ministers. The last few days were filled with brilliant sunshine; on the final Sunday it was estimated that five to eight thousand people were in camp. The Reverend Dr. Guard preached in the morning, with the Reverend Cleveland and Norris taking the afternoon and evening sessions. Without the rain meetings could be held all over the grounds, inside and out. The YMCA tent was never empty. The young people had meetings of their own, guided and supervised by elders. Lay preachers were sent out to work the crowds on the fringes of camp, too. On a crowded Sunday the young adults would themselves be sent to the fringes to help prevent the buying or selling of anything on the Sabbath, an act so heavily proscribed as to rival the ingestion of spirits as a sin. The general enthusiasm continued even after the big Sunday congregation, and the YMCA tent garnered many converts on Monday and Tuesday. A tradition which was to continue for several years was established on the closing day's evening—the YMCA evening sermon stretched out into a continuous exhortation, a kind of Christian filibuster, that went on all night. "There was but little sleep on the ground" that night, according to the *Sentinel.* Many a tired camper packed up for town the next morning with a ringing in his ears.

The first camp closed that Wednesday morning leaving a large cleared space that looked empty yet was filled with rich memories, new traditions, and a firm base for the new community. The physical legacy was the clearings and paths, the wells with their pumps removed and covers in place, a few enclosed buildings for storage and next year's concessions, platforms for large tents and speakers, and a simple railroad depot sitting where Railroad Street and Grove Road now meet. On a more spiritual level there were the one hundred converts created by the camp, the memories of the ordeal of the rain and the joy of the nearly two hundred and fifty tenters, the enormous gratitude of the organizers for the success of their venture, and, especially considering the 141 new shares pledged during the course of the meeting, the bright hopes of the leaders who would go on to build an enduring summer community as well.

The original form of stock certificate.

THE ASSOCIATION

PROFILES I: BACKGROUND

A community like Washington Grove does not exist in a vacuum. Its life can be recorded as a series of events caused by direct stimulation, but this would be an incomplete record for it would ignore the larger social forces that shape all human endeavor in any age. The Grove began at a specific point in time in 1873, but it was a product of its entire environment up to that moment, and its survival as an Association for the next 64 years would continue to be influenced by the waxing and waning political, social, technological, and economic forces to which it found itself subjected.

Washington, D.C. was heavily Republican in the 1870's and, though its citizens had no vote in national elections, they were at the epicenter of the country's dominant Republican party. Abraham Lincoln had brought them the prize of the Presidency for the first time—they were to hold it for the next 24 years. (Andrew Johnson, Lincoln's second vice president and successor on his death in 1865, was in fact a Democrat. But he was never an elected President and while in office he headed a thoroughly Republican administration.) The Democratic party was the party of the South; the South had been defeated and the Democratic party divided. Like other protestant religions of the United States, the Methodist congregations were divided into Church North and Church South along political lines, with Republicans usually choosing the North and Democrats going with the South. Washington was a Northern Methodist city.

War hero Ulysses S. Grant was first elected president in 1868 after the political brawl of the Johnson years. He was re-elected in 1872 over Horace Greeley, the outspoken founder of the New York Tribune. Grant's presidency was involved with many important issues of the day, including the ongoing Indian wars in the west, a paper currency crisis, and negotiating a new treaty with England, but it was radical Reconstruction for which his administration is best remembered.

RECONSTRUCTION

Lincoln's view of Reconstruction was to get the rebellious states back into the Union as quickly as possible, and to allow their prewar governments to resume functioning as soon as 10 per cent of the electorate (white males) would sign a loyalty oath accepting the the inviolability of the Union and the abolition of slavery. Tennessee was accepted back into the Union in 1862, and both Arkansas and Louisiana had been re-admitted by the president before his death. Andrew Johnson continued this policy and in fact all of the rebellious states except Florida and Texas had met the requirements and been accepted before the end of 1865. Hardliners opposed this conciliatory approach and it quickly developed that the southern legislators intended to defy emancipation and return the blacks to a new form of slavery under a set of repressive laws called the Black Codes.

Fighting Johnson's policy, Republican legislators passed radical reconstruction laws. This led directly to three legislative accomplishments—incredible in light of what we know followed: the 14th amendment, the 15th amendment, and the civil rights act of 1875. Taken together these seemed to give blacks full equality under the law. In addition, the state governments which had been readmitted under Lincoln and Johnson were suspended, and most Southern whites were disfranchised pending proof of their loyalty. Federal troops were sent to maintain order in the state capitals, and to insure that blacks would be protected under the new laws. The actions taken on behalf of full freedom and equality for blacks were amazingly far-sighted for the time, but within a short time the radicalization created or gave momentum to a powerful backlash against black freedom. The object of Reconstruction, the re-building of Southern society, was lost forever in the turmoil. In 1873 the carpetbaggers and scalawags were at the peak of their power, the Grant administration was rocked with scandal, the railroads were running on borrowed money and the economy on borrowed time. Full freedom and equality for black Americans had been written into the lawbooks, but it was not to be exercised in the land. Radical reconstruction was a bold experiment, but its legacy was to lead to the legal segregation of blacks in America.

SEGREGATION

The Civil War ended slavery in this country, but its successor was the post-war phenomenon of segregation. It took a long time to perfect the odious web of law and custom that segregation was to become. The first Methodist churches were fully integrated, but in time they began to take on a political aspect. In 1784 the church denounced slavery but declined to enforce the doctrine. Afterward, they backed away from the question: abolitionists failed in several attempts to get the church to take even a mild anti-slavery position, even after the war had begun. In 1873 the church openly supported Grant's reconstruction but did not actively seek a reunification with its southern counterpart. The church seemed to hope that blacks would achieve equality, but were not active in promoting the concept from within the congregations.

Maryland was to have an altogether different role in the promotion of segregation. As a slave state sharing all the evils of the institution, Maryland nevertheless had different demographics and therefore a different history. Slave importation was prohibited in 1783. Free blacks had voted in many states, but lost that right in Maryland in 1810. Before the Civil War, Maryland had the largest free black population; in 1830 there were 291,000 whites, 103,000 slave blacks, and 53,000 free blacks. All slaves were freed in Maryland by act of the 1864 legislature, but the state failed to ratify the 15th amendment for universal (male) suffrage. And it was in Maryland that a high court decided that the 14th amendment (which provided for equal protection under the law) applied only to Federal law: this took all the teeth out of the law and led inexorably to the era of Jim Crow.

In 1860 Montgomery County had a population of about 7000 blacks, 5421 of whom were slaves owned by 770 masters. A typical master held 9 or fewer slaves; twelve large farms in the County had 30 or 40 slaves each. In November of 1864 with no homes, few possessions, and no food put up for the winter the nearly 5000 remaining slaves—men, women, and children— were told that they were free to go. Most migrated to the free black settlements which existed at odd corners of the county—Tobytown, Laytonsville,

Scotland, Martin's Lane, and Beantown were among the dozens of communities which were established or embellished by this exodus.

The Methodists had always had sizable black congregations and at first they were integrated with the whites. Their unique outreach programs knew no color barrier, and blacks participated to a degree in the governance of the church. Several county black communities were predominantly Methodist, among them Brooke Grove, Etchison, and Howard Chapel east of Damascus, Stewarttown on Goshen Road, and Emory Grove, near the mineral springs on the road from Gaithersburg to Laytonsville.

The form that such communities would take was an uncertainty to whites. Their primary purpose was to be home to blacks, free and newly-freed. It remained to be seen whether they would become wholly different from white communities—say like African villages transported and updated, with unique collectivist cultures—or whether they would mimic European institutions either by habit or in imitation of the formula that gave whites their apparent superiority.

These communities did grow, and even thrived for awhile, but in the end they were all stunted by the lack of real opportunity for blacks as a group and the fear and distrust of the surrounding population. In Montgomery County, in a state neither liberal enough to be northern nor courageous enough to be southern, the dominant and unabashedly Democratic *Sentinel* constantly kept the population in fear of Negro crime or revolt, reporting one-sidedly all the most bizarre incidents, real or rumored, of the Reconstruction era.

THE ASSOCIATION

EMORY GROVE

The land in Emory Grove was purchased by blacks in the years 1864 to 1870 from the comers of farms owned by Woodwards, Bowmans, Cookes, and Talbotts, and finally totaled over 300 acres. In 1871 there was a mission of the Washington Conference of Methodists there; a congregation was established and by 1874 the first church building built. Camp meetings were a popular method of gaining converts, black or white. The black Methodists began a camp meeting tradition at Emory Grove which endured almost 100 years, and long outlasted the Washington Grove Association.

Emory Grove was small and insular until the coming of the railroad. Though "free and equal" by law, Emory Grove would never rival Gaithersburg or Laytonsville on economic or political grounds, but when the railroad came at least it opened the community to Washingtonians, providing access to Emory Grove as one of the few suburban retreats of that time available to blacks. The existence of the new Washington Grove summer community and the conversion of Gaithersburg from a sleepy crossroads to a central agricultural depot expanded opportunities for outside income to Emory Grove's fulltime residents whose main occupation had theretofore been a combination of subsistence farming and day labor.

A black public school system was inaugurated in 1872 in the county—the white system dated from 1860. Soon an elementary school was built in Emory Grove and named the Washington Grove School, apparently after the nearest railroad stop. With these institutions in place—home ownership, church affiliation, and a school

PROFILES I

building with teacher—Emory Grove did thrive and might have survived as a community forever. But urban renewal erased most of its heritage and its history is all underground. Now it is only a name on a map, a suburb of the city of Gaithersburg.

\

GAITHERSBURG

Gaithersburg was much more likely to survive for a long time. At the beginning it was a crossroads like Cracklintown, Goshen, Offutt's Crossroads and Redland. Cracklintown became Laytonsville, Goshen disappeared, Offutt's is now Potomac Village, and Redland is still a crossroads. Originally Gaithersburg was called Logtown, but by a turn of fate it was included as a stop on the Metropolitan Branch of the B&O, and bigger things were in store for it. William Gaither was the first resident, and the name Gaithersburg had become affixed before the civil war. But the name Forest Oak was preferred by certain influential people, and for a time the post office address was officially Forest Oak. When the railroad came through it chose the founder's name for its depot, and Forest Oak was dropped.

Gaithersburg, though not yet a chartered town, became commercially aggressive with the opening of the railroad. In a short time several entrepreneurs established agriculture-related businesses along the tracks. Soon three freight stations were located within Gaithersburg's present city limits. Earlier in the century tobacco was the cash crop and com whiskey the trading commodity, having a value of one shilling to the gallon in much the same way tobacco had been valued at a penny a pound. But now tobacco was less valuable, and

Gaithersburg area farmers had added wheat as a crop.

The population of Gaithersburg grew rapidly from 170 in 1860 to 313 in 1870—the 1870 census lists 64 free blacks in the city. Guano, advertised as genuine Peruvian, came north on the trains to be used as fertilizer for the com, wheat, and tobacco to be grown and shipped south to the consumer. The train was a bright hope for Gaithersburg, if urbanization was in fact a desirable end. The last rail of the single set of tracks was laid in Gaithersburg in February, 1873. A second track was intended to be laid out to Gaithersburg, and two major embellishments were planned which if completed would thrust Gaithersburg into urbanity far earlier that its boom of the 1970's.

The first of these improvements was a wye: locomotives in those days drove only in one direction— if a locomotive were to haul a train only to Gaithersburg or thereabouts it would still have to go on further to a turntable or, worse yet, to the end of the line. A wye was a great Y-shaped piece of track grafted with its top against a straight section of mainline track onto which an engine would pull forward then back up after a switch was thrown to face the opposite direction. The coming of a wye to Gaithersburg was a signal that it was strategically important as an outer terminus for certain kinds of traffic.

The other big event planned was the construction of a branch railroad from the B&O line at Laurel over to Gaithersburg, to serve as a sort of outer beltway for the county. It would establish Gaithersburg as a railroad center, and make it the preeminent commercial crossroads in the county. But events later in the year eliminated this plan forever, denying Gaithersburg's emergence as a hub, but preserving it for the role of corridor city it was to take on a century later.

Technology

Railroading was high technology in 1873. The gravel roadbeds and oak or chestnut crossties, and even the steel rails (before 1856 they had been made of weak and fast-wearing iron) were not such technical wonders, but consider the engines: massive steam furnaces on wheels, with boilers that could reach 200 pounds of pressure, driving fine-machined pistons connected directly to steel trucks holding six to ten large forged wheels. All the brass dials and gauges with high-pressure fittings, the controls for steam pressure, waterflow, and firebox draft, and the intricate lubricating system—even the steam whistle itself—were technological developments of only a few years before, yet taken together they were by far the most complex transportation system yet developed by man.

Other modes of transportation were contemplated in the technological rush of the 1870's, too. A rigid- frame airship had been demonstrated in 1852. Hot air balloons were used extensively for reconnaissance in the Civil War. There were experimental automobiles in the 1870's and the first experimental flying machines were only 20 years away. Intra-city public transportation was still exclusively by horse-drawn trolley or cab (in many cities the system was better known for the intensity of competition than for the quality of service rendered), but it would be only a decade until the electric trolley would be inaugurated in Washington, D.C. Even the bicycle— a novelty in the 1840's—was brought to nearly its present state of sophistication by 1884 with the invention of the pneumatic tire.

In the science of substances, chloroform and ether had been developed as anesthetics, and dynamite and nitroglycerine as explosives. DDT came in 1874, but treatment for diphtheria and tuberculosis would have to wait until the 1890's—and penicillin didn't come along until 1929. Radioactivity was discovered in 1896, and radiation sickness the following year. Cyanide was isolated in 1905.

Communications and media were in a mighty state of change. Photography was invented in 1826, and both metal-plate and glass-plate technologies were perfected during the Civil War, though paper prints were unavailable until the close of the century. The telegraph was in broad use in the 1830's, and the long anticipated telephone was on the verge of becoming a reality. The microphone led to the practical disc phonograph in 1877, as the invention of celluloid in 1870 led to the invention of the moving picture machine in the 1890's. Electricity was known to be useful for motive power by this time, but the real push for electric distribution systems came with Edison's electric lamp in 1879. The discovery of electro-magnetic waves in 1888 would lead eventually to radio and television.

Life in 1873 was neither primitive nor technology-dependent. Items that might be found in a typical Washington household include fruits and vegetables put up in Mason jars (invented by J. Mason!), a sewing machine in the spare room, linoleum on the kitchen floor, a player piano in the parlor, and a lawnmower in the cellar. Not to be found anywhere were a fountain pen, rayon stockings, a safety razor, or a zipper. Some Washingtonians might have an icemaker, a luxury not available to those away at camp.

THE FINANCIAL CLIMATE

All this furious inventing and manufacturing took money for development and working capital. The second half of the nineteenth century was a time of great capital expansion that followed a period of broad swings in the economy; a crippling recession in the mid '50's, paper currency printed in quantity to finance the Civil War, and a brief collapse in 1869 when the gold market was cornered for a short time. Enormous sums were tied up in railroad construction, while at the same time railroad competition was so keen that very little freight moved without some form of cartel or kickback scheme—even the Washington Grove Association had negotiated a rebate on excursion tickets. When 1873 brought the Grove's first summer of camp, there was financial trouble in the air—trouble that would not keep. On September 20th the failure of a major investment banking firm in New York triggered a financial panic and a series of explosive failures that sent the economy into a meltdown. When the smoke cleared the nation's financial system was paralyzed from the pocketbook down. Less than a month after its successful opening season and four months after the first passenger train chugged past its grounds the Washington Grove Association and the railroad that had brought it there were looking forward into a business depression that would bring such organizations to consider their very survival.

THE ASSOCIATION

3

Building Traditions

THE FIRST CAMP CLOSED ON a sunny day almost too bright for the sleepless eyes of its all- night revivalists, but the sun was nonetheless welcome among those for whom a week of rain was too recent a memory. There was sunshine for the founders, too. A flawless first camp meant a larger and better second camp and more enthusiasm for stock in the corporation. The 141 shares pledged at camp brought the total spoken for to over 500, equivalent to a capital base of $10,000, and half the total shares available.

A meeting was held at Metropolitan Church on Tuesday evening the 16th of September 1873, to review the first camp meeting and make an initial plan for the second. Many of the preachers who had organized the camp and several of the incorporators were there, including E.F.Simpson with his stockholder record book. Some of the original shareholders purchased additional shares at the meeting, and seven new names were added for a total of 33 new shares subscribed that evening.

The following Thursday America's economic bubble burst. The New York office of Jay Cooke and Company, a highly respected financier to railroad and industrial interests, announced its insolvency and closed its doors. The fall of this prominent house began a panic and led to a deep depression that featured bank and business failures, unemployment, strikes, and labor violence barely matched by the Great Depression of the 1930's. Investment capital vanished, and with it personal wealth diminished for everyone from the shrewdest railroad tycoon, to the out-of-work steamfitter, to the dirt farmer whose produce prices fell by more than half. Washington's Territorial Governor Cooke, a tycoon who had channeled family money into the city's commercial development on a grand scale, came to a great fall.

Although the trains kept running into and out of Washington even without Cooke money, and the impact of the depression on the railroad was cushioned by the growing federal government, nevertheless service was reduced and improvements held off. The Metropolitan branch still had only a single track for its whole length, which made back and forth scheduling difficult and dangerous. The planned second track was postponed indefinitely, and the station-houses promised for all the stops in Montgomery County, including Washington Grove's, were also postponed.

Washingtonians, rich and poor alike, husbanded their money in the fall and winter of 1873-74 against the financial uncertainty that lay in the wake of the stock market crash. Many pledges for shares in the Washington Grove Association went unredeemed, and others failed to meet the second or third installment and forfeited the money they had already paid in. Some stockholders even sold their shares, usually to existing shareholders and undoubtedly at a discount, creating a secondary market that competed with the Association's

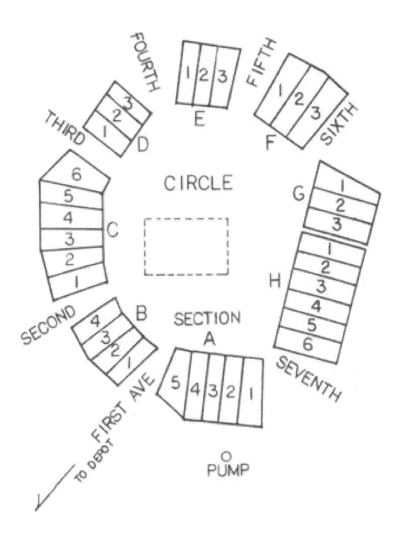

The first numbering system for Circle-area tent lots was established in the mid-1870's before the first cottage was built. But it would be revised several times before the turn of the century.

shares. But those who remained stockholders— roughly four-fifths—were enthusiastic about the coming prospect of a second camp meeting, and about getting a start on the summer community. The Maryland General Assembly approved the Association's charter application in its session of 1874, and the Board of Trustees and its several committees held numerous meetings to decide which features of the first camp should be retained, which should be redesigned, and which should be eliminated.

Almost every feature of the first camp was retained or enhanced, but a big exception was the layout of tent sites and streets, which were so radically altered that few campers could identify the sites they had occupied the year before. The biggest difference was that the square had become a Circle (or really more of an irregular heptagon). The only tent sites kept from the original plan were a row of eight sites along the east side of the Plaza behind the speaker's platform, and a row of five sites along the south side. A new pattern of avenues led out radially from the circle. The original main path from the depot received the name 1st Avenue from the circle to the edge of camp, and five new avenues, 2nd through 6th, were named clockwise from 1st Avenue; all along roughly the alignment they have to this day.

The tent sites clustered immediately around the perimeter of the circle were laid out in Sections designated A through H, with three to eight numbered sites in each. Sites on the avenues beginning behind the Sections on the circle were laid out in blocks and numbered in ascending order from the circle, alternately with odd numbers on one side and even numbers on the other. There were also sites on the east side of

Broadway, a wide avenue aligned along the "old county road," and now called upper Grove Avenue. There were also a Preacher's Court, Annapolis Court, and a 7th Avenue, whose exact locations history has temporarily misplaced, but 7th Avenue was probably aligned with what was later platted as Frankland Street running due east from the gap at the lower east side of the circle. Milliken's dining tent, said to be near 7th Avenue, was located in that area.

The facilities were similar to those of the first camp, though surely much improved after a year's reflection on their utility. At the depot (an open shelter, nothing more, for the promised station-house was a victim of the hard times), the Adams Express Company was set up to receive the campers' goods. At the left of the entrance to camp, roughly at today's Center Street and 1st Avenue, was a market house for perishables, and beyond it were stands for straw and furniture, a carpenter's stand, the two dining tents run by Milliken and Baker, a barber shop, a confectioner, a bedstead rental, and (let the rain fall!) two enormous meeting tents 24 by 40 feet each. The horse pen at the northeast comer of camp was operated by Mr. Suter, whose farm lay just south of the tracks.

The meeting itself was unexpectedly successful in view of the poor economic climate. The cost of camping had gone up slightly from 1873; a ground rent of one to two dollars was charged to non-stockholders for the first time, and the cost of renting a tent ranged from $10 to $15, up from $9 the year before. Other expenses were collected by the Association for straw, boards (for flooring and bunks, cut to order by the carpenter), and cartage, and amounted to an average of around $16 for the two week period. Cots and mattresses were handled by Bates of Baltimore and Singer of Washington, respectively. Costs for the vendors were high, too: Milliken and Baker each paid $150 ground rent for their dining tents called boarding saloons (saloons in which food, not alcohol, was served), and the confectioner, who provided such luxuries as candy, gum, ice cream and sodas, paid $300 for the period. For some reason, the barber's ground rent was a paltry sixteen dollars and 34 cents. But higher costs were not enough to discourage the zealous campers, who returned in great numbers, both stockholders and not. Among the returnees were most of the ordained ministers including Reverend Burris, Reverend Cleveland, and Dr. Wilson, several if not most of the lay preachers, the original trustees W.R.Woodward and Dr. Howard, and a corps of regulars who would go on to build the first cottages on and near the Circle.

It had been decided to hold a full two-week camp with the first few days reserved for getting settled-in and preparing for the heavy schedule of activities of the big first weekend. Camp began in earnest on Wednesday, August 5. The *Sentinel* reported that the grounds were "elegantly laid off, and the large number of tents looks like an encampment not of soldiers with glittering bayonets and grim sentinels...yet it is an army engaged in a far different warfare...against vice, immorality, and crime...and the leaders are messengers of the Prince of Peace." This was an unusually warm reception by the rabidly Democratic Rockville newspaper for an effort which, though religious in nature, was 98% Republican. This tone may be accounted for in part as an endorsement of the railroad. The *Sentinel* had been vociferous in promoting its construction before the fact and, once it began, vituperative in pursuit of its completion. The *Sentinel* hoped that the Railroad and the institutions which would grow up around it would establish Montgomery County as the flagship county of Western Maryland. The *Sentinel* article went on to support the idea that the Grove was, if not exactly a virgin forest, at least a "grand old woods."

Camp meetings were the primary purpose of the Grove's existence as described in its promotional literature and as spoken about in its public meetings. If an Association like this one could be called successful it would need no more credentials than the statistics of its second meeting, a meeting taking place in the worst of economic times. In addition to the tenters, which met or exceeded the number of the year before, there were the improvements in the form of a new layout of tent lots (a plan which has been altered only slightly to the present) and a new set of service buildings (some of which survived for fifty years but which are all gone now). To sell its stock the Association wanted to be perceived as successful, and a successful meeting at this worst of economic times would be just what it needed.

Success it got. The number of tenters exceeded that of the first year, but the incredible statistic claimed by the *Sentinel*, which would go on to be cited many times over during the camp meeting era, was the gathering of a crowd—a largely welcome crowd—of nearly 10,000 persons meeting, praying, singing, playing, eating, drinking, buying, and selling in the camp proper and just outside it in the area between the depot and the Circle, all concentrated in about a fifth of the present developed square footage of the Town. The press also reported favorably on the new layout of tent lots, and the set of new service buildings, some of which would survive

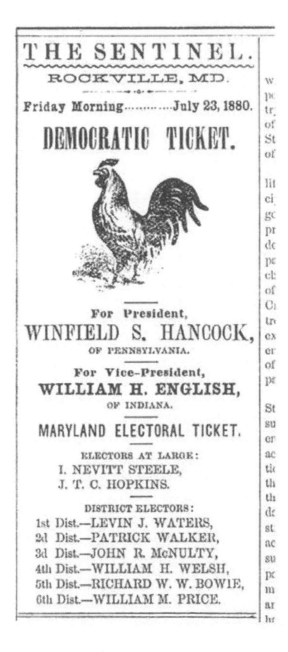

THE SENTINEL.
ROCKVILLE, MD.
Friday Morning............July 23, 1880.

DEMOCRATIC TICKET.

For President,
WINFIELD S. HANCOCK,
OF PENNSYLVANIA.

For Vice-President,
WILLIAM H. ENGLISH,
OF INDIANA.

MARYLAND ELECTORAL TICKET.

ELECTORS AT LARGE:
I. NEVITT STEELE,
J. T. C. HOPKINS.

DISTRICT ELECTORS:
1st Dist.—LEVIN J. WATERS,
2d Dist.—PATRICK WALKER,
3d Dist.—JOHN R. McNULTY,
4th Dist.—WILLIAM H. WELSH,
5th Dist.—RICHARD W. W. BOWIE,
6th Dist.—WILLIAM M. PRICE.

The *Sentinel* was a strident and powerful political voice in Montgomery County after the Civil War.

well past the camp meeting era.

It was a successful camp from the economic point of view—there were now sufficient shares bought and pledged to insure the present and future solvency of the corporation, from an attendance point of view—a steady 250 campers and up to 10,000 visitors, and from a religious point of view—over two hundred converts were garnered in the first two years. This combination would continue to be successful for many years to come but not, unfortunately, without some of the evils that accompany man in even his highest endeavors.

AN INTOLERANCE FOR INTEMPERANCE

In the first camp there had been only one incident of a serious nature that was reported in the press—a disorderly man "under the influence of rum," was arrested. In the second camp this particular evil had recurred, and it was reported that "two 'sports' from Washington, Clark and Smith" were arrested on the campgrounds for selling liquor. This crime was a significant threat to the perception of order that was essential to the existence of the camp meeting, and a cruel slap in the face of the Methodist organizers, for it was done on a Sunday, a violation of religious law as well. Drinking—and selling the liquor that was to be drunk—remained a problem for the camp for many years. The *Sentinel* was waxing philosophical about the closing of camp after the season of 1877, describing the empty avenues and the turning leaves, when it added that not until next year was a "

"manish youth to steal away far down the fence and look suspiciously around him as his hand grasps down around a post to bring forth the well-hidden bottle there."

Buying, selling, or consuming liquor was not seen as just a matter of breaking a charter rule of the Washington Grove Association, nor even simply a case of desecrating the Sabbath by doing other than the Lord's work on the Lord's day, but rather these acts by both sellers and consumers were in violation of one the more fundamental tenets of Methodism: abstinence from alcohol.

The position of the Church has its roots in the essence of Protestantism itself—the throwing off of the perceived evils of Roman Catholicism, one of which was the selling of Indulgences, but another of which was the over-use of alcohol which was common among the church hierarchy. Intoxication was inconsistent with the concept of fundamental piety that had inspired Wesley in England and driven Asbury in America that man should not indulge himself with wasteful and wanton things. And alcohol was growing from a mere self-indulgence to a social evil just at the time that Methodism was growing from an inspiration to a social force.

The art of distillation of spirits was developed in the Mediterranean basin, and spread into Europe during the middle ages. Northern Europeans embraced the habit in rapidly increasing numbers until by the 1740's drunkenness was perceived to be a pressing social problem, and many a promising young man and woman fell victim to ruin through its unchecked allure. In the second half of the 18th century the opposition was organized into the Temperance Movement with a proliferation of militant societies. The movement spread to the United States, first in New York and New England, though the consumption of alcohol was still light by England's standards. Early in the nineteenth century prohibition was adopted by the Methodists as a missionary goal.

A rapid increase in per capita consumption followed and in 1840 had reached over four gallons per year. Interest among Americans to do something about the problem broadened. In 1851 prohibitionist Neal Dow led a successful battle to get the first statewide ban on the manufacture, sale, and consumption of alcoholic beverages in Maine, and prohibition legislation came to be known as Maine Laws. Similar bills were introduced in many other states, but few were passed into law; in 1860 the per capita rate had risen to 6.4 gallons. The Civil War interrupted the progress of prohibitionist legislation, but did not slow down the increasing use of alcohol, so the struggle was taken up with renewed vigor shortly after the war ended. The Prohibition party was established in 1869 to identify and endorse prohibitionist candidates for elected office and to field its own candidates where no existing ones were satisfactory. The Methodists expanded their work against intemperance, too, but chose to work for "local option" legislation instead. It was hoped that in this way a town, city or whole county could vote itself dry through referendum.

At first these efforts were rebuffed, but the epidemic continued. In 1880, when the annual consumption rate hit 10.8 gallons for every man, woman, and child in the U.S., Maryland finally passed a local option law, and later that year Montgomery County subsequently voted itself dry, and it remained legally dry for another fifty years. The Methodist church was given the major share of the credit for getting the law passed, and in Montgomery County much of the organization and many of the rallies were held in the Grove.

Despite the proliferation of local option laws that followed, both local and national liquor consumption figures continued to soar, setting the stage for a bitter battle. At the end of the century the Women's Suffrage and Prohibition movements combined in the common cause of a national prohibition law, and twenty years later they got it.

SETTLING IN WITH THE LOCALS

A Methodist-backed "local option" law did become effective in Montgomery County at the end of the Grove's first decade, but this effort would not have been so successful if the Methodist camp meeting had not taken some trouble—perhaps more than it bargained for—to form a neighborly relationship with local people.

During the second season the Association had successfully reached out to county people for the camp itself-nearly 10% of the 1874 camp was from the areas of Montgomery County immediately surrounding it, and nearly another 10% was from a wider circle that included Annapolis and Frederick. And now its stockholder list included twelve names from the county, including Gaithersburg businessmen Ignatius T. Fulks and Henry C. Ward.

Some changes needed to be made, though, to deal with the problem of liquor. The '74 camp had no sooner wound up with its now-traditional all night revival than the planning began. A chief feature of the plan that emerged was the construction of a perimeter fence to enclose the grounds. When camp opened in August of 15 it was to the Grove's old friend rain, and to a sour review of the fence by the *Sentinel*: "Meeting began August 4th to bad weather. A drawback is the inaccessibility of the camp grounds to carriages...a post-and-rail fence erected around the grounds makes it difficult for those visiting for just a day or two who expect to use their carriages as a rendezvous." It did go on to say that the fence "makes the grounds excellent for promenading by persons from the city."

The weather cleared and camp went on as usual, the *Sentinel* reporting that on the first Sunday "several long trains of cars brought visitors from the District cities, Frederick and other points." There is no record of the number of campers, but several additional shares were sold, and it seemed that all was going well. Unfortunately this was not entirely the case. There had been some trouble on the grounds involving local boys and liquor. The incident was quickly over, but it incited a brawl among the print media.

The *Sentinel,* which had been generally supportive of the camp, was suddenly very negative. After the close of camp it reported: "The camp was in many respects a failure. Our people from the County manifested little or no interest in it during its progress." And, "An idea has gone forth, unfounded we hope, that the country people were not welcome to participate with their brethren from the city...on such terms of equality as they alone would accept."

The *National Republican,* a Washington newspaper of a similarly narrow but opposite viewpoint to that of the *Sentinel,* had reported that on the last days of camp "there was considerable rowdyism on the grounds and the roughs came from Rockville and Laytonsville." The sensitively Democratic *Sentinel* took this up as a political battle and retorted in a separate column that

"On Monday night last the religious experience meetings were prolonged into the late hours of the night," then quoted the *National Republican,* and went on to say, "We hurl this foul slander back in its teeth and are forced for the sake of the truth to say that the only disorder we perceived at the camp was perpetrated by Washington bullies."

Local pride, at least in the eyes of the *Sentinel*, was deeply wounded. The *Sentinel* reacted by boycotting the 1876 camp meeting entirely. There was no mention of the camp in the paper that year, before, during, or afterward, nor did they run the usual paid advertisement.

There was another potential conflict with the *Sentinel* and proponents of its viewpoint that year. If the *Sentinel* chose to react to it with silence, that was perhaps for the best in that indelicate time. Emory Grove, the community of black freedmen to the north of Washington Grove, was an active Methodist community with a camp meeting tradition of its own. It was part of the same Methodist Conference and was in harmonious purpose with Washington Grove. Its camps were scheduled to avoid conflicts with the Grove's; in 1875 they opened on July 29 and were finished in time for the Washington Grove camp to open on August 4. Things did not go so smoothly for Emory Grove in 1876.

Emory Grove held no camp at all in 1876; they had lost the right to use the campground that had been been the scene of the two earlier camps. Apparently there was a dispute with one of the adjacent landowners, and whether it was an economic or political problem is not recorded, but it seems to have involved a deed, lease, or other right-of-use that was called into question.

The *Christian Advocate,* the official newspaper of the Baltimore Conference of Methodists, listed the camp meetings to be held that summer as usual, with no listing for Emory Grove. Instead it noted, "May we not hope that at the approaching 'Washington Grove Camp Meeting', which takes place in August, the liberal men of Montgomery will restore to their African neighbors and friends a little sanctuary, which may long be an honor to that grand old county?" The Advocate may have been suggesting that the Grove offer its grounds to the Emory Grove camp. What specific response Washington Grove made to the difficulty in '76 or '77 is not known; but as blacks were free to come to camp during the day (as were all citizens) it is likely that in those years there was a sizable contingent of blacks at camp services.

The problem was still unresolved in 1879, and the Grove issued a specific invitation to the Emory Grove Association to come and worship, which the *Sentinel*, now on speaking terms again, reported without comment. Camp meetings were finally able to resume in Emory Grove in 1880. A large advertisement appeared in the *Sentinel* that July announcing the camp, without reference to color—the *Sentinel* made note of the ad in an editorial column, and made certain there was no doubt that it was to be a blacks' camp meeting.

IMPROVEMENTS

Irrespective of the smallish camps of the period (the worst three years of the depression were 1875-77) there was considerable activity among the core of dedicated campers and eager summer residents-to-be to establish a permanent settlement. A post-and-rail perimeter fence was added in 1875; in 1876 the fence had been remade into a continuous wall of chestnut boards. On opening

THE GREAT CAMP MEETING!

The Rockville Camp Meeting.

Of the Washington Annual Conference of the M. E. Church, Washington District, will begin in Mrs. Hamilton's Grove, this Montgomery county,

On Saturday, July 31st,

1880, and continue until Monday August 9th.

SPECIAL RATES

From all stations on the Metropolitan Branch of the B. & O. R. R., to and from Washington Grove Station.

This Grove is beautifully located one mile North of Washington Grove; it is well watered and shaded. Persons coming by way of the above named road will leave the cars at Washington Grove Station.

N. C. BROWN, Pastor,
jy23-2t   W. C. COOPER, P. E.

Advertisement for the Emory Grove camp meeting. Nothing was mentioned about race, but the editor made certain that his readers were aware that Emory Grove was a black community.

day August 10, 1877 there were 90 tents pitched (with more expected to be put up on the weekend) around a handsome new Tabernacle in the middle of the Circle.

As the Grove's first building for worship, the Tabernacle also brought a finishing touch to the Circle which, as a center for prayer, was like a cathedral under a crown of oaks in good weather but a sodden and abandoned ruin in foul. Though functionally it was like a tent-top made of wood perched on sticks above an open-air theatre, its sturdy proportions and rustic materials gave it more the feeling of an open-air church. It was a full seventy feet from its outermost west side benches to the enlarged speaker's platform on the east end, and forty-eight feet from north to south; it was said by the *Sentinel* to seat 500 persons. (A standard movie theatre seat today occupies less than five square feet, so this estimate is well within reason.) It was completely open along the sides with approximately 12' between posts of about 5 inches square.

The roofline sloped up from each of the four sides at a pitch of about 36 degrees from the long sides, and about 30 degrees from the short ends so that the four sections met at a point in the center. This roof design required fewer internal supports than a simple gable roof with ridgepole, yet it was still suitable for supporting the highly unpredictable snow load of Washington's winters.

Later a belfry was added at the peak into which the original camp meeting bell that "first hung from a tree" according to Page Milburn (and now hangs at McCathran Hall) was installed. The bell was used to call worshippers to prayer at camp meetings and was traditionally rung on the last evening after the benediction to signal the end of camp. The Tabernacle was quickly a revered fixture of Grove life, and was well attended-to in the off-seasons. In 1884 a wooden floor was added and then an enclosure of removable panels made for its protection during the winter months. In 1899 its deck was raised by about two feet and extensive repairs were made. But by this time it was inadequate for the crowds that were by then visiting the Grove not only for camp meeting but also for the Chautauqua-like activities which had begun to be a part of Grove life. In 1902 there was much debate about whether to enlarge the tabernacle and enclose it, to move it, or to build another building elsewhere on the grounds. In spite of a widespread desire to keep the Tabernacle, or at least to use its now-sacred posts and beams in a relocated building, and even though more repairs were made in 1904, it was replaced by a grand new Auditorium in Woodward Park in 1905. The old Tabernacle was unceremoniously hauled away by the contractor, its heavy posts and roof timbers to be recycled into some probably untraceable but possibly still-standing building in Gaithersburg or Laytonsville.

The charming cottages for which Washington Grove is now best known also came into existence during this period, having been planned from the start but delayed during the fiscal hard times. It is debatable which cottage was the first to be built in either the Tent Department (Circle area) or the Cottage Department (Grove Avenue), but only because two authorities of the period make conflicting statements about the subject, neither of which squares with other evidence. By examining contemporary plats and lists, and working backward to 1877 when there were no cottages, and relying on the July 19, 1878 report in the *Sentinel* that the "Reverend Mister Burroughs is erecting a handsome (implying that someone had seen it) cottage which will be finished by the commencement of camp," the author concludes that Rev. William Burris of Dumbarton Church, built the first cottage in 1878. Burris, who had bought his shares at the first camp and attended every camp from its inception, located his cottage on his tentsite, #2 in Section A, 50 feet from the southwest comer of the Tabernacle, in the grassy side yard of what is now 2 The Circle. [It is possible that 2 The Circle is the original Burris cottage.] His cottage was clearly considered by many to be a desirable improvement, and there were five or six others built by the end of the

The Tabernacle as seen from 3rd Avenue. The lamp in the foreground is probably a kerosene model. This may have been taken just after the turn of the century.

The Tabernacle and cottages on the east side of the Circle as seen from 1st Avenue in 1898.

season. The next year there were sixteen cottages arrayed around the Circle, and one built for Miss Kilgour out on Second Avenue. A year later there were at least fourteen more, extending down First Avenue on the left and right and spilling over onto 2nd, 5th, and 6th Avenues.

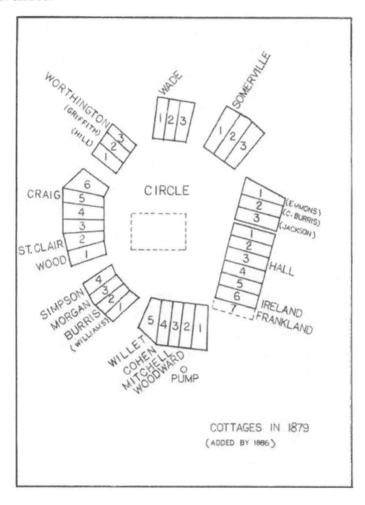

The original Circle cottages and their inhabitants in 1879. Cottages added by 1886 are shown with their owners' names in parentheses.

The Circle occupants were a Who's Who of the Association's officers and directors: President Thomas P. Morgan, Vice President W.R. Woodward, Secretary E. F. Simpson, Trustees R. H. Willet and J. T. Mitchell, Rev. Burris of the Executive Committee and S.Worthington and George Hall of the Committee on Grounds and Supplies. At any point in the summer one needed only stroll across the Circle to convene a meeting of most any committee. The committee rosters were so overlapping that it may have been difficult to remember at times just which committee was in session. The indefatigable E.F.Simpson seems to have acted as Secretary for most of them.

The Hotel as seen from Broadway (Grove Avenue) near McCathran Hall. The two trees with the pipe seat between them survive today with peculiar lumps where the pipe had been attached.

The cottages themselves were simple structures: wooden platforms on low pillars, exterior walls with just enough 2x3 or 2x4 studs to keep the exterior skin of wood panel together, with high-pitched gable roofs sometimes joining at a ridgepole and sometimes not (relying in the latter case on the roof sheathing to hold the roofline true), with occasional stringers high across the rafters to keep the roof from pushing the side walls out under a load of snow (though the steepness of the roof made this less a concern than in more conventional designs). The cottages were remarkably uniform, though they came with a choice of dimensions: 14x20, 14x25, 14x30, or as with the R.H.Willet cottage (still standing at 1 The Circle), 14x40.

The element of individuality was achieved by the selection of door and window styles, and the gingerbread trim, rather than by the shapes or exterior dimensions of the cottages. The Preacher's Lodge on 6th Avenue was a little grander than most, having "bedrooms, study, and washroom and will accommodate all the ministers" according to the *Sentinel.* The *Baltimore Methodist* of September 4, 1879 described the cottages as "very simple in architectural style and finish, and put up with reference to comfort and convenience, rather than show. They are all one story, only one of them having sleeping quarters above the first floor." This would have been a loft; while it is not known to which cottage the passage refers, the front half of 17 The Circle, now a house made up of two cottages, did at one time have a loft in it.

Wash B. Williams was the holder of a tent site on the Circle between 1st Avenue and the Burris cottage, but he never built on it. In an interesting maneuver, the full story of which may never be known, J.T.Mitchell took over the site (Section A, #1) in 1880 and moved his 14x20 foot cottage from its location about 150 feet away. What makes this intriguing is that his cottage had been moved from what had been the Rev. B. Peyton Brown's choice tent site, one of the few sites surviving the 1873 first camp layout. Apparently Brown thought that it was his site permanently, but a regrettable decision had been made in his absence to give it to Mitchell. Brown, whose return to the camp in 1879 was heralded by the *Baltimore Methodist,* which reported that he was "in constant attendance at all the devotional services," must have expressed some displeasure in finding a cottage where his tent belonged.

In 1880 the Mitchell cottage had moved and Brown was back in a tent on his original site. Later there would be a peculiarity with J.T.Mitchell's stock that would add to his discomfort, but the concept he pioneered of moving a cottage from one place to another took hold and eventually became almost a sport in Washington Grove—a great adventure, one suspects, for those contracted to do the moving, and a game for the summer residents who could only guess what cottage would be where when the next season rolled around.

Wash B. Williams, who had been displaced by Mitchell's movable lodging on the circle, was a prosperous furniture merchant from Washington who had proudly provided White House furniture for President Hayes. His main business was in the city at 7th and D streets NW but he had rented and sold inexpensive camp furniture from a building along 1st Avenue in the Grove since the first camp. In the waning years of the depression he made his own ambitious improvements at the Grove. His original furniture stand on the path from the depot had been steadily improved but by 1878 was inadequate for the level of business he was doing. In the official announcement for the camp of '78 the Presiding Elder noted that "Wash B. Williams has built a new wareroom with lodging rooms attached and a barber shop." The *Sentinel* reported on the first week of camp that "attendance was estimated at 5000 on Sunday" and that "The first floor [of William's store] is used as a post-office and furniture store, and the second story is carpeted."

Williams continued to rent rooms above his store until the demand far outstripped the supply. Inspired by his success, the trustees commissioned him in 1880 to build a hotel building to be placed in the area west of Broadway where the Woman's Club now stands, and he was franchised to operate it for the summer season of 1881. The old furniture store, which sat in what came to be known as the Triangle—the ground between 1st Avenue and Grove Avenue that slowly narrows to a point at Center Street—was not dismantled, but began another of its several incarnations, this time as the Young People's Hall. In 1881 *the Baltimore Methodist* reported that "the new hotel has all its rooms engaged." Williams had designed the building and supervised its construction, but it was owned by the Association and leased back by Williams.

In 1883 he bid low and lost the franchise—the building was rented instead to a Mr. Noyes, who kept it for two years. Williams, not previously a stockholder, petitioned to purchase 5 shares of stock in May of 83, apparently in the hope of retaining the hotel lease, but the Williams entry in the stock book is marked 'cancelled', and his name never appears on a list of stockholders. By 1884, it was reported, the Annual

Meeting of stockholders was held "in the Dining Room of the Hotel," an annex that had been built over the previous winter to "feed the multitudes". The minutes also state that it had by then separate privies and a cesspool; the cesspool was probably across the street where the Washington Grove United Methodist Church now stands. The hotel building went on to be called the Albany Hotel and was at one time listed among the finest resort hotels of Maryland.

No sooner did the first cottages appear on the Circle than holders of five shares or more of stock began to think of building more substantial summer residences in the Cottage Department, which at that time consisted entirely of the lower half of Grove Avenue. A subdivision plat was filed in Rockville showing 40 lots, 20 on a side. On the left side, walking north from the depot, was a gap (where lot 30 should have been) for a cross avenue exactly halfway to what would become Center Street. On the right side there was no gap. The Avenue was 50 feet wide, the lots 50' wide by 150' deep. But the plat was a mere legalization of what was already established—in 1881, Dr. Lanahan of Foundry Church, Peyton Brown's mentor and his successor as pastor of Foundry, was already "building a $1000 cottage" on lot 23, now 202 Grove Avenue.

But there is some uncertainty about whether Lanahan's was the first cottage on Grove Avenue. Page Milburn reports that "the first cottage to be built in the Cottage Department was the 'Pioneer' erected by the Rev. William Burris" at 124 Grove Avenue—if so, it was built during 1881, for it was not present in 1880 and, also if so, it would mean that Rev. Burris was the first to build in each Department. Milburn lists the Wadsworth house at 112 Grove Avenue as being the

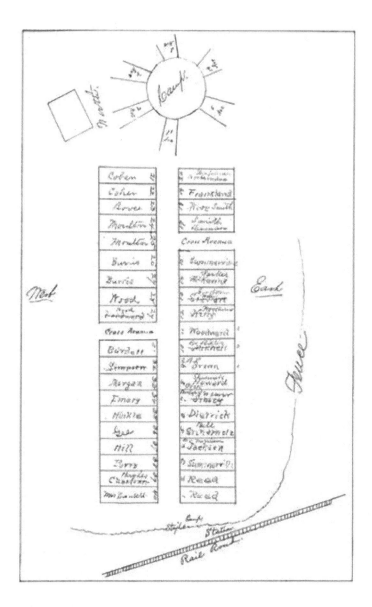

Plat of Grove Avenue showing site owners in 1886, with names later changed to show the 1893 owners. By the end of 1886 there were ten large cottages completed.

second large cottage, but in fact there was no cottage there as late as 1886.

It may be instead that Major Thomas P. Morgan's 14x30 cottage was later moved from its origins on lot 3 of Section A on the Circle to the Wadsworth plot on Grove Avenue, in which case the house would indeed have been constructed before Lanahan's and Burris's (Cottage Dept) cottages, but would not predate their location on Grove Avenue. In 1893 Morgan is shown as owning and occupying 114 Grove Avenue. But while we cannot be absolutely certain about which was the first large cottage, an E.F.Simpson document definitely lists Lanahan's, Burris's, and two others—W.J.Sibley's and H.A.Singer's—as being the first four on Grove Avenue. Three of these are still standing—at 113, 124, and 206 Grove Avenue—the fourth occupied 202 Grove until it was dismantled in 1939 or 40.

By 1885 the annual meeting minutes listed eight large cottages; the Lang survey a year later showed 10 built, and another planned. On the left side coming from the depot there were none until after the cross avenue, then J.W.Wade's on lot 28 (122 Grove), Rev. Burris's on lot 27 (124 Grove), a shed or outline of Robert Cohen's (never completed) on lot 25, now a part of Oak Street, Dr. Lanahan's on lot 23 (202 Grove), and H.A. Singer's (to become Rob Cohen's) on lot 21 (206 Grove). The right side was more popular, perhaps because a well-worn service road already existed behind it. From the depot the first cottage was Reed's on lot 2 (103 Grove), then Dietrick's on lot 6 (111 Grove), and Dr. Sibley's on lot 7 (113 Grove), then a gap to W.R.Woodward's on lot 11 across from the cross avenue (119 Grove), then a gap to J.W.Somerville's on lot 15 (127 Grove). Lot 16 was reserved for another cross avenue (Oak Street), followed by the Bearman cottage on lot 17 (201 Grove). There were no others until Grove divided at First and Broadway; beyond the pump at 1st Avenue the smaller cottages reached out from the Circle.

The Grove began its ascent out of the depression of the 1870's by building a Tabernacle on the Circle in 1877 and went on a building spree that eight years later could boast eight large cottages, 60 small cottages, a Hotel and Preacher's Lodge—all with a combined net worth of $43,720—by 1885. The transition from tent city to summer colony would leave some people behind—most notably Dr. Flodoardo Howard who was then in his 70's and ailing—but many of the people, some of the structures, and most of the traditions that were to figure heavily in the turbulent decades ahead were firmly in place in the early 80's. Contention and enthusiasm competed for attention in this dynamic period—and the sprouts of the controversy that was to dog the Association to its death in the 1930's were clearly evident by the time the first whitewash had dried on the Lanahan cottage.

4

Confronting Reality

THE DEPRESSION OF 1873 was left behind as the Grove entered a building boom that sustained itself for many years. Each new season's improvements reinforced the idea that the Grove was headed for prosperous maturity, when all the cottage sites would be sold and built upon, and the high point of each season would be a large and lively—but well- disciplined—camp meeting.

Of course neither lives nor institutions sail as smoothly or predictably through the course of time as we would have them do. External forces work against such orderly passage in both subtle and cataclysmic ways—great events can shove us roughly out of our channel, while currents of fashion, manners, and mores push and nudge at us in more subtle and clever ways. A fragile craft is more vulnerable to shifting forces the longer it sails; if it must be constantly repaired and rebuilt it can change from its original design; if it survives to get where it is going at all, it may have become something different by the time it arrives.

As the summer community aspect of the Grove's existence grew, and the cottages began to be occupied earlier and longer, the stockholders and residents began to confront issues they had not anticipated. Meetings of the Board of Trustees and their supporting committees, (especially the Committee on Grounds and Supplies) became longer and more frequent. Uniformity of opinion on the new issues was not assured, either. The Annual Meeting of Stockholders became more serious as the installations in the Grove became more valuable—some stockholders began to think of the capital stock as a right of ownership or a certificate of investment, rather than as a contribution to a worthwhile cause. At the root of all this was the success and vitality of the venture itself. The Grove had become an active and social summer community.

Time had healed the injured pride of those few county people who had been offended in the fight between the city newspaper and the county newspaper in 1875—even the *Sentinel* was satisfied and able to report in 1878 that the best of order was maintained "and the present management must make Washington Grove the most attractive camp in the country. We notice also that now our county people are treated with proper courtesy which is a great improvement over the rudeness and even insults of former years."

Campers were coming out earlier in the summer, even before any permanent cottages had been built. The *Sentinel* reported in July of 1878 that "many from Washington are at present quartered on the grounds and propose staying until camp breaks." In early August of 1880 it reported that 29 families were present well ahead of the opening of camp. And in July of '81 "there were over 250 people on the grounds" two weeks before camp; among them was Dr. Lanahan, who preached on Sunday the 29th. Sunday School services were also held. The *Sentinel* attempted to capture the tone of those weeks before camp meeting opened: "The discipline of Meeting is not yet in force, and though there are religious services at stated intervals the campers are now a sort of merry pic-nic party." The same author noted: "A good many people are on the grounds already—the grove being a most delightful summer retreat."

Call it a picnic or a delightful retreat, certainly the Grove was a lively place during those post-depression years. During the camp meeting weekends the Sunday crowds were breaking the attendance records established by the early camps: in 1879 there were 8000 on one Sunday, and in 1880, another new record high. Of course if the weather were bad attendance could drop to below a thousand—in 1882 there were 12,000 on one Sunday and only 1000 the next. The camp of 1883 brought 16,000 visitors for the two Sundays combined. The *Sentinel* characterized the crowds as being made up of "all nationalities and grades, all classes and all creeds fully and largely represented. Some went for pleasure, some for show, some from curiosity, and many to enjoy the religious exercises of the day."

Grove activities were not confined to the religious service of camp. In August of '79 there was a large wedding, "all parties from Boyds." In the fall of 1881 the Grove was a refuge for victims of typhoid under the care of Rockville's Dr. Stonestreet. In spite of competition from the new Summit Hotel in Gaithersburg, Wash Williams' hotel was booked full every weekend of the summer. On June 24, 1881, the *Sentinel* noted that on "last Friday evening the guests of the Washington Grove Hotel and their friends enjoyed a most delightful evening's entertainment consisting of recitations, music, and reading." Later that summer there was another entertainment "of music, reading, etc" by Washington talent, "mostly guests of the hotel. The interior of the building was handsomely decorated."

On a sad note, what is most likely the Grove's first death was reported in July of '82 when Erasmus H. Weaver, the infant son of Lt. and Mrs. E.H.Weaver, died suddenly in the night at eight months of age. Tragedy came again the next summer, this time to ebullient hotelier Wash B. Williams, who had moved on to manage the Summit Hotel in Gaithersburg. His son Robert was struck with "paralysis" and died at the Summit Hotel in midseason.

The Grove was a desirable spot for meetings of the larger community of Christians, too. Many prohibition meetings and rallies were held at the Grove both during and out of the camp season. In 1884 the Grove was host to a massive celebration of the centennial of the Christmas Conference—the 1784 meeting in Baltimore that launched the Methodist church of America.

Liquor traffic continued on the periphery of the Grove but at great risk to the sellers: in 1879 Rezin Offutt was arrested for the crime on the first Wednesday of camp, and "Charles Mobley, white, and Patrick Warren, colored" were arrested and held on $600 bail the following Sunday. As noted previously, selling liquor on Sundays at camp was considered a heinous offense. But selling anything on Sunday was considered Sabbath-breaking and not to be taken lightly. Consider the case of Mr. C.W. Thompson who was caught in 1880 selling goods in the Grove on a Sunday—he was arrested under a 1725 law against violating the Sabbath and fined 200 pounds of tobacco, which had been legal tender at the time the law was enacted. The very next

Tuesday the entire community was shocked when Officer Miller, the Association's hired policeman, arrested a Mr. Seitz, the man who had leased and was operating the official camp store, on reports that he had sold cigars and other articles on Sunday. His defense was that the committee (presumably the Committee on Grounds and Supplies, and not the Committee on Religious Services) had given him permission. While we will never know whether it had in fact, or to whom the cigars were sold (a member of the Committee?) we do know that the charges were eventually dropped.

To what degree the Sabbath must be kept holy has been a subject of controversy since before the Old Testament was reduced to writing and will continue to be for some time to come. The argument flares up among those with secular aims as a question of whether, and among those with religious aims as a question of how much; that Mr. Seitz was able to get away with selling cigars on Sunday (once) indicates at least some degree of debatability on the subject even at camp meetings. But a much larger issue of Sabbath-breaking was to confront the Association and force it to take a hard look at its own identity—was the Grove a religious encampment or a summer retreat?

THE REBATE CONTROVERSY

The issue was one that was faced by several of the camp meeting organizations in the eastern United States—all of them, in fact, which were accessible by train: If a person were to drive to camp meeting on Sunday in the family buggy, he would not break the Sabbath, nor would he if he bought a ticket on a regularly scheduled train. But if he were to buy a ticket on an excursion train serving only the camp meeting, the railroad would be profiteering and therefore breaking the Sabbath. For the Grove this was no small problem since most of the thousands who came to camp each Sunday came by train. The issue first surfaced at the Methodists' Annual Conference in Baltimore in 1879. While condemning the practice of running excursion trains, the Conference was not ready to blame the camp meeting itself:

"The question of Sabbath desecration [by the railroad] at camp-meetings has been very generally discussed by the preachers and people, but no satisfactory remedy for the evils has yet been suggested. The Camp Meeting Committee cannot stop the running of trains on the Lord's Day any more than they can stop the people from all parts of the country from attending in such modes of conveyance as they can command. They have not the means to enclose the grounds and its an open question whether they ought to do it if they had the means."

The Association was represented at the meeting by Dr. Lanahan and Reverend Brown. Dr. Lanahan argued that the Grove Association was doing its best in the matter:

"We at Washington Grove have made an earnest effort to ... outwork the devil ... by bringing our many talented lay workers, and sending them among the crowds on the outskirts of the camp, to preach the gospel, and persuade sinners to repent."

The following year the matter was again a topic at the Annual Conference. Baltimore's Emory Grove Camp Meeting (not the Montgomery County Emory Grove) announced that it would remain closed during the 1880 season, ostensibly in protest of the B&O's excursion trains. Actually, it may be that the gesture of closing "in protest" was a bit opportunistic, as the Emory Grove Association was also declared bankrupt that year, as a result of "severe financial mismanagement." In March of 1882 the excursion issue was still unresolved, but a larger problem had been placed, politely but firmly, on the table of the Conference—it seemed that not only was the B&O making money on Sunday excursion trains to the Grove, but it was passing back a rebate to the Washington Grove Association on each ticket sold!

It had been easy to argue that the camps could not regulate the means by which their visitors arrived, and even that they should not try to do so, since more visitors meant more opportunities for conversions. But when it was discovered that the Association received a rebate on each ticket to the Washington Grove station the debate heated up considerably and the formerly general discussion began to focus on the Grove. After the report of the Committee on Sabbath Observance was read there was "considerable discussion" in which the Reverends Lanahan and Brown participated. The tone of the meeting can be inferred from the fact that at one point Dr. Lanahan called for a point of order to put on the record that they were talking about all camp meetings, not just the Grove's. The point was sustained, but the outcome of that meeting was an "unqualified condemnation of all Camp Meeting Associations which agree to receive rebates from railroad Sunday travel."

The following week the discussion continued. Rev. Brown argued that running the trains was not Sabbath breaking because the extra cars were only sections of a regularly scheduled train through the Grove. Brown lost the argument—and a bit of dignity as well—when it was revealed that on at least one occasion there were three separate excursion trains each with its own locomotive and a "well-filled train of cars" that arrived after the regular train had left. Feeling was so strong that many believed that camp should be abandoned until the situation could be definitively corrected. In a final argument at the next week's session Brown insisted that the Association had done its best; he also revealed that in a meeting with the B&O in 1873 that pre-dated even the first sale of stock, he had negotiated the rebate and made a contract that no excursion trains would be run on Sunday except by Association request. The Conference ended with the Association still refusing to relinquish the rebate; at 15 cents per ticket, the rebate yielded as much as $700 a year.

The controversy would not rest, however. The Annual Conference met just once a year, but the Preacher's Meeting was a monthly forum that went on meeting all year long. The Preacher's Meeting took up the issue and urged the Association not to hold the 1882 camp. It went on to demand that the Grove's campground be enclosed to discourage the fringe crowds. The Association declined to discontinue camp for the season, but did agree to take up the matter at its annual stockholders meeting the next May. The preachers were incensed that the issue would have to wait a year to be resolved, if then, but they did not have the power to stop the Association.

In fact, the matter was not taken up by the annual meeting at all, but apparently was kept in the hands of the Board of Trustees. During the year they voted to enclose the grounds, and by year end had erected 500 panels of chestnut fencing for the purpose. They did not take up the rebate issue itself until just before camp was to open. On July 25 of 1883 the Executive Committee of the board finally voted not to accept the rebate for Sunday tickets. A blue-ribbon panel made up of Dr. Howard, Major Morgan, and Thomas Somerville was appointed to convey the decision to the railroad offices.

Whether the rebate stopped as a result of this action is not clear, but the excursion trains certainly did not. In 1887 Thomas Somerville was dispatched to the B&O again to say that "unless the trains on Sunday are discontinued we will have no camp meeting on Sundays." The Preacher's Meeting requested that Sunday camp meeting be discontinued, but again it was not. In May, 1888 the B&O was requested again to stop the trains, and this time the Annual Meeting backed it up by voting to lock the gates of the Association to all vehicles and horses of visitors on Sundays. This time the trains stopped coming. Sunday camps continued, but were never again the circuses they had been.

In the midst of this wrangling over rebates another aspect of the personality of the Association came to light. Though it was easily smoothed over it led to an unsettlement about just how the Association should be governed and by whom, and shifted the focus of its existence forever away from Washington and toward the state and county in which its assets lay.

THE CHARTER CRISIS

The crisis in question arose from the discovery that under Maryland law a charter corporation had to hold all its business meetings in Maryland. In the winter of 1881-82 the Association was considering a new charter and bylaws; by February a committee had met with two attorneys and the dreadful fact had been discovered that since the Association had failed to comply with the law of Maryland in this regard it no longer had a legal existence. By this time the Annual Meeting of Stockholders, at least, was being held regularly at the Grove. It was decided to go ahead with the 1882 meeting and to work out a revision to the charter and bylaws which would solve both problems at once, and then to submit a new charter to the Maryland legislature at its 1883 session.

An amended charter was quickly agreed upon and submitted to Annapolis, where it was accepted, but many details had not been fully resolved. A new revision effort, undertaken almost immediately, forced the Trustees to take a closer look at the large undeveloped areas within the corporate limits, and attempt to clarify its vision for their future use.. Before this time there had been a survey and plat of the Tent Department, but it was not filed with the county land records in Rockville. The Cottage Department consisted only of the 40 lots on Grove Avenue. The Trustees contracted with civil engineer J.C.Lang to undertake an extensive survey by metes and bounds of the entire grounds on the camp side of the tracks, and had him subdivide the unused land into more tent sites, more cottage sites, and for the first time, some common areas for recreation.

THE LANG SURVEY

The Lang survey, completed in 1885 and printed in early 1886, was an extension of the land uses that existed at that time, but had some striking new features as well. The tent department with its tiny lots 17' wide by 40 to 70 feet deep were extended in six long fingers up either side of 4th, 5th, and 6th Avenues to a cross street at roughly the site of McCauley Street today. Across Grove Road extended (then unnamed but aligned with the old mineral springs trail) was an expanded Laundry Reserve where the Men's Walk and the Ladies Walk (to the privies) were located and, further into the woods, the trenches for burial of waste, including "soap suds and stew slops," were placed. Further out Grove Road on the right side also, was an extended carriage park to accommodate the coaches, buggies, and wagons which bore the hordes of Sunday visitors who did not come by train. The low lying area south and west of McCauley, below the tents on the east of 6th Avenue, was divided into a parking area and a horse pen.

The area west of Broadway and behind the cottages on the west side of Grove Avenue over to the Laytonsville Road had been cleared land, so it was less attractive for tenting and development than the land to the east, which was elaborately divided by the Lang plat into cottage department lots. Unlike the existing cottages on north-south running Grove Avenue, the new cottages were to be oriented along three long east- west streets: South Avenue (roughly Brown Street) near the depot, Oak Avenue taking off east from the lot 16 gap on Grove Avenue (now Oak Street), and Park Avenue running east from 1st Avenue along the present alignment of Center Street. No street ran west from 1st Avenue, there being instead a continuous park from the Singer (Cohen) Cottage on lot 21 to the Hotel. A small part of the park had been appropriated to build the Singer cottage (now 206 Grove Avenue)—as it happened, Singer was unable to locate his cottage within the 50' lot without cutting trees, so the trustees extended the lot 29 feet into Chapel Park. The house sits mostly in the 29' segment, for which Singer was assessed $40,

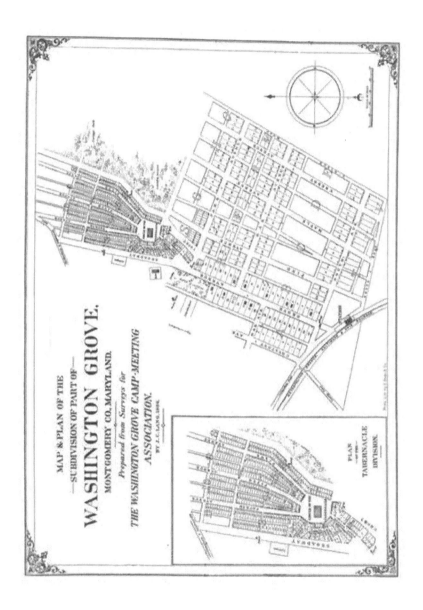

The Lang subdivision plan of 1886. Few of its features were adopted.

but which he never paid.

Three 50-foot lots and three 20-foot lots were added to the Grove Avenue corridor opposite Chapel Park and filling the space up to First Avenue. Three lots had been established earlier by the trus tees along South Avenue (Brown St.), facing the railroad. These were retained and Pine, Maple, and Cherry Avenues were set roughly as they are today but behind the row of lots on Brown Street a large common, five hundred feet deep, stretched east from Grove Road all the way to Ridge. On the other side Chestnut Avenue was established parallel to Grove, but shown with a few lots on one side only, and the Avenue itself faded off into the superintendents garden at its north end.

What doomed the Lang plat in the short term was the lack of an aggressive enough cottage-building program which would have established it permanently as soon as a few of the oddly distributed lots were built upon. In the long run it was not a desirable plan anyway, having clusters of three lots facing north or south then two facing east or west in a herringbone pattern, with several odd lots scattered about and a peculiar wedge driven down its middle.

With its subdivision plan at least temporarily described by the Lang plat, the Association adopted a new charter at the annual meeting of May 1886, and a committee was appointed to inform the Maryland legislature. The elements of the new charter included an increase in the Board of Trustees from nine to 25 members, the removal of the Executive Committee which had previously done much of the board's work, and the publication of an annual list of stockholders. At the annual meeting the election of so many trustees took several hours and in the end embraced nearly everyone

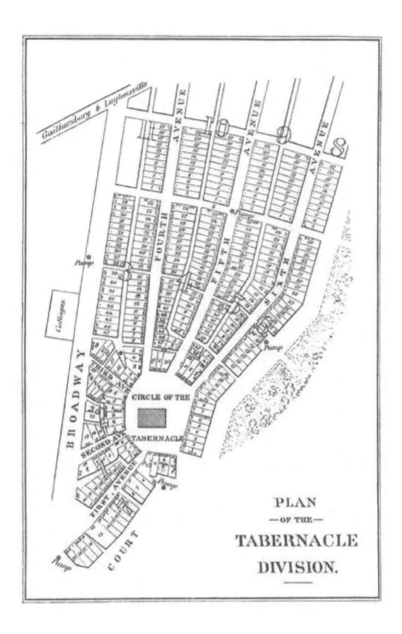

The Lang plat showed the Circle and its immediate vicinity the way it had developed on its own.

of voting age present. Two other provisions of the new charter were to have a far-reaching impact on the Association, in fact to bring it to its knees a few years later. One was the shift in the tax burden ("assessments") away from the stock and onto the lots and improvements. The other was the authority to issue leases to the owners of improved lots—but the lease was a relatively new concept in real estate law, and it was facing a long future in the court system.

THE LEASE CONTROVERSY - ACT I

It was a problem that began at the beginning, though no one seems to have recognized the potential trouble it could cause. The original flyer announcing the sale of stock in the Washington Grove Camp Meeting Association of the District of Columbia and Maryland said only that "The capital stock has been fixed at $20,000, divided into 1000 shares of $20 each, and is now offered to our friends." The expression "to our friends" was social code of the time meaning that only persons acceptable to the trustees would be allowed to purchase stock. There was no mention of what rights would accrue to a shareholder, nor did there seem to need to be, for in the beginning there were only well-meaning friends on the stockholder list.

At some point before the first charter and bylaws were sent to Annapolis for ratification, the idea of separate tent and cottage areas for campers and summer residents, respectively, was clarified and then fatally linked to the ownership of shares by the concept of "located stock." In exchange for one's $20, then, one was to be issued one share of stock which allowed the owner one vote at stockholders' meetings. One share also entitled the owner to select a tent site, after which the share was said to be "located". Five shares allowed the selection of a cottage site. There was no definition of what "locate" meant other than the obvious inference that it entitled one to tent indefinitely on the located tent site or, in the cottage area, build a cottage and occupy it indefinitely.

This seems workable enough if one assumes that each new share issued would immediately have a tent site assigned and the site number written on the certificate, or each five share multiple would have a cottage site assigned and recorded. Under this system one could imagine a set of stock certificates of one- and five-share denominations pre-printed with the block and number of a building site. The number of certificates would be exactly equal to the number of building sites. The certificates could then be issued as shares were purchased, the choicer sites going to the earlier subscribers. Buying into the Association would then be a matter of finding which sites were for sale, and selecting from among those privately held or those still in the hands of the Association. Certainly it is true that this system could not have been implemented ahead of time—the land was not platted in any detail for several years—but several possible versions of such a plan could have been implemented later.

In 1880 such a system seems to have been in effect in the minds of the trustees, but it was only informally administered. When stock subscriptions were first offered they were bought in 1 and 5 share certificates in great numbers, but also 2, 3, 4, 6, and even 12 share lots were subscribed by a few buyers. There was also some stock trading during the depression years of the mid-

70s, so other stockholders also wound up with odd numbers of shares. Stimulated by the first serious building on the Circle (and possibly forewarned by J.T.Mitchell's unfortunate placement of a cottage on B.P.Brown's lot) many stockholders were moved to secure building sites and began to round out their shares into one and five share certificates by buying, selling, or trading for odd shares. Beginning in 1879 new shares were recorded in the stock book with a notation as to lot selected, though all too often the notation was vague: for example, "Lot __, Grove Avenue," would indicate the purchaser had not decided on a lot.

What this loose approach failed to anticipate was the development, over only a few years, of a nightmare of classes of ownership interest. Instead of one-share, one-name, one-vote, one-site, stocks and lots began to be traded without proper records being kept, and soon there were leaseholders without stock, stockholders without lots, and lots without leases. There was also outstanding stock for which the owners were unknown. The impact of this was two-fold: first, it muddied the concept of ownership, or "vested interest," and second, it made the equitable distribution of the tax burden or "assessments" difficult or impossible.

As noted previously, one cause of this confusion was that the tent department was not fully platted, and at this time the only cottage department area laid out at all was Grove Avenue—and there were only 38 lots there (two now reserved for cross-streets). The Lang plat was six years away and would be a disaster anyway. So whatever good intentions the Trustees had in 1880 were also difficult if not impossible to implement. There were chances later to rectify the problem, but each year that passed added to the number—and diversity—of people who would have to agree to whatever was decided.

Ownership of the stock had a clear enough value at the annual meeting: it was still one share, one vote. But the value of the stock for any other purpose seemed to depend on whether it was located stock, and where it was located. The value of the stock began to be confused with the value of a lot, then with the value of an improved lot, and finally with the value of the improvements themselves. The cost of annual maintenance and the division of responsibility for it had been simple when all stock was equal, but in time it became a matter for repeated adjudication.

The first recorded attempt to solve the problem of vested interests, legally, occurred at the 1882 annual meeting in the Grove at W.R.Woodward's cottage on the Circle. The main business of the meeting was the consideration of a new charter and bylaws, the Association at that time working without legal existence. Section 14 of the new bylaws called for 99-year leases to be issued "renewable forever upon condition the lessee conform to the ByLaws of the corporation." The section was adopted without amendment, but there followed an agonizing attempt to define at what point one would be eligible for such a lease. It was finally decided at that meeting that a vested interest existed and therefore a lease could be written, (1) if a tent or cottage department site had at least a wooden tent or cottage, respectively, built on it, and (2), if the owner held or purchased five shares of stock in addition to the 1 or 5 shares he was already required to own to have located on the site. This created an immediate problem: it defined a second class of stock, one which could not be located. On top of that, no sooner had the measure passed a vote, but an exception was made, for unstated reasons, for Reverend E. D. Owens.

In the meantime, the meeting had taken up so much time with the entire charter and bylaws to consider and all the debate about leases, that it had to be continued during the trip back to Washington; it was too early in the season for the cottages to be occupied overnight. The meeting adjourned from Woodward's cottage for the sylvan walk to the depot, where it reconvened in a railroad car. It was here that the new trustees were nominated; there was a formal call, so they had to be elected by ballot. The meeting was then adjourned from the car to the Washington Grove station, where the executive committee was elected, and Thomas P. Morgan was returned to the Presidency, William R. Woodward to the Vice Presidency, and Edward F. Simpson to the position of Secretary. In a contested race, the first such on record, John T. Mitchell was elected Treasurer. The train must have been ready then for the meeting adjourned during the short ride to Gaithersburg, and reconvened in the station there. (Since there was only one track, the cars had to be pulled to Gaithersburg to wait for an engine which would pull them back to Washington.) After a brief session in Gaithersburg it finally adjourned *sine die*.

A lease was written that would comply with the wishes of the annual meeting, the first of many forms it would take. The lease, as an instrument of title, seemed to be working, but the collection of annual assessments from the leaseholders was still uneven. By 1883 the situation was so serious that a committee was established to amend the bylaws again. Their report of September 14 was presented to a special meeting of stockholders at Foundry Church on November 23. Out of the meeting came the call for a new lease form, and some very tough provisions for those who failed to pay. Under Forfeiture of Stockholder Privileges, persons indebted to the Association for any of several reasons were to become ineligible to be trustees, to be officers, and even to vote; no^ would they receive railroad passes to the meetings, select or occupy lots upon the grounds, or enjoy any other privileges upon the grounds. It also provided that a list of delinquent stockholders be published regularly, and that the list be read aloud at each meeting of the stockholders.

At this same meeting the bylaws were also amended to limit ownership: "noperson shall be entitled to occupy and have a lease for more than one lot in each [department]," and gave the trustees authority to levy assessments on unoccupied cottage department sites as well as on all improved lots in either department. This was to prove an especially contentious issue in the future, but for the moment it seemed to work. Whether out of respect for the new rules, or in fear of having their names read at the annual meeting, the stockholders and leaseholders were paying their dues.

* * *

So a problem which had existed from the start had come to light, and been dealt with. The Association had survived an identity crisis and a legal crisis by making some small adjustments to its structure. The need for an instrument of ownership had been neatly solved with a system of perpetual leases, and by 1888 the delinquency problem was being attacked successfully with tough new rules. What the Association did not know—and probably could not have known—was that these two concepts, vested interests and collections of assessments were becoming inextricably intermingled in law so that every flaw in one was compounded in the other, and in making rules about either the Association was dabbling in areas increasingly reserved for democratic governments. The ultimate test of such rules would lie not within the Association but in the public courts.

THE ASSOCIATION

PROFILES II: CAMP NOTES

Camp Meeting meant an idyllic excursion for the majority of Washington Methodists who made the day-trip from the city. For some others there was a seamier side to it. Some stories from the *Sentinel* illustrate the point.

8-24-83: "Excitement on a Train"

"On Sunday eve whilst the excursion train from the Washington Grove Camp was returning to the city, over the Metropolitan Branch of the Baltimore and Ohio Railroad near Tuscarora Station, a report was circulated that a colored woman had fallen between the cars and had been killed. The train was stopped and backed, but had gone but a short distance, when some one started a rumor that an extra train was following and a collision was imminent. A general stampede took place, men, women, and children rushed from the cars whilst they were in motion, some from the windows and other from the doors. Things soon quieted down and the train started for the city arriving on time with a large number of passengers more frightened than injured."

8-29-84: Item

"Frank McGlathey attempted to whip a negro man for insulting a lady friend of his when the negro cut him across the abdomen with a knife. The negro afterward ran and made his escape."

8-28-85: Items

"At Washington Grove Camp on Tuesday the carriage of Mrs. Reed was nearly demolished by the horse which was attacked by a swarm of bees near where it had been tied."

"Mrs. Edward Thompson was thrown and killed on the way home from camp to Rockville."

5

Changing The Guard

THERE HAD BEEN A FLAW OR two in the foundation of the Grove and a misstep or two on the part of its administrators but it was not after all a utopia they were after, but simply a summer community that could combine the spiritual assets of Christian principles with the healthful aspects of country living while at the same time incorporating a program of active witnessing for Christ.

That the pious purpose of the camp meeting was often mocked by "red-eyed dandies" and that the community was thought of by outsiders as something between a picnic and a summer resort did not discourage the insiders—the ministers, shopkeepers, doctors, lawyers, husbands, widows, wives, and a growing population of young people for whom the Grove was a second home. With a firm basis in their common beliefs they turned to building a society with common interests and activities, and lasting institutions and traditions. No longer was the search for converts the Association's sole purpose nor the camp meeting its single event. The community was opened to a variety of Christian endeavors and to events which ranged from the purely religious to the largely recreational. The population of summer residents grew and began to spread out from the clearly-defined areas around the Circle and along Grove Avenue. As new areas began to develop a more serious long range plan for development was soon needed.

Pushing Out

The Lang survey of 1886 had incorporated the earlier plats of the Circle and Grove Avenue areas with all the modifications that had accumulated up to that time, and appended an imaginative but impractical platting of lots for the area to the east. But on the west side it showed only a few lots on Chestnut Avenue backed up on undivided space. The west side of the property had access from the railroad and Laytonsville road at its southwest comer, and South Avenue was platted to run into it from the east. A cross-avenue through one of the Grove Avenue lots had been established earlier to connect the area with foot traffic from Grove. The high ground near the railroad was as desirable as the center of the grounds, having larger trees and good drainage. Moving north from the railroad the land dropped off and became open and less well drained. In the extreme northwest lay the superintendent's fields and feedlots, and a formidable collection of outbuildings. Across Laytonsville Pike at the north end lay the newly relocated horse pen and carriage park.

Interest in the west side of the grounds had been expressed by several stockholders, because of its easy access and good drainage. Some stockholders had asked that their stock be located there. The more southerly part needed considerable work before it could be developed, and the first order of business was to move Chestnut Avenue thirty feet to the west and redefine the lots to be 50 by 150 feet, the same as on Grove Avenue. This was not difficult, for not even a path existed yet to define Chestnut Avenue, and no lots had actually been laid off. The new avenue was then graded, the first of many times, and lots were marked off. A program of tree planting was announced, and the first shares of stock, officially located on what is now 111 Chestnut Avenue, were issued to a Melville Lindsay in 1891. He applied for a permit to move his cottage on the Circle to his new lot, but it was eventually determined for reasons of safety not to allow the move.

Those wishing to locate or relocate on Chestnut were at first asked to pay all assessments on those lots back to 1886 but in the face of a swift protest the Trustees rescinded the ruling. Robert Bains established a cottage half a block north of Lindsay, and by 1897 Irving Fulks had taken the comer lots at Laytonsville Road and South Avenue with the intention of building a store there. The future implications of the trustees approval of a commercial enterprise there was lost on the residents and stockholders of that time. Development of the Chestnut Avenue and Switch Road areas proceeded slowly over a protracted period; it was not until the present era that Hickory (Switch) Road was put through to Center Street.

On the east side of the grounds, Lang's plat had appended a herringbone pattern of lots to fill the space between the alley back of Grove Avenue and Ridge Road, lanes which were then being used by the farmers in the area of the mineral springs north of the Grove. There was an ill-fated scheme announced in the Spring of 1889 to sell the lots east of Maple Avenue by auction on the upcoming Fourth of July. But that was the only attempt to develop the Lang plat as it stood. The same plan included other improvements on the east side, one of which was the clearing and grading of Grove Road, which had hitherto been a wandering track, and clearing the underbrush in what later became the ball field and tennis courts. This was the most poorly drained land in the Grove; it was mostly a thicket with a bog at its bottom. One can see why it was Ridge and Maple—the high ground—that had been selected for auction at that time, but it was a widely held view that even the soggiest ground would drain and dry if the underbrush were cut away and the sun allowed in. In fact, an extensive system of ditching, and very probably some landfill, would have been required before that ground could be habitable for cottages. The present land use stands in testimony to the impracticality of building there.

In 1886 there was agitation among the trustees to clear underbrush from all the land to the east for sanitary reasons, and, though some work was done in that direction, it was a larger job than the Association had resources for just then; that work did result in the removal of the horse pen from the east side of 6th Avenue to the west side of Laytonsville Road.

The Lang plat subdivided the grounds south of South Avenue (Brown Street), though not in the vicinity of the station because the drainage was poor. Local drainage had not been carefully considered when the railroad was first put through, and the area just west of the depot tended to pool in a storm. But in August of 1890 the B&O constructed a new culvert under the tracks at the Association's request, and the following summer the

Ridge Road watershed area was able to drain under the railroad bed and out through Oakmont to Muddy Branch.

It was at this period that the park around the depot was first recognized as the front door of the Grove. Motions to subdivide it were defeated, and attempts by outsiders to establish a thoroughfare across it, or a commercial development within it, were defeated. Wagon traffic from the farms on the northeast comer of the Grove desired a shortcut across the association grounds; they petitioned the County Commissioners for a road which would bisect the ballfield and come out at the freight platform, which was then at the east foot of the bridge. In the face of heavy lobbying by the Grove the road was defeated, but the wagons were still able to use Ridge Road and a new lane was cut outside the Grove fence approximately where Railroad Street now is.

The privacy and physical integrity of the Grove was at issue in the disputes over thoroughfares, but an equal concern for the trustees was the maintenance issue— each year much of the intellectual effort and a large part of the fiscal expense of the Grounds Committee went to maintaining the avenues and alleys in good order. The great volume of foot traffic in the summer would undo almost any preparatory work done in the spring, and the trustees were constantly in search of a better surface.

The Avenues had originally been placed directly on the forest floor without preparation. They were first covered with cinders donated by the B&O, but the heels of the masses would force the cinders to mix with the earth, making an unpleasant mud when wet. Board walks were built and then rebuilt on Grove Avenue, First Avenue, and on the Ladies Walk, but with the absence of wood preservatives they rotted out in a season. In the early 90's Grove Avenue was cut down almost 24" at its high point, and the excess earth was used to fill in the low spots. Later, soapstone chips were imported for the avenues because they made a hard surface when rolled; but they were also very slippery when wet. In the mid-90's a complex new system was tested on Grove Avenue: a bed of clay was laid between side timbers and rolled to a crown, then a cover of crushed stone was laid on top. The stone allowed the walks to drain while keeping the clay packed down. This system was eventually used on most of the walkways.

In 1888, the trustees declared that the area south of South Avenue should be "held and used forever as a public park and that no intoxicating liquors shall ever be kept, sold, or given away...and no building shall be erected and no mercantile, mechanical , or other business shall be conducted or carried on upon the ground." They also designated the road (Railroad St.) to the common use of the County and Association—this apparently to maintain a single station at the Grove, for without access to the Grove station the people of Laytonsville and vicinity would have argued for another stop just outside the limits. In 1890 the area in front of the station was officially decreed a park.

CUTTING CORNERS

It was in this era that the Association began to sell off odd bits and pieces of its original purchase. There was the land across the tracks, some odd triangles on the north end, and the old farm across Ridge Road, outside the fence. The triangle of Suter land orphaned on the

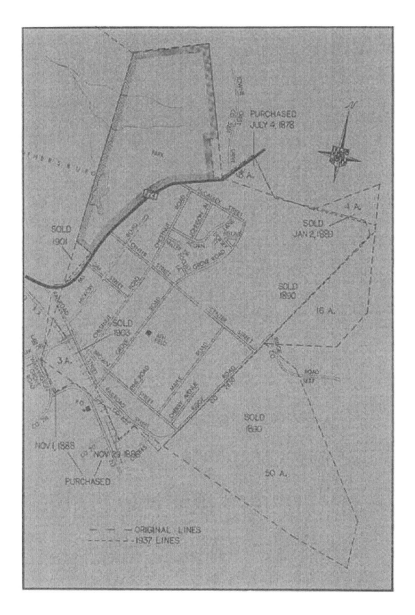

The original boundaries of the Grove included land south of the tracks, and a 50 acre "old farm" on the east side.

Grove side of the tracks east of the depot had been purchased by the Association in 1886. In 1878 the trustees bought the 3 acres on the northwest comer that give Boundary Street its off shape, and in 1889 3 acres on the east end of Boundary were sold off. In 1888 there was an aborted attempt to sell the Grove's holdings, about 3acres, on the other side of the tracks and in 1890 an agreement was signed to convey it for $1000, but that also fell through. Again in 1893 a motion to sell it was defeated, but it finally was purchased by E.A.Eakle a decade later for $1200 cash, there being reserved only a 75 x 100 foot piece for the long promised new station house. The old farm, a 50 acre tract at the east end of Brown Street, was offered in 1890 for $50 an acre to help pay off Association debt. There was quite a battle among the trustees about this, and the matter finally was settled at a special stockholders meeting.

When the freight siding was moved from the east side of the bridge to the west side of the bridge, a triangle of land remaining between it and Railroad Street was sold to J.B Diamond for $500; this thin triangle became the subject of many disputes, and remains so right up to the present. The ground across Laytonsville Road—the cleared land across from Fulks' and the wooded land containing the springs, and later known as the West Woods, was half-heartedly offered for sale if the price were right. Fulks bought the first acre across the pike at its intersection with Railroad Street, and a few adjacent lots were sold later. But there was no serious effort at the time to develop or sell the springs. Twenty-five years later the entire west woods would come perilously close to subdivision and development.

Cars and carriages pick up arriving passengers. The old depot sits in what is now Railroad Street, at its intersection with Grove Road.

The first instance of the Association's trying to buy back a lot occurred in 1892 when H.B.Moulton's (the Association President for one year in 1889-90) lot number 25 on Grove Avenue was desired by the trustees so that Oak Avenue could be continued across Grove Avenue to the west.

Lot #16 had originally been a building lot but was reserved on the Lang plat for Oak Avenue to connect to Grove. They solicited the feeling of Moulton on the matter, but (for reasons which shall be explored later) he sent back word that he "would not sell for $1000!" Later, he accepted a counter offer of $500, but only, he stipulated, if it could be paid in cash by the end of May, a condition he knew to be next to impossible. So ownership of the lot remained private, but the feud over its use was a public matter for the rest of the Association's life.

THE MADDOX SURVEY

During its brief life a number of revisions were made to the Lang plat. Chestnut Avenue was moved eastward and the lots were enlarged; in November of 1890 the name Broadway was abandoned and the walkway became simply an extension of Grove Avenue; and in January of '91 all the lots in the southeast corner were re-platted to conform with the pattern and size of those on Grove Avenue. It was clear to everyone that a new survey and subdivision plat was needed, and soon. Several times individual trustees had offered to supervise the work, but no action was taken on their offers. Finally a new Maryland law made a resurvey and subdivision of the grounds a necessity. C.J.Maddox, the County Surveyor, bid the job for a $60 flat rate fee on

The Maddox subdivision plan closely represents the Grove of today. The undeveloped areas were divided into cottage department-sized lots in imitation of the Grove Avenue pattern. A shortcoming of the Maddox plan was too little land devoted to open space. Another was the lack of a cross-through for Oak Street.

the proviso that the Association would furnish him with assistants. The land survey was quickly accomplished, but the subdividing took almost two more years.

The Maddox subdivision plan is almost indistinguishable from the present town plan, a testimony to both its sensibility and its adaptability. In the plan the Grove is almost evenly divided north and south of Center Street, which is shown for the first time running all the way from the Laytonsville Road to Ridge Road. The lots below Center are all on the Grove Avenue pattern of 50x150 foot lots, the only exception being a row of lots along South Avenue, which had now become Brown Street. Oak Street replaced Oak Avenue on the east side of Grove and, after being interrupted by Moulton's lot, continued on the west side to the pike.

North of Center Street the traditional camp meeting area was preserved as it had come to stand, but on all the land west of Grove Avenue, north of McCauley Street, and east of Grove Road the larger lot pattern is established. The west woods was undivided but the east woods was completely given over to large lots. Woodward Park was established where the ball field is now, but it was narrower; where it now abuts Grove Road there was shown instead a row of lots with Pine Avenue as their front walkway.

The sensibility of the plan was in its large, accessible cottage lots placed on a rectangular pattern around the well-preserved camp meeting and small cottage area on the sacred Circle. Its adaptability was in the placement of common areas spaced around the Grove; a pattern of usage was allowed to develop on its own. Not to argue that this was done with foresight—if all the lots platted had been sold the first year there would have been no east woods and no field large enough for baseball—but through an accidental provision of the charter, with only a thousand shares authorized and five shares required to secure a cottage site, it would have been impossible to fill the lots anyway!

SANITATION AND HEALTH

The problem of drainage was a big factor in the preservation of the east woods and the larger-than-intended Woodward Park. And good drainage was directly linked at that time with basic sanitation and health. Louis Pasteur's discovery in 1878 of the relationship of bacteria to disease had a profound effect on sanitary practices in America. It was already well known that disease flourished in packed cities and that epidemics could be caused by contamination of food or water by sewage. Those who could afford to leave the city in the summer did so for reasons of health as well as comfort. Summer camps, whether religious or not, provided an inexpensive alternative to more distant health spas or resorts. But as health-conscious parishioners flocked to the camps they concentrated into small spaces with temporary sanitation facilities and therefore were exposing themselves to epidemic should the food or water become contaminated. So while the inhabitants of Washington Grove were more highly educated about personal hygiene than the average Washingtonian they were still susceptible to the poor habits of others.

The bacteria described by Pasteur made these sources of disease easier to picture, which helped raise the general level of consciousness about the consequences of poor sanitation. In a presentation to the

1886 Annual Meeting, Association President Thomas P. Morgan issued a strong admonition to the stockholders:

"I would recommend that the drainage of the grounds be continued until every wet spot shall disappear. The open ditch now in use except the main ditch should be replaced by blind- or underditching, so that there may be no break in the surface of the ground. The clearing out of undergrowth and debris of every character should be continued, so as to give a free circulation of good, wholesome air at all times.

"I would urge upon the attention of all persons interested, the utmost care in regard to the sanitary conditions of their own premises. There is no more important subject to which our attention could be called. Living as we do—many of us—in closely built avenues, one careless and uncleanly family might cause serious trouble to all. It should not be forgotten that the secrets of one sick person near the town of Plymouth, Pennsylvania poisoned nearly the entire community— such was the fatal effect of the typhoid fever epidemic engendered by the carelessness of the attendants of the patient referred to, that more than 300 persons died from the effects of the disease, and a thousand in all were stricken with it. All sanitarians agree that there is nothing so important for continued health as good drainage, free circulation of air and pure water. We have an abundance of good water, fair drainage, pure air, but not much of it, it is too much obstructed especially in the east side of the grounds by low bushes, dense thickets of briers, and scrubby pines."

Over the next four years increased attention was given to clearing out the low areas. A wide swath from the railroad all the way through the grounds to the mineral springs was in thicket. Woodward Park had been a field at one time but it was now grown up in brush. The clearing efforts led to the drainage improvements under the railroad bed, and to the construction of an elaborate closed storm sewer network beginning at the Circle and ending in the lake woods. Cesspools were forbidden, so most of the cottages had privies with buckets or boxes which had to be emptied daily by a scavenger, a service usually provided by black men from nearby Emory Grove. Originally the buckets were wooden, but metal cans had replaced the last of the wooden ones by the turn of the century.

The scavenger gained access to the buckets or cans through flap doors on the alley side of each cottage. One feature of the Maddox subdivision was to provide a ten foot alley behind all cottages for this purpose—most of these alleys were legally abandoned later and incorporated into the lots. The public toilets— the Men's and Ladies' Walks—were converted from a system of stationary pits to a system of moving trenches. Instead of putting a privy over a pit and moving it when the pit was full, they installed buckets under the privies and hauled the buckets daily to trenches in the east woods, applying lime over the offending matter as required. Then when the trench was full they would dig another, topping off the former with the dirt dug from the latter. J.H.Nugent was the scavenger for many years and was apparently a popular figure in the Grove.

SEGREGATION

The last quarter of the century saw amazing advances in science and technology; many useful inventions made factories more numerous and farms more productive. Developments in medicine were making disease less deadly and treatment less painful. But for black people the social conscience was taking mincing steps backward. The people who were made free and equal in 1865 had not been assimilated into the population, as some had hoped and others had feared. Their suppressed cultural heritage, their lack of education, and their increasingly dubious legal status had shunted them away from mainstream American life and into a separate, though overlapping, society.

Racial stereotypes invented before the Civil War and meant for a certain class of black were now being applied to all blacks. A set of differentiated characteristics including slothfulness, criminality, and uncleanliness was being ascribed to a whole race of people and the image was being promulgated by every medium: orally, in the popular press, and even in scientific journals. What a consensus of white people was concluding by the mid-90's was that black people, while certainly possessing the same right of freedom as other races, probably were incapable as a race of becoming their absolute equals. What this view endorsed was the concept of separation of the races into their separate endeavors and the legalization of what was *defacto* true by this time anyway—the racial segregation of society.

In Washington Grove the effect of this slowly emerging national consensus was small. The Methodist Church had formed its own rather advanced form of segregation years before the civil war. It was a practical matter to them, not an evil design, for these were not cynical people and the twin communities of Washington Grove and Emory Grove had existed for 23 years before Plessey vs. Ferguson was heard by the Supreme Court of the land and segregation became U.S. policy. The

On any given Sunday, and especially during Emory Grove's camp meeting, black people from Washington would leave the train at Washington Grove and make their way to Emory Grove via Grove Avenue and Broadway.

effect on the Grove was small but it was significant.

W.A.Scott was a young black man who lived in the area when the Grove was being founded. He may have worked on the railroad, but more likely he was a hand at the Cooke or Suter farms, or did odd jobs for many.

He was probably born a slave. He may have been at the Grove during the first clearing work in 1873 but he first appears in the treasurer's records in 1878. He is described by Milburn as having been a "pioneer cottage builder" in the early 1880's. By 1883 he had become Superintendent of the grounds. He lived and worked in the Grove for the next eight years. He built his own small house and several of the cottages on the avenues near the Circle which the Association would offer for rent in the summers. He cleared brush from the old fields east of Grove Avenue and Broadway and along the Laytonsville road and raised vegetables and grazed stock for food. He built fences, barns, and other outbuildings for himself and the community, and cut 50 to 100 cords of firewood each year for the Association to sell in the fall and winter. He dug ditches, cut brush and trees, graded avenues, and picked up the cuttings, leaves, and branches year round.

The official records of the town offer neither praise nor criticism of Scott, though, then as now, one can be certain that there was some of each. He seems to have been a satisfactory employee (though there would be many successors who were not!), but when new voices joined the trustees in 1889 there were several discussions about replacing him. In May of 1890, just before the annual meeting, the Grounds Committee was authorized over considerable opposition to seek a new superintendent. One vote on the matter was a 7 to 7 tie. They did not actually fire him that year, but Scott's role was successively reduced over the next three years. He was finally replaced altogether when A.T.Tracy took over as President in 1893.

Whether this action was tied to the mood of the country cannot be known for certain; statutory segregation was by this time quite common in the South, and tensions between the races had increased since the founding of the Grove. Under those circumstances the firing of Scott could have been triggered by this unrelated incident: in December of 1892 one Jesse Lancaster, an Emory Grove resident, broke into and ransacked twelve Grove cottages in a reckless spree. The Association offered a reward for his arrest and he was subsequently captured, tried, and given a long sentence. Scott did continue to be associated with the Grove after his dismissal, but in 1895, as the low bidder for the winter grounds cleaning, he was passed over in favor of the next higher bidder, a white man.

In 1897, in response to whatever real or imagined fears may have driven them, the trustees voted to close the gates of the Association during the Emory Grove Camp Meeting. It seems likely that participation by blacks in the Washington Grove Camp Meeting must have declined sharply after this, if in fact it was still active. Jesse Lancaster served six years for his crime, but the trustees joined with leaders of Emory Grove in 1899 to petition for his pardon and release.

A CLASSIC STRUGGLE

The establishment of a consensus on a basic subdivision and land use pattern, the heightened sensitivity to matters of sanitation, and the extensive improvements to land and the avenues were achievements made in the midst of a changing of the guard. The Grove was founded by clergy and pious laymen cut from the same cloth as Asbury and Foxall, but there were differences in the atmosphere of the 1890's; the 1870's had been a period of reconstruction and renaissance, but by the 90's people had been using the inventions of the 70's for 20 years and had grown to expect even more. They were a little tired of piety and ready for some practicality—and fun.

These changing values combined with the ever present potential for enmity between the generations to bring forth a classic struggle for power in the government of the Association. It was a struggle of the old versus the new. When a governing body begins its work its ideas are new: it desires and expects to make changes. When it has been a successful governor for a time, the changes have all been made and its ideas are no longer new. There is a danger inherent in this process, for in a changing world new ideas must constantly evolve. If a governor governs too long he will, like France's Napolean or Mexico's Diaz, eventually be denounced and replaced for doing pretty much what he was revered for doing in the first place. Washington Grove had grown and changed after twenty years, but an entrenched old guard left little room for the fresher ideas of its newer residents.

Some earlier problems with stormwater management, surfacing of the avenues, and sanitation had caused grumbling, but the continuing uncertainties about the value stock and leases were to bring a confrontation with the old guard. It is impossible to say when the first verbal shot was fired, but the discontent which triggered it began a few years earlier, in 1886, when the new charter took effect. A key provision of the charter had expanded the board of trustees from 9 members to 25, and removed the Executive Committee, an inner circle of trustees, from existence. This was a well-intended but unwieldy arrangement: the election of the 25-member board alone took most of the 1886 annual meeting's time, and thereafter in trustee's meetings every point had to be debated by as many as twenty-five members. The same new charter also stripped stockholders who were indebted to the Association of their rights as stockholders, denied them the right to hold office or to occupy their lots, and added the word "delinquent" next to the names of those in arrears on the annual list of stockholders, which was to be read aloud at annual meeting.

By the annual meeting of 1889 the impracticality of working with 25 trustees had been brought well home, and the stockholders voted to rescind that provision and return the Board to nine members. This would have been fine but for the awkwardness of determining who would remain on the board and who would depart, and the inevitable conflict that eventually resulted. The balance of old and new that had begun with the increase to 25 members was shattered when the stockholders returned the older conservative group to office.

It was also at that meeting that an incident occurred which was not to be resolved for several years: J.T.Mitchell's right to vote was called into question, not because he was delinquent in his assessments, but because he apparently no longer owned any Grove stock—he had sold it all the year before. It was not legitimate to own and occupy a cottage without owning the requisite number of shares of stock, and he did claim to own 14 shares; but the records show that he had sold them. A committee was formed to determine the truth of the matter, but the following year they reported that they could not make any definitive finding, but "as he has occupied a tent site for many years it recommended he be accepted as a stockholder."

In another action the annual meeting voted to lift a long-standing restriction that limited the number of sites a stockholder could control, and the amount of time he could hold them before building. This would have deep significance to the Grove a decade later, and probably changed its course irrevocably, though no immediate problem was apparent.

This was also the year that Secretary E.F.Simpson stepped down from the office of secretary to the board of trustees, a significant date for anyone studying the history of the town through its minutes of meetings, for Simpson had such a nearly illegible style of writing that each word in his records must be studied like a hieroglyphic. He was succeeded by the youthful Warren Choate.

Over the winter the trustees recognized that in going from 25 to 9 members they had created some undesirable friction, so at a called meeting of the stockholders at Foundry Church the stockholders (the few present, anyway) voted to return the board to 25 members. The Maryland legislature was contacted but the Association was informed that it was too late to change its mind, that the action was already taken and the bill signed into law. An attempt was then made to enable the composition of the board to represent the residents more fairly, that is, to allow non-Methodists to serve on the board. It was moved, seconded and passed that only six of the trustees must be Methodists. After this action, H.B.Moulton, a long-time resident, was elected president and Dr. Frank Ritter was added to the list of trustees. Dr. Ritter took the position of designated dissenter for the next twenty years, expressing freely his strongly held views on most subjects. His first dissent came over a motion that the old farm be sold to help the retire old debt; Ritter was very much in favor and got into a loud dispute with Reverend Rice, one of the original stockholders and organizers, who was staunchly opposed to the sale. This was the first of many head-to-head disputes between the old and the new.

In 1891 a Washington Grove Advisory League with one Alvan T. Tracy as president was formed independent of the Association government to make the views of the dissenters known. When in September they requested information from the board about assessments and disbursements they were told that no such information would be given to any organization "unknown to the Charter." Eventually some information did flow to the League, but tempers flared at a meeting in February of 1892; the minutes report that a discussion was held between Carlton Hughes and Alvan Tracy about finances, "in fact quite an animated discussion was held in which the trustees came forth more than conquerors."

Again the following March the stockholders met at a called meeting and voted to amend the bylaws. Although such meetings were legal, they were irregular, for they tended to be accessible to those who called them on short notice and actions were sometimes taken that would not necessarily be approved of by the larger body. While we do not have the details, apparently a change in the nature of the leases given cottage owners was made at the meeting. The dissenters were beginning to get their way. Reverend Rice strongly objected to the procedure, and left the meeting in protest. In response, the remaining trustees adopted this landmark resolution establishing a commission to consider the whole question of leases:

"Whereas certain differences of opinion have arisen among stockholders of this Association upon questions regarding leases which have been granted by the Association, and the effect of the same as between the said lessor and lessee, and also in relation to the question as to what constitutes a lease, and the conditions in law which are essential to be contained in a lease executed on the part of the Association, and also as to the title upon which certain lots are held by occupants thereof where no lease had been executed by the present holder thereof, then therefore ..."

The annual meeting that followed in May of 1892 was thrown into disorder. At it, J.T.Mitchell moved that the last meeting be ruled illegal, though he did not say on what grounds. Animated discussion followed on whether it was shares or shareholders which voted, whether it was one vote per man or one vote per share. This was a crucial question which should have been settled in the original charter. Rev. Brown admonished the stockholders to be careful "lest the stock and not the people control the affairs of the Association." Rev. Rice objected again and notified the meeting of his intent to introduce a due notice provision that would prevent a few stockholders from making an end run at a special meeting. B.S.Platt introduced a complicated motion which would provide a means for both individual voting and voting by stock. In the divisive atmosphere it took eight ballots to elect the nine trustees for the year.

During the summer Dr. Ritter took the Association to court on the voting issue. In February of 1893 Judge

Vinson ruled in favor of voting by shares, citing state law that "each person present shall vote the number of shares he owns at corporate meetings and elections." This did not answer the question of whether voting by proxy would be allowed, so a lively debate on that point was assured. The old-timers were against it, and for the time being, they prevailed.

A month later the special committee looking into leases (and any other controversial matters that might come up) reported that under Maryland law stockholders have a right to vote by proxy, that the number of shares any one shareholder can vote cannot be limited. They also concluded that the leases presently being issued were not soundly based: according to the law at that time, a lease is simply a contract to rent for a period; further, long leases are breakable at ten or fifteen years with 6 months notice by either party. Clearly, those who were concerned about the quality of their tide were not going to be happy with the current lease situation.

At the annual meeting the rebellious Dr. Ritter and his sympathizers pulled off a coup—they elected A.T.Tracy to the presidency. But an embarrassment occurred immediately after the balloting was complete: quoting from the minutes, "At this juncture of the meeting Wm. J. Palmer rose and stated that one of the stockholders said to be elected to hold one of the offices of the Association is indebted to the Association for assessments, and under the bylaws was not legally entitled to hold office." None other than Tracy himself then arose and said "I am the man referred to, Mr. President, I promise if elected to pay the assessments levied against me." The matter was permitted to drop. It was at this time that an offer was made for Moulton's lot, but former president Moulton refused to deal with the interlopers.

The leadership controversy continued into the camp meeting period. Apparently the Presiding Elder, Dr. Naylor, sided with the conservatives and "declined to hold the regular annual [camp] meeting for reasons he did not give." Dr. Peck and Warren Choate were dispatched to Baltimore to persuade Dr. Norris, an early supporter of the camp meeting, to operate Washington Grove's meeting this year. He did so, but camp was shortened to ten days.

Tracy, himself a lawyer, presented a new lease form in March of the next year, but it was not warmly received by the other trustees. He went into the annual meeting with little resolved in his year in office, and he was neither nominated nor elected to another term. His name still appeared on the assessment delinquency list, too, though it is not clear whether this was his original delinquency or a new one.

Some election shenanigans occurred at this meeting: the bylaws called for five trustees to be from the state and four from the city, and for legal reasons, all voting for trustees had to be done at once, then the top five Maryland nominees would join the top 4 D.C. nominees to form the board. After the voting was held, Tracy made a move that shocked even the secretary who wrote, "Then by some strange inherent right vested in the chair, the President then proceeded to fix and change the residence of Brother Warren Choate from state to city thereby striking off the name of the one getting the lowest number of votes and therefore creating a vacancy in the list of state trustees, announcing that Brother Palmer being the next highest to the one to be stricken off was not eligible [being from the city] but intimating that he the president was about to become a resident of the state." This move by Tracy to appoint himself to the board in the waning minutes of his presidency, when he had not been nominated and was ineligible to serve, quietly failed when G.T.Woodward's motion that Choate be declared a resident of the state, which in fact he was, passed. Fred Gee, an older man associated with the old guard, was elected president.

Carlton Hughes, who was elected with Tracy and re-elected with Gee, was a Secretary of some extraordinary style. At the end of each year he wrote a History of the Board and recorded it in the minute book. For the year just ending Hughes offered this assessment:

"Coming into power after a struggle of two years between rival factions, and with the avowed purpose of changing a policy that had been in vogue for twenty years engrafted into the very spirit of Methodism as believed by many members of the Association, the new Board resolved to do all things that in its opinion would be for the betterment of the association both in a temporal and spiritual sense.

"Its accomplished work was a thorough overhauling of its stock records, correcting errors therein, and issuing stock to those entitled to it. Through the labor of M.D.Peck and C.Hughes principally this work was done, running through the entire life of the Board.

"The sanitary conditions of the Grove were radically changed for the better. The old manner of permitting the fecal matter of the closets to remain upon the ground until absorbed by the earth or washed away by the winters rains, was changed to a bucket-service, under control of a scavenger whose duty it was to empty and carry away from the grounds all such matter. Printed rules of Sanitation for cleanliness were made laws and distributed among the dwellers of the Grove.

"A camp meeting was held under adverse circumstances. Outside assistance was necessary to conduct the meeting as the Presiding Elder Naylor refused to officiate, and Rev. R. Norris was called at a cost of $100 and expenses.

"Chestnut and Grove Avenues were graded and opened. A reduction of annual expenses of over $1000 was brought about, the records of the Association were collected and classified, a newer, fuller and better arrangement made with the R.R. authorities and an impetus given to improvement."

Hughes was right to take credit for cleaning up the stockholder records, and his act of gathering up the Association records preserved some valuable documents which might otherwise have been lost (unfortunately, they were unable to find minutes of any stockholder's or trustees meetings for the Grove's first 8 years) but in general the other accomplishments were ongoing in nature and some credit for those should have been allocated to earlier boards.

During Gee's term the fight over proxies continued, with the traditional view prevailing, even though it had been established that not recognizing proxies was in contradiction to Maryland law. A new lease form was introduced by trustee Talbott, and another one by Gee himself. Gee poisoned relations between himself and most of the other trustees in the first meeting by attempting to appoint himself to the job of railroad agent. Bickering between Gee and the rest of the board continued all during the year, but by year-end a modified version of the Gee lease, which cured a significant flaw in previous leases, had been adopted.

Carlton Hughes

Carlton Hughes, outspoken Secretary of the Association from 1893 through 1900, was also a prolific poet.

The year ended with an annual meeting that was refreshingly uneventful until it came time to read the list of delinquent stockholders: Mr. Tracy rose and objected to the reading (for his name was surely on it again) and the chairman acquiesced, saving Tracy the embarrassment of a third consecutive mention. Carlton Hughes saw the year this way:

"The former board having assumed power after a protracted struggle thought it best to open its ranks and take into it a representative of its opponent. F.A.Gee was selected and made President of this Board of 94 and 95.

"The experiment was not a success as the President was imbued with the ideas of the old management and was not in accord with the progressiveness of the new.

"In consequence of this condition the year was passed in routine work and nothing new accomplished save the framing of a new form of lease.

"There seemcd to be a feeling of hostility between the old and new which prevented that spirit of progress so necessary.

"The President made the mistake at the organization of the Board to arbitrarily take to himself the position or office of R.R. agent and was opposed and beaten, thereafter destroying that confidence that should exist between members of the board.

"Entirely by the efforts and supervision of M.D.Peck a new or revised contract with the R.R. authorities was made from which this association derived benefit."

Gee was re-elected at the 1895 annual meeting, but not without incident. There had been a slate of trustee candidates printed in an apparent effort to prevent the re-election of Gee, or at least of certain other trustees. This was the first time there is any record of candidates running on slates, and Gee objected to this procedure. But then he countered the slate with a printed list of candidates of his own. The election proceeded as usual, but the ardent Secretary, Carlton Hughes, was outraged by the incident and promptly resigned when Gee was re-elected. He was persuaded to stay on, but relationships were strained and the conduct of business was affected. By early September it was clear that Gee could not work with the board. Finally Hughes introduced a motion that would effectively prevent the President from carrying out his duties. Gee requested that the motion be withdrawn, but when it was not he refused to put the motion to the board. Then Hughes asked that the president vacate the chair; Gee substituted a motion to adjourn instead, whereupon Hughes walked out, breaking the quorum.

Perhaps the president's ill-humor was the result of poor health; Gee never again met with the board. The vice President called a meeting four days later, and sent a messenger to invite the president to attend, but Gee was too ill to attend. Board meetings continued without Gee, whose condition rapidly worsened until his death in early November. Vice President Dr. M.D.Peck was elected to fill the chair, and the board returned to a harmonious and productive relationship that was to last for several years.

* * *

Growth and change occupied the trustees during the waning years of the century, as they confronted more practical aspects of operating the Grove: land division and use, maintenance of the streets and avenues, sanitation, and meeting the needs of a new breed of summer residents—a widening mix of people who had survived the years of tenting and who now had cottages, with those who had merely discovered a good thing and bought into it. These were people who had a sizable investment in the Grove, and wanted to be sure that some careless action of the board would not sweep it away. There was a new breed—a hybrid of the survivors and the discoverers—and though it was forged in controversy it emerged in unity. It was this breed that soon brought the best to Washington Grove, a unique mixture of the reverence inspired by a fundamentalist religion, the intellectual curiosity attendant with Chautauqua, and the robustness of competition on the playing fields. These virtues conspired to create the essence of modem Washington

Grove, a spirit which would flare brightly for the next dozen years, and then bum down to the enduring flame that would carry the Grove through its coldest and darkest hours.

PROFILES III:
PASSING THE TORCH

Several of the brightest lights among the Grove's founders were called to their creator in the period of transition from 1895 to 1905.

Dr. Flodoardo Howard was a founding trustee and first President of the Association, and was many times elected a member of the board of trustees. He was first brought to Montgomery County by his father from a farm in rural Virginia to the Quaker community of Brookeville, Maryland at the age of eleven. He apprenticed in medicine there with his uncle, Dr. Henry Howard, but moved to Washington at the age of 18 and studied pharmacy. He owned and operated a pharmacy until at the age of 41 he reentered the medical profession, eventually to be one of the founders of Georgetown University. At the age of 56 he returned to Brookeville in poor health, where he farmed and practiced medicine during his long recovery. He returned to Washington and Georgetown a distinguished- looking gentleman in full beard and moustache. He was married to Lydia Robertson, with whom he produced three sons and a daughter; he remarried in 1885 following her death. Always a prudent investor, he took the unusual action of entering into a pre-nuptial agreement with his second wife. They were soon taking their summers in Rockville, where he held a considerable amount of real estate, beginning in 1878, and became permanent residents there in 1885.

Howard had a cottage on the circle, and later he located his stock on a Grove Avenue lot, but he never built on it. He was associated with the Grove for over twenty-five years, and was active in meetings of the board of trustees until his death in January of 1888, at the age of 77. When the new subdivision plan was made up in 1896-7, the open ground adjacent to the hotel was named Howard Park in his honor.

* * *

William Ryland Woodward, founder and original trustee, vice president of the Association for its first 15 years, was born in 1819 in Georgetown. He attended Dickinson College in Pennsylvania and went on to study law at Cambridge University. He married Mary Redin, the daughter of a prominent Washington attorney, and set up a practice in Washington. He was a pioneer in the legal specialty of title investigation and perfection, and a founder of the first title insurance company in D.C. He acted as a trustee for the D.C. public school system and was appointed to a commission in 1862 to consider the emancipation of Washington's slave population, later serving on the board that compensated their owners. In 1879 he inhabited one of the first circle cottages, next to B. P.Brown's, and later built a cottage at 119 Grove Avenue. He died in 1903 in Washington.

Woodward's brother, G. Thomas Woodward, and his sister Roszel, were active in Grove affairs, as were his son William Redin Woodward, and his daughter Nanny Redin Milburn, the wife of the Reverend Page Milburn. Only in his early forties, W. Redin died suddenly and unexpectedly in the cottage on the circle on an evening in the last week of July 1898. Carlton Hughes dedicated this poem to his friend and neighbor:

Quiet had fallen upon the Grove,
So every leaf was still;
Only an echo heard now and then,
The call of the whip-poor-will.
The sweet, glad laugh of the little ones
Was hushed, though the night was young;
The songs of a merry, happy youth
For once were left unsung.

'Twas an unsought, uncalled visitor
Had come in this moonlit night
To summon a soul we could not spare
And bear him from mortal sight.
Not a footfall of this messenger
By the listeners was heard
And as he passed through the sylvan Grove
Not even a leaf was stirred.

He called but we could not hear the call,
Not e'en the watchers hear;
Our friend had gone with the messenger
Before we knew he was near.
We deemed the work in God's vineyard here
As urgent, and just begun;
The Lord of the harvest summoned him,
He knew that the work was done.

His sheaves are garnered in "Beulah Land,"
The worker is with the Lord'
The labor he did in the vineyard here
Is bearing a rich reward.
He builded better than e'en he thought,

His mansion is in the sky;
He has learned how the dead may live again,
The living may never die.

The footprints left by our Christian friend,
Are plain in the ways he trod;
They always have had the upward trend
And leading straight up to God.
Then peace, sweet peace to the one now gone,
To his honored ashes rest:
His memory for the good he's done
By every one is blessed.

In his "Reminiscences", Page Milburn writes that Woodward Field was named for G. T. Woodward, but it seems more likely that it was named for founder W. R. Woodward, his brother.

* * *

Benjamin Peyton Brown, founder, organizer, financier and self-styled business manager for the Association, never held office in the Grove beyond that of trustee, but was involved in every aspect of its existence. Born in tidewater Virginia in 1830, he was the youngest of six children and the only one to reach the age of fifty. He started at Dickinson College in 1849, but left soon thereafter because of diminishing eyesight. Two years later he was converted to Methodism by the Rev. John Lanahan, and joined the church. He was licensed to preach in 1852, became a deacon in 1855, and was elected an elder in 1857. Highly respected in Washington, he was appointed to a presidential commission which traveled to Montana to negotiate with the Sioux Indians. He and Rev. McCauley, a president of Dickinson College, made an official call on President Grant when he first took up residence in the White House.

Brown was many years the pastor of Foundry Church and twice a Presiding Elder of the Baltimore Conference of Methodists. He married twice and was the father of three children by each wife. He maintained a tent site on the circle for many years; like Dr. Howard he had a lot on Grove Avenue, but never built on it. In his later years he was often the voice of caution, admonishing the stockholders not to forget the purpose of the Grove.

Brown died in the winter of 1896-97; that spring South Avenue was renamed Brown Street in remembrance of his role. Homer Calkin's history of Foundry Church characterizes Brown as "clear and logical in his statements—earnestly expressing his convictions. His conversation was noted for its humor, wit, and anecdote."

* * *

Major Thomas P. Morgan, a founding trustee of the Association who succeeded Dr. Howard as its president, was born in Alexandria in 1821 of Quaker parents. His father died when he was eleven and the boy was taken in by a Montgomery County family. He worked the farm in the summers and went to school in the winter. At 15 he was apprenticed in the apothecary of Dr. Howard and later took up manufacturing and commercial enterprises. In 1847 he was elected to the common council of Washington and in 1851 to its Board of Aldermen. During the Civil War he was Army quartermaster in charge of water transport.

In 1873 Morgan was appointed to the D.C. board of Fire Commissioners and, in 1878, to the post of Major and Superintendent of the Metropolitan Police. He was active in church and Sunday school work and a President of the YMCA. He had an original cottage on the circle which survives at #2 The Circle, and later spent his summers at 112 Grove Avenue. He died in May of 1896.

* * *

Also taken in that period was Fred A. Gee, who had accepted the Presidency of the Association in a conciliatory role in 1894, and who was re-elected by the stockholders in 1895, but who was taken ill almost immediately thereafter and died that November. He was replaced by the Vice president, Dr. M.D. Peck, who finally calmed the troubled waters on the board of trustees and went on to serve five years as its president. But he, too, was ill and was increasingly distracted from Grove affairs until his death in October, 1901.

Thomas Somerville was a well-known Washingtonian and founder of the National Brass Works, a brass foundry which cast metal parts particularly for pipeline and plumbing connections. He died in 1898 but his cottage still stands as the front half of #17 The Circle, and his name is carried on by the Montgomery County distributor of plumbing supplies, Thomas Somerville and Company, Inc.

Another prominent Washingtonian whose life touched the Grove was William J. Sibley. He was born in Prince George County, but moved into Washington as a youth and went into the lumber business. In the 1840's he was appointed to serve as an assistant to the Postmaster General, and is credited with originating the postage stamp system in this country. His hardware business made him a fortune during the Civil War, and in later years he gave of his fortune to establish Sibley Hospital, originally the Lucy Webb Hayes School for nurses, which was eventually incorporated into American University. He attended the first camp meeting at the Grove, and others, and later bought several lots on the comer of Ridge Road and Center Street where he hoped to build a home for retired nurses in need of care. He built one of the first four large cottages which is still standing at 113 Grove Avenue. Sibley died on his 86th birthday in March of 1897.

Two other substantial Washingtonians in continuous association with the Grove were R.H.Willet and B.H.Stinemetz, whose cottages were on the Circle. Willet operated large lumber yards in the District of Columbia and Maryland, and Stinemetz kept a first class haberdashery in Georgetown. Willet was paralyzed by a stroke in January, 1902, which led to his death that year. Stinemetz died that October.

Each of the foregoing men, along with their families, had made important investment in the Grove- not by buying a share of stock, for each could easily afford to spend the $20, but by appreciating the Grove and believing that the Association could make it work. They, and the others like them, had built a foundation that would outlast their era.

THE ASSOCIATION

6

Bringing Chautauqua

THE YEARS FROM 1894 to 1904 were among the best of the Association's lifetime—everything seemed to fall into place. Peace had come to the board of trustees, a new subdivision plan was approved and filed with the county records, the number of residents who stayed all summer had grown to over seven hundred, and control had been passed to a younger group for whom the Civil War, Reconstruction, and the depression of the 1870's were second-hand memories. It was a period in which problems were solved, or if not solved, at least put away for a time. The best years were the busiest, as the new breed brought new facilities, new activities, and new traditions to the Grove, and finally brought it Chautauqua.

THE ASSEMBLY HALL

Before the turn of the century there had been no formal place of worship in the Grove other than the Tabernacle, except for the prayer tents which were erected during the camp meeting. In the early years there wasn't sufficient demand for a church building, as there was no congregation to meet in it. Among the few families who were present outside of camp meeting time there were always some preachers, either ordained or laymen, willing to lead a service, and the tabernacle was the logical spot to have it. By 1890 there was some interest expressed in having a chapel for use by the residents, and Wash Williams warehouse in the Triangle was proposed as a possible site. When the hotel opened and the warehouse was no longer in use, however, it was remodeled instead into a facility for Sunday School and other youth activities, and named the Young People's Hall.

By this time many families were staying in the Grove until the cold weather came in November or December, and some were even braving the winter months. In spite of some bad financial years during the mild depression that followed the Panic of 1893, the pressure grew to establish a Grove congregation and build a hall in which it could assemble out of the open air. Some fundraising was done during that period by the young people but the amounts collected were too small to inspire the planning necessary to bring a building to reality, and the lack of planning did not inspire more serious fundraising. In 1900 the Young People's Hall had become "a nuisance and an eyesore" and it was proposed to move it to the corner of Chestnut Road and Railroad Street and to sell the land under it to the adjacent residents, the money from the sale (about $100) to go to the chapel fund. The Hall, the store, and some sheds and stables were to be rearranged to accommodate a chapel to be located at the northwest corner of Chestnut Avenue and Center Street. Chapel Park had been set aside for a church building, but on reflection it was deemed by the trustees to be too close to the residential area. A committee was formed to map out a subscription program and secure plans for a building.

The financial climate was improving, and by the first of April, 1901, the young people had raised $1130. The building committee had procured a plan, they said, "that fully meets all requirements of a commodious, symmetrical, and substantial place of worship." By the first estimates the new hall would not exceed fifteen hundred dollars in cost, but upon review it became necessary to authorize an expenditure of $2000. An ambitious building schedule was

The Assembly Hall was built for a chapel and used for Chautauqua, but it was also the site of most stockholder meetings after 1902. The Hotel can be seen in the background.

announced by a committee made of William H.H.Smith, Dr. J.N. Bovee, and Irving T. Fulks: the building was to be complete and occupied by the 4th of July—the entire job would take only two months!

The miracle that would have been represented by the completion of the chapel in two months was not to appear, but good progress was made during the months that followed. By the end of April a plan was approved for the relocation of the motley collection of outbuildings on that side of the street. By mid-June the plan for reconstructing them all into the superintendent's barn was scrapped, and a third revised design of the chapel, to include a lower hall, was circulated and approved; it was presumably also at this meeting that the proposed location of the hall was brought back across Chestnut Road to its present location, and the lower hall added to the plan. The annual meeting minutes refer to the new building as the Auditorium, a name which had also been given the tabernacle from time to time. The name did not stick, and when it was completed in September (a miracle by modem standards, anyway) the building had already come to be known as the Assembly Hall. That name held until the 1950's when the building was rededicated in honor of Mayor Irving Leroy McCathran.

The Assembly Hall fronted on Grove Avenue and consisted of two sections: the main hall was an octagon 20 feet on a side or 48 feet across, with windows all around except for two double doors on the front which let out to a short uncovered porch. The lower meeting room area was a 20'x20' square section the width of one side of the octagon and attached to the back wall, and was accessible to the main hall by two narrow staircases on either side of a speaker's platform in the main hall, and from the outside by a door on the Center Street side. There was no plumbing, heat, or electric lighting. The foundation was cedar posts on pads of stone or brick; the main hall stood over two feet from the ground, its unattractive underpinning hidden by an attractive latticework. The outside and roof were of cedar shakes. It is possible that the Young People's Hall was remodeled to make up the lower section. At a glance, the building does not seem to have changed in these 85 years; in fact the only obvious changes are the widening of the lower hall to accommodate bathrooms and the addition of a covered porch with a belfry that houses the tabernacle bell. The original foundation proved to be unsuitable as the freezing and thawing cycles of winter pushed the walls and floors out of true, so eventually a block foundation was installed. The cupola, like the one on the tabernacle which topped the apex of its roofline, disappeared in time.

THE COMMERCIAL CORNER

It was not inevitable that the Grove would have a commercial zone on its southwest comer. Commercial ventures existed elsewhere on the grounds from the first picnic in 1873, but they existed only to satisfy the needs of the Grove, and they existed at the pleasure of, and under the tight restrictions of the board of trustees.

They included Wash Williams' furniture store, a food market, a barber, and , during camp meetings, a host of special goods and services. The hotel was also a commercial venture, rented each year to someone who would operate it for what he hoped would be a profit... The trustees closely controlled the nature of the merchandise offered in all the shops in the Grove and kept them corralled in specific areas. All these facilities were located in the area across Broadway from the tent department, in the public area where the Women's Club and McCathran Hall now stand.

What may have set the southwest corner apart from the rest of the Grove initially were its appearance—it was open ground—and its location on the Gaithersburg-Laytonsville Road. It is even possible that the road ran across it in an earlier time. The existence of the Washington Grove stop on the railroad brought traffic in

Hershey's store (c. 1900) was operated by J.L.Burns in the 1880's and 90's and contained the Grove's first chartered post office

from the pike; and thus a public lane was established through the private Association grounds, which left a triangle of land isolated against the railroad and put a public way on two sides of the comer lot. When the bridge wasbuilt in the 1880's it connected Railroad Street with Central Avenue, then a small county road on the other side of the tracks; in addition to more traffic, the earthworks from the bridge cast a shadow down Chestnut Avenue.

The Lang subdivision plat did not attempt to define that comer at all and, by abandoning it, seemed to exclude it from the useful grounds of the Association. The Maddox plan of 1897 showed it laid off in lots consistent with the rest of the Grove, but the slow development of the Chestnut Avenue corridor left it isolated and empty for many years.

The triangular piece across Railroad Street was sold to J.B.Diamond in 1896 for $805. It was not included, therefore, on the Maddox subdivision, and had been used for a variety of commercial purposes ever since. In 1897, at the same meeting of stockholders which approved and adopted the Maddox survey and subdivision plan, Irving T. Fulks sought to locate his ten shares of stock on lots 1 and 2 of Block 1—the commercial comer—for the stated purpose of building a store. After much discussion he was given permission to erect a store there, provided "that nothing objectionable was to be kept for sale or sold in such store."

A store has occupied the comer more or less continuously since then. Its freedom to operate as a commercial area has been repeatedly challenged since that time, but without serious curtailment until the 1980's. Fulks went on to purchase an acre of Association ground across the pike from his store (also excluded from the 1897 subdivision plat) in 1900, perhaps to expand his enterprises; but in the 86 years that followed there were no serious business enterprise established there.

A POST OFFICE

One of the facilities that best helps put a place on the map is a post office. Of course there has not always been a tight association between the existence of a post office and the place it purportedly serves, witness that Gaithersburg's post office was stubbornly called Forest Oak for years; and in the case of the Grove the post office lay outside its limits for most of its history.

Postal service in the Grove was available as early as 1878 in a comer of Wash B. Williams's store, though there was no official post office and no postmaster. A Grove post office was officially inaugurated in 1886 with the appointment of Sarah LaFetra as Postmaster. Mrs. LaFetra had leased the hotel for the season and held her post for only two months. In 1887 the post office was opened again in the hotel, this time for four months. Roszel Woodward, the sister of William R. and George T. Woodward, was Postmaster in 1888, and this time it was open through the end of September.

In 1888, the Association requested that a permanent office of the Post Office Department be established in the Grove, but the following summer a temporary office was again established in the Grove, but the following summer a temporary office was again maintained in the hotel, this time for six months, through November. Finally Jesse L. Bums, who operated the store just across the tracks, was appointed year-round postmaster in December. At the request of the Association the postal service was operated independently of Bum's store and on the Grove side of the tracks, in the little store on Broadway operated by Miss Woodward.

Bums was among the Grove's first year-round residents, but in 1890 he announced that he was moving the office back across the tracks to his store in the new subdivision of Oakmont. A strong protest was lodged by the Association, which said that it "would not consent under any circumstances to locating the P.O. across the Railroad tracks from the Grove side." It voted "to inform the Postmaster...that it insists upon the removal of the office to this side of the tracks" and "that in the case of failure of the Postmaster to comply, the Secretary be directed to lay the matter before the Postmaster General."

The matter remained unresolved and under protest until 1894 when the Post Office Department settled the argument in favor of Bums, and commissioned his store as the official location for the post office. Apparently a compromise was reached whereby Bums would operate a satellite post office in the hotel during the summer season. But in April of 1897 he again refused to open on the Grove side and more protests followed, again to the Postmaster General, this time including a petition from the residents. But Burns prevailed. In 1905 the trustees attempted to establish a rural free delivery route for the Grove, but this, too, failed, and the Washington Grove Post Office stayed outside of the Grove for another seventy-five years.

ILLUMINATION

At first the Grove was lighted by candle and coal oil (as kerosene was then known) both in the cottages and in the tabernacle. In the 1880's kerosene also illuminated Grove Avenue and the walkways radiating from the Circle. By 1889 a more highly refined liquid fuel, gasoline, was being widely used for outdoor lighting because it made a much brighter light, though it did require a much increased volume of fuel. In 1890 gasoline lamps were installed in the Grove as street lights and used for several years. But the price of gasoline increased more quickly than kerosene, and soon kerosene was again the more practical fuel. All the Association's gasoline lamps were sold at public auction in 1895.

Gas light had been used in Washington since the 1850's, and was by far the safest, brightest, and least expensive fuel. But it required a generating plant and pipelines that were impractical for the Grove. But in 1891 Grove resident C.E.Cissel offered to install "one of his patented gas lamps" in the tabernacle at no cost, in exchange for its advertising value. The lamps used acetylene gas released from calcium carbide crystals in a small cylindrical generator. The following month he added five more burners, and charged the Association 25 cents a night for the service. Gas became the preferred fuel for the Association's lighting needs.

Another form of energy, electricity, had become a common source of motive power in the cities with the invention of coal-burning dynamos in the 1870's, and electric lighting became practical with Edison's invention of the "improved electric lantern" in 1881. By 1890 the nation's capital was extensively wired, and gas gave way to electricity for lighting public buildings; many of the streets in Washington were illuminated at night for the first time by electricity.

In 1889 electric power lines came to the suburbs;

electricity powered the Rockville Electric Road, a trolley line that ran from Georgetown to Rockville. The Association was eager to have the trolley, and therefore the electricity, extended through the Grove to Gaithersburg. A delegation from the Grove received assurances that it would, and in 1906 a formal announcement of the extension was made. But the line went bankrupt before the extension broke ground.

In 1900 the Potomac Electric Power Company was formed by the merger of several competing firms. PEPCO offered to wire the Grove, but for unstated reasons the trustees declined; it is likely that the amortization costs would have been too great for the small, seasonal community to absorb. The Grove's buildings and walkways remained lighted by gas for another thirteen years.

FIRE SAFETY

Washington Grove was founded in the wake of the great Chicago fire of 1871. In spite of the perils of wood-fired cooking and coal-oil lighting, the Grove successfully avoided a damaging fire during its first twenty-five years. Several disastrous theatre fires shocked the world in the 1880's, however, and it may have been in response to these calamities that fire protection began to be a serious matter in the Grove. In 1888 the Grove purchased its first pump apparatus at a cost of approximately $100. In the early 1890's a form of individually operated extinguisher, called a hand grenade, was purchased; in 1895 an experimental new version using soda and acid was tested in the Grove.

Many residents expressed concern over the closeness of the cottages, and an amendment to the bylaws that every other cottage be removed for fire safety was seriously proposed. In time this spreading- out of cottages did occur, for a variety of reasons including the fear of fire but without the impetus of law. The only serious Grove fire of the last century occurred in 1897, in the hotel, where a heating unit caused damage to two rooms. The damage was quickly repaired and it was reported that the hotel suffered no loss of business over concern about its safety. At the next annual meeting the post of Fire Officer was established with the powers and duties "to see to the fire safety of the community."

ATHLETICS

One of the great benefits of the industrial revolution was the windfall of leisure time for those not of the leisure class. All over the world men and women began to use their free time to invent, learn, and play games. This worldwide movement culminated in 1896 when the first Olympic games of the modem era were played. Many existing games were imported into the United States in this period, and many new games were invented, including baseball (1839), tennis (1874), golf (1888), basketball (1891), volleyball (1895), and field hockey (1901). To help keep the devil away from their newly idle hands, the Methodists embraced athletics of many sorts. Baseball and tennis were to hit the Grove in a big way.

Baseball's origins are uncertain, though it may have come in part from the British game of rounders, played in colonial America, or from a game called One Old Cat, that was first played in the early 1800's; but the modern version of baseball is said to have been invented by Abner Doubleday in Cooperstown, NY in 1839.

Common rules were adopted in 1845 and the first national meet was held in 1858. Baseball was a gambler's game, and an accumulation of betting scandals forced a major cleanup in 1867. The modern league structure was designed at that time, and the Cincinnati Red Stockings became baseball's first professional team.

By the early 1870's there were several amateur baseball teams in the Gaithersburg and Rockville areas, and it is possible that some of the boys from the Grove's camp meeting crowd went off to play with them. By the mid 80's the game had become a summer obsession in the county, with every community fielding at least one team. Competition with teams from Washington and even further away regularly took place in the better county ball parks.

At this time the only cleared areas in the Grove were the fields farmed by W.A.Scott, the superintendent. When W.A.Scott lost his job in the early 1890's his fields could have lain fallow had not the seeds of baseball been sown on them instead. It was there in 1893 that the trustees first gave permission for the game to be played in the Grove. When Woodward Park was cleared of underbrush in the spring of 1896, the boys sought and obtained permission to set up a diamond there, and baseball has been played on it ever since.

In the peak Chautauqua years baseball came to be a consuming passion of the young men in the Grove, and the Washington Grove ball diamonds were the regular site of many county league games. A grandstand was added after the turn of the century, and baseball on a grand scale lasted in the Grove well into the depression of the 1930's.

The town's other athletic passion was tennis. Tennis

is ultimately derived from an ancient game, but today's version was invented in 1874 by a Major Wingfield. He called it Sphairistike, a name which fortunately did not stick, and played it on an hourglass-shaped court, which happily was also changed. The rectangular court was adapted to tennis in 1877, the year of the first tournament in Wimbledon. Lawn tennis, whether played on grass, clay, or asphalt, was always a game with a sparsity of rules—the racket still has no restrictions as to materials or dimensions. Tennis is played today essentially as it was in 1881, only the strategy employed having undergone profound changes.

In the Grove the first courts were authorized for the area between the Women's Club and Chapel Park, and also in Morgan Park. The trustees authorized that "the committee on grounds be authorized to locate and lay off lawn tennis and such like grounds upon the lower part of the hotel park and the park near the depot...granting the use of such courts to such persons as shall request them and will further prepare them for use." It is not recorded whether courts were actually prepared that summer, but a tradition of tennis was established with that act.

Tennis courts were next laid out in peaceful coexistence with a croquet court on the then-empty building lots at 118 Grove Avenue. However, the game was not considered peaceful enough by Mrs. Alfred Wood, of 122 Grove Avenue: in 1896 she filed a protest which successfully brought the playing to a halt. The following month a Mrs. Rerick was occupying the same cottage and was persuaded that the tennis should be resumed; on her advice the trustees lifted the stop order. Courts were built on the unoccupied lots north of McCauley Street at the end of 5th Avenue in about

1900, and continued in use for many years. The public courts that exist today on Grove Road were probably built in 1903 or 1904; they, too, were set on buildable lots, but those lots were incorporated into Woodward Park in 1905. In 1904, Mrs. Wood was again able to persuade the trustees to close the courts next to her, this time permanently.

Young Roy McCathran on one of the Grove's many private tennis courts.

Other private courts were built which more than made up for the loss of those on Grove Avenue; there are said to have been 20 or more courts active at one time, scattered about on otherwise unimproved lots, the comers of town parks, and tucked into narrow strips between cottages. There were courts at 401 Brown Street, 104 Pine Avenue, 103 and 112 Chestnut Avenue, 405 6th Avenue, and one somewhere on 4th Avenue near McCauley. There were as many as four public clay courts, and the Girl's club built at least one court north of the men's courts in Woodward Park in 1910, on which the girls played regular tournaments with teams from all over the county and Washington. The Great Depression and World War II slowed tennis down, and the private courts were slowly retired, but enthusiasm for the game returned with vigor in the late 1940's.

The third most popular sport in the Grove in those days was croquet—played on grass—or roque, a game with the same principles but played on a thirty-by-sixty foot hard-surfaced court with a raised border. Croquet courts could be set up anywhere there was grass—their shape could vary with the terrain. Prior to the Civil War, croquet was a game that was played primarily by small children, but by the end of the century it was also popular among adults, among whom croquet strategy could become a topic of intense discussion. Roque courts were located in the lot next to Mrs. Woods, in Chapel Park, and on Brown Street. Association President Williamson had a covered court in his backyard at 110 Grove Avenue.

Croquet, tennis, and baseball were played all summer and into the fall (though not yet on Sunday, for that would be Sabbath-breaking), but two holidays—the 4th of July and Labor Day—came to be devoted to athletics in the Grove. The 4th of July was a very big holiday throughout the country, with picnics, baseball, and fireworks, and celebrated with perhaps a little more spirit in that time of fewer holidays than it is today. A 4th of July picnic had been the Grove's first tradition, and when baseball came to the Grove the 4th became baseball's day.

Labor Day was a new holiday, first declared in New York City in 1884, having evolved from a traditional parade staged there by the Knights of Labor. In 1887, Colorado became the first state to set aside the first Monday in September as a holiday. The first nation-wide Labor Day did not occur until 1909, but in Maryland it was made a holiday each year by proclamation of the governor. In 1902 the Grove began a new tradition, the Labor Day Field Day. The games included in that first field day are not recorded, but in time a complete track with regulation courses and distances was set up opposite the diamonds on the baseball grounds. The annual Labor Day ritual was held regularly for the next thirty years.

For the less organized athletic enthusiast, the bicycle offered a pleasurable form of exercise. J.K.Staley invented the modem bicycle in England in 1885, and in 1890 the bicycle was still an imported luxury in the U.S. But by 1893 they had proliferated through the miracle of mass production, and were already a nuisance on the walkways in the Grove. Complaints of their speed and danger were made frequently during the 90's, with the trustees urging the riders to keep to "a moderate pace." In 1898 bicycles were banned from the walkways on Sundays. By 1900 bicycles were being produced in the hundreds of thousands annually and America was then exporting them. Bicycle racing and touring were popular among the Grove's summer residents and there came a time when you could tell whether someone was home by the presence or absence of his bicycle on the front porch.

CHAUTAUQUA

America's deep religious feeling had inspired the camp meeting movement, and its need for freedom from city heat and pollution had brought it the summer resort. The Grove had expanded from a camp into a summer community with the requisite institutions and traditions, but it shunned the frivolous vices of the resort in favor of the more wholesome entertainments of choir, bible reading, sermonizing, and other story telling-with-a-message. But the whole country was getting a taste for popular culture, and the residents of the Grove were not exceptions. By the turn of the century it was ready for Chautauqua.

The origins of Chautauqua were in the pre-Civil War Lyceum movement, which had spawned a number of self improvement societies with the purpose of literary and scientific study outside of the universities. Chautauqua itself was established as a Methodist Sunday school training camp on Lake Chautauqua in New York, in 1874. It was not a part of the Lyceum movement, nor was it a camp meeting, the only similarity being that the teachers were housed in tents the first few years. There teachers were rigorously trained in bible stories and holy land geography. In 1878 a new venture, the Chautauqua Literary and Scientific Circle, was formed by the founders of Chautauqua to be a university of the home—a correspondence school for classic and scientific study. Meanwhile on Lake

Chautauqua program, cover page, 1905. McCathran Hall before the cupola was added.

Chautauqua, the teachers school added courses in math, science, music, and foreign languages and, though still operating only in the summers, declared itself a University—The Chautauqua Institution.

Except in the form of its home study correspondence courses Chautauqua never left western New York, but imitations sprang up all over the country. There were two types, the independent Chautauqua, which operated at a fixed location, and the tent- (or circuit-) Chautauqua, which toured. Chautauquas were not always cultural, either—the name was borrowed for carnivals, a poultry show, a farm equipment exhibition, and the Ku Klux Klan once threw a 'Klantauqua'. Many were patterned on the Chautauqua Institution and occupied camp meeting sites. By 1886 there were 38 other Chautauquas, and by 1904, 150.

The circuit Chautauquas were organized by several independent producers, the largest ones by a Janies Redpath; circuits operated from as little as a week to the entire summer. The more serious ones ran from five to nine days long in each location and were tightly scheduled; before the last lecture was delivered in one town an advance team would be putting up the tent in the next. By 1910 the circuit Chautauquas were leaning away from education and towards entertainment, and some were clearly breaking the Sabbath. The peak years for Chautauquas were 1921 to 1924, with estimates of participation of up to 40 million; but by 1933 the last Chautauqua tent had folded.

Chautauqua first came to the Washington area in the form of a chapter of the Chautauqua Literary and Scientific Circle in 1883. Interest in establishing a local Chautauqua was centered in the Methodist community, and in January of 1891 at Foundry Church a meeting of those who wanted to bring Chautauqua to Washington combined forces with another group which was working to establish a "People's College". The college group had sixty acres and an auditorium that seated 2000 located at Glen Echo on the Potomac. The resultant organization, the National Chautauqua of Glen Echo, opened in June of 1891 with hopes of eventually becoming a liberal arts university. It operated continuously until May of 1903, but the venture failed financially and, in the spirit of the times, the hall was sold for an amusement park.

A child's ticket for the Chautauqua season of 1902.

Chautauqua in the Grove had as its antecedents the evenings of recitation, music, and reading at the hotel which had begun under Wash William's sponsorship. Also, camp meetings had brought speakers who addressed topics of social and political significance in concert with, but somewhat beyond, the purely religious. A tradition of music performances at the Grove had begun as early as 1889 when a large choir performed at the 4th of July ceremonies. Its director was Percy Foster, who was later to become a president of the Association, and whose avocation was directing large choirs—he once directed a choir of 1500 voices at a Washington Monument ceremony. During the summer season of 1900, there were regular Friday and Sunday evening lectures which often involved the use of a stereopticon, or slide projector. Finally, in 1901, the trustees—some of the same people who had worked on the Glen Echo project—authorized that "a Chautauqua committee composed of W.H.H. Smith and two members of the board be appointed to investigate the feasibility of a Chautauqua Course."

There were apparently some feelings of competition among the camp meeting leaders, for a month later an organization was established which would spread out the work and expense of the camp meeting, in order to expand the meeting and advertise it more widely. But Smith's Chautauqua committee came back to the board the following March with an "exhaustive report," according to the minutes. They swept the trustees off their feet and pulled the rug out from under the camp meeting committee by the boldness of their program. Rather than merely investigating its feasibility, the committee had planned a complete season of Chautauqua programs, and incorporated the camp and temperance meetings into the Chautauqua schedule as well! The program was to run for two full months, and aside from the camp meeting services there were to be "twenty-five pay events for week-days, forty free Sabbath services, and thirty-five free week day events, making one hundred services and events in all." The camp meeting committee grudgingly consented to the camp meeting schedule.

The trustees expanded Smith's committee and named it the Chautauqua Assembly Committee of the Washington Grove Camp Meeting Association. They recommended "that this committee and the Chautauqua plans be considered as a part of the work of the Washington Grove Camp Meeting Association, and not as an independent body," and the resolution went on to say that all disbursements should be the responsibility of the Association and the receipts accrue to its benefit, but that the committee should operate independently during the season. It was unusual to allow this degree of autonomy, but the resolution was granted unanimously by the board.

The Grove's first Chautauqua season began on the 4th of July, 1902 with a dedication of the Assembly Hall and patriotic services, and continued through Labor Day with a potpourri of events which included social sermons, musicals, pronouncing matches, spelling bees, illustrated lectures, and Chalk Talks, lectures from the blackboard. Special topics were to be emphasized on Temperance Day, G.A.R. Day, YMCA Day, and YPSCE Day. Sprinkled in with all this secular material were sermons, Sunday Schools, and Bible lessons taught by prominent clergy from various protestant denominations. The prices for tickets were $2.00, or $1.00 for children, per season, or reduced amounts for shorter times.

The acceptance of Chautauqua was immediate and enthusiastic. Its income more than covered its expenses, and the excess was applied to furnishing the Assembly Hall. At close of season the Chautauqua committee was enlarged in proportion to its endeavors—and for a while its endeavors were to include most of the camp meeting, athletic, and cultural events of the community. Its plans for the 1903 season were to expand on the most popular events—and these happened to be the more secular ones.

Chautauqua was planted under the calming influence of the years that M.D.Peck was president of the Association. In 1902 it blossomed under a new generation of officers—Henry Strang as president, John Bovee as vice president, David Wiber as Secretary, and Robert Cohen as Treasurer. A record number of residents—915—occupied the Grove in a record number of small and large cottages, a summer population nearly 20% greater than that of the present era.

7

The Walker Years

BEFORE THE TURN OF THE CENTURY the Grove was a reverent and quiet place, except during the two weeks of camp-when thousands came to praise the Lord aloud. When Chautauqua came, it spread the celebration out over the whole summer. The streets were busy six days a week, eight weeks a year. Carriages and two-seater buggies came from all over the county. A second track on the B&O line had been added in the 1890's, facilitating weekday train service for both camp meeting and Chautauqua. In 1906 a commodious new station-house—promised since the 1870's—was finally built. It featured separate men's and ladies' waiting rooms, each with a pot-bellied stove, separated by the ticket office a window each for the men and ladies and one outside for blacks. During the Chautauqua era the Grove reached its peak if busyness.

The Chautauqua experience fell about halfway along the path of the Grove's journey from a private religious corporation with a public purpose to a public municipal corporation with some very private features. This time in the life of the Grove was like the midpoint of a pendulum swing; when a pendulum reaches the bottom of its swing it is at its highest velocity but it is just beginning the deceleration to the end of its arc. For the Association, its midpoint was the time of its greatest prominence, but also the beginning of its end.

Major Sam Walker, himself at middle age, was the Grove's most prominent personality during this period—the Walker Era.

MAJOR WALKER

Samuel Hamilton Walker was born in Washington, D.C., in June of 1844 into a large and entrepreneurial family with roots in prosperous and aristocratic Prince George's County. He was named for his uncle, Samuel Hamilton Walker, a celebrated adventurer who fought in Mexico at the battle of Vera Cruz, later became a captain of the formidable Texas Rangers, and was the inventor of the Walker Colt, a formidable weapon of the times. Samuel's father Jonathan was originally an Episcopalian but was swept into Washington's enthusiastic Methodist community and joined Foundry Church. He is said to have founded—and helped build—McKendree Church on Massachusetts Avenue. Sam Walker attended college at what is now George Washington University, and went to work in 1862 as a clerk at City Hall, in the office of land records. He made a successful career as a land developer and builder, and accumulated capital in his own right. In 1872 he married Sallie Brady of Annapolis and built a grand house on Capital Hill, at 420 B Street. That house, and many of the other structures he built, are still standing.

Walker's talent with capital and finance led him into the bonding and insurance business, in which he founded four insurance companies, and then into banking, where he was among the original incorporators

180

of two Washington banks. His keen business sense carried him through the depression of the 1870's, from which he emerged a wealthy and prominent citizen. In 1886 he was named Superintendent of Police (of the District of Columbia)— a political appointment which he was to keep only a short time, but after which he was forever known as Major Walker. Family lore has it that he was asked to resign because of his excessive zeal on the job— specifically because he refused to tolerate congressmen's visits to Washington's flourishing houses of prostitution. Another reason given was his insistence that the police wear white gloves, and carry canes instead of billy clubs, that brought his police career to an early end. His official biography merely says that he resigned to give more attention to his business interests.

Whatever the case, Walker was certainly a devout Christian and an active Methodist. His family worshipped at McKendree Church, and he was for a time the superintendent of the Sunday School his father had built at Waugh Chapel. He was a founder and first president of the Washington branch of the Anti-Saloon League and is said to have paid the salaries of its staff. He often gave lodging to visiting preachers and regularly entertained clergy in his home. Among his friends in the Methodist community were several founders of the Washington Grove camp and, according to his granddaughter Rosalie Shantz, he began bringing his family to the Grove in the early 1880's, where he lodged them in the hotel for the season.

In around the year 1900, chronic illness is said to have taken hold of Major Walker—a daughter describes it as kidney trouble—and he decided to take a cottage at the Grove in order to rest and recover. The cottage he chose was located at 202 Grove

Walker family portrait in 1911. Rob Walker is at far left, the Major and Sallie at top right, and Rosalie Hardy Shantz is in front row center.

Avenue, one of the grander houses in the Grove, and competing with Percy Foster's large cottage at 111 Grove Avenue for Victorian grandeur. The house had been built by Hosea B. Moulton, a past president of the Association and the man who had bitterly refused to sell his side lot back to the Association for the Oak Street cross-over. Moulton died in the 1890's, and his widow sold her ten shares of stock and cottage to Walker in 1903. It was a big house with a square tower at its left front and had many gables and porches, with extensive gingerbread trim. He named the cottage Service, and added a water tower and indoor privy on the back, and eventually added several outbuildings, including a stable and cook's quarters.

The Walkers came out for the whole summer. Eight of the eleven Walker children had survived the perils of childhood disease and had grown to young adults. The two oldest were already married. With the Walkers came their doorman and cook from the B Street house, who lived during the summers over one of the outbuildings. The Walkers were one of the first of the Washington families to have a carriage at the Grove, in which they traveled widely into the county. In July of 1904, Walker accumulated another ten shares of Grove stock from among several stockholders, and in August his eldest daughter, Lucretia Hardy, purchased ten shares herself. All the Walker family shares acquired until that time had been bought from previous stockholders; the market price for Association stock was then below the $20 par value of the shares being offered from the Association's treasury.

The aura of vitality that Chautauqua brought to the Grove also brought Major Walker in search of a cure

Three views of Major Walkers cottage, Service, at 202 Grove Avenue.

for his illness. But once here Walker saw something else in the Grove—a place to establish his branch of the family, and a good investment opportunity as well—and he began to stake out a claim. The first years of the Walker era were like a courtship— Walker and the Grove began to do things together, and slowly their interest in each other grew. The period from Walker's first stock purchase in 1903 to his election as president in 1909 were very busy years in the Association's history, and Sam Walker had a part in most, though not all, of it.

STAKING A CLAIM

Chautauqua had fielded a rich and varied program with appeal to nearly everyone. There were purely scientific explanatory lectures, moral and social exploratory lectures, and politics, travelogues, and music—every kind of music from solos to orchestras, from harps to washtubs. Much of the talent was local, but there were the famous, too, including William Jennings Bryan. For children there was an array of programs from the purely educational to the trivially entertaining.

The Chautauqua Committee took over McCathran Hall as it did nearly everything else in the Grove, but soon it found that the Hall did not have enough available space for the number of events or the size of the audiences. After the third Chautauqua season a committee was appointed to study moving, enlarging, or enclosing the tabernacle. But it was quickly judged that the tabernacle, however modified, would never be adequate for the Chautauqua program. At a special stockholder's meeting in February of 1905 it was decided instead to build a new and enclosed tabernacle, away from the crowded Circle. A committee soon submitted its plans for a large building with floor dimensions of 80 by 100 feet, an overall height of 36 feet, and a seating capacity of 1400, "to accommodate the largely increasing patronage of our own people and those of the surrounding country in attendance of the regular Camp Meeting and Chautauqua events."

The old depot (left) was used for storage and a covered waiting area when the new station (right) replaced it in 1906.

The debate on where the new building should be located was lively. Major Walker thought it should be put in the vicinity of the tennis courts on the east side of Grove Road, but there was some opposition to this, since the entire length of Grove Road was platted for cottage lots on both sides, and the tennis courts next to Oak Street were considered to be but temporary occupants of the Grove Road lots. After more discussion, however, it was decided that Woodward Park should be extended out to the edge of Grove Road, so as to incorporate those building lots into the athletic fields. Major Walker's original suggestion was then adopted: the Auditorium, as it was soon to be called, would be located immediately behind the tennis courts. In an act which altered the ultimate layout of the Grove and contributed greatly to its long-term appeal, the stockholders then went on to declare the two blocks south of Oak and north of the building lots on Brown Street as officially "set apart for Athletic purposes and to be known as Athletic Park, and that hereafter no lot or lots shall be leased or sold for any building for private use," and "that the primary purposes for which this Park was set aside are...Base-Ball, Lawn Tennis Courts, Running Tracts, and such like purposes."

The following month local builder Hezekiah Day was selected from among several bidders to build the new Tabernacle at a contract price of $3700. Day declined to use any of the materials from the old tabernacle; he paid $100 for the privilege of taking it down and hauling it away for salvage.

The Auditorium was a handsome building. It was eighty feet across the front, with five 8x10 foot openings each with a double sliding door, each door having 6 large glass panes. There were five openings with the same sized doors down the hundred foot length of each side as well. With the doors opened it was an open air pavilion; closed it was transformed into an indoor arena or theater, depending on the seating arrangement. In the back was a shallow but adequate proscenium stage which connected with men's and ladies' dressing rooms and storage areas, one on each side. There were nine high windows at the back of the stage and stairways on each side of the front from the stage to the floor.

The floor was gently slanted from the front entrance to the stage at the back, which enhanced the building's

The Singer cottage, built 29 feet into Chapel Park to avoid cutting trees, was later home to the Cohen and Myers families.

The Foster cottage at 111 Grove Avenue was probably the most-gabled cottage in the Grove.

use as a theater, but which was distracting for playing certain games, such as basketball, where one's right leg would seem first a little shorter, then a little longer, than the left.

A long gable roof, with windows in its flat front and dormers, four to a side, provided a high ceiling over the center of the interior and contributed to the light and ventilation. The windows could be raised and lowered by a system of ropes and pulleys. Along the galleries seating was less desirable since there were six inch steel columns every 16 feet, and the ceiling tapered off to about ten feet at the outside walls.

The Auditorium was first lighted by gas, with an acetylene generator purchased for the purpose. There were four large chandeliers, each with twelve arms and one burner per arm, down the middle of the seating, and ten small chandeliers with three arms each mounted along the side. There were two large outdoor gas lamps near the front door. Later the building was wired for electricity. There were two wells with pumps, one at the left front of the building and one at the right rear.

A board walk was laid on Oak Street from Grove Road, and a stone walk connected Oak to the front of the Auditorium. The following summer the stone walk was continued northwest along a diagonal path from the front door to the comer of Grove Road and Center Street, where a path followed Center up to Grove Avenue and the Assembly Hall. A post and wire fence enclosed the Auditorium grounds. Except for its steel columns the building was entirely of wood, including its cedar shingles on the roof. The full cost of the building was just over $4000.; a note for that amount at 6% interest was signed with the National Capital Bank, a

The Auditorium at its inaugural celebration in 1905.
\

The interior of the Auditorium (c. 1905) shows its custom-made gas chandeliers and original benches. Later, many of the benches were broken up and burned, though a few survive today.

bank where Major Walker was a director

For the Auditorium's first season Percy Foster provided a grand piano from his Washington showroom. Funds for curtains and carpeting were appropriated from the treasury. The following summer an eight by ten foot porch was added in front of the middle door. The Auditorium was soon the focal point for all public activities, including camp meeting and Chautauqua, of course, but also a host of other religious, fraternal, and political meetings. A three-by- six foot billboard was placed at the Laytonsville Road corner to announce Chautauqua and other public activities at the Auditorium.

Percy Foster, talented musician and President of the Association from 1906 to 1909.

During this period of adjustment to Chautauqua, H.L.Strang was president of the Association. After eight years as treasurer, he had been elevated to the post in 1901 when Dr. Peck died in office. Like former Secretary Carlton Hughes, Strang was an amateur poet, and he contributed an annual poem in tribute to those who had died during the year past. Oddly, Strang was an extraordinarily poor speller for someone otherwise competent with both the English language and bookkeeping. He seems to have been neither allied with nor opposed to Major Walker's undertakings, but as Walker became more involved in Grove affairs, Strang seemed to become less so. In 1906 he was passed over for the presidency in favor of Percy Foster, but was elected vice president instead. This was apparently an insult, for Strang resigned immediately, and was replaced by John P. Davis.

Davis had a cottage just off the circle on Second Avenue, and later built the house at 103 Grove Avenue. He seems to have been a fiesty person by nature; he is often mentioned in the minutes of various meetings, often in an adversary role. Davis had not been an officer before the 1906 election but he had been chairman of the Grounds Committee, a demanding post with hard work and few rewards; no sooner was he vice president than he was enmeshed in fresh controversy. He wanted the path to the Auditorium along Oak Street to remain a boardwalk, but there was discussion of paving it in gravel instead. He threatened to resign if the trustees overrode him: they did, so he did. Dr. E.D.Huntley was elected to replace him.

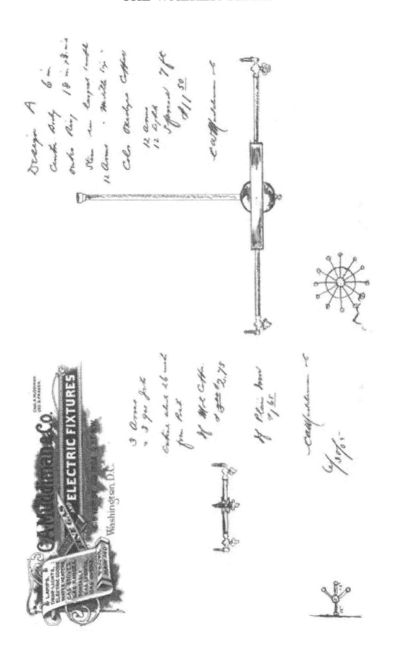

Original sketches of the gas chandeliers. They were later dumped in a landfill behind the Auditorium.

One of the effects of Chautauqua and the new Auditorium was to shift the focus of the Grove away from the Circle. Just the other side of the Auditorium were Maple Avenue, Maple Road, Cherry Avenue and Ridge Road. With the improvement of Oak and Center Streets these areas would be open for new cottages. It was decided to encourage development on the other side of the park and, by selling lots on Maple and Cherry, to offset the Auditorium loan.

The shift away from the Circle had one very practical aspect. It had long been thought that the closely packed cottages in the tent department constituted a health hazard for the spread of communicable diseases as well as a safety hazard for the spread of fire. While cottages had been moved before, the absence of the Tabernacle on the Circle and the new open areas to the east of the Auditorium and west of Chestnut Road gave new impetus to the relocation of cottages. In 1905, the cottage which stood next to 15 the Circle was moved to the southeast corner of Oak and Maple, where it stood until the 1960's. In 1906, the Teepe cottage at the north end of Grove Avenue in the yard of #413 was moved all the way to the other end of Grove to #105, where it stands today. Major Walker's daughter Lucretia and his son-in-law, William B. Hardy, bought and moved a cottage from the backyard of 1 The Circle to 102 Center Street. Walker bought the two lots adjacent to the Hardy lots, and eventually the Walker family owned the whole block between Center and Oak.

In 1906 J.K.McCathran moved the cottage that he and his father-in-law J.T.Harrison had built on lot 11 of 6th Avenue to Maple Avenue, where it stands today at #119. He may have purchased the required five shares of stock in annual installments, for the stock was not

The new station showing the freight loading platforms.

The new station in a wide angle view. The men's waiting room was on the left, the ladies' on the right. There were indoor and outdoor ticket windows.

issued to him until 1911. In 1907, the Ladies Guild decided to unburden itself of the two cottages it had maintained since early camp meeting days for camp officials: the Preacher's lodge and the Presiding Elder's cottage. The Presiding Elder's cottage had been on the Circle in the side yard of 402 Fifth Avenue; its move was authorized in 1908 and it was relocated to upper Maple Avenue, north of Oak Street. Tradition has it that the cottage at 205 Maple Avenue (lots 1 and 2) was moved there in 1905; if so, it seems likely that the presiding elder's cottage was located on lots 3 and 4. The Preacher's Lodge at 403 6th Avenue was donated to the Men's Athletic Association in 1910 and moved to the athletic field where it became their clubhouse. In 1911 the Rolfe cottage was moved from lot 17 of block 9 on the Circle to 418 Oak Street, at the corner with Ridge Road. Later, a cottage on lot 9, in the yard of 15 The Circle, was moved to lot 11, now 405 6th Avenue.

Other Circle area cottages were merged to make larger and more spacious dwellings; the houses at 404 4th Avenue and #8 and #17 The Circle are compound cottages, the one at 17 The Circle formed by joining the cottage on lot 2 end-to-end with the one on lot 4. For a time there was another double cottage on the circle—a cottage was connected by covered walkways to the house now at #2 the Circle. Two cottages were moved from near the circle and combined on the lot at 112 Chestnut Avenue, until they were taken down in the 1940's. One cottage, at 406 Grove Avenue, was turned 90 degrees and a front and back were added to it. Later, the Superintendent moved a cottage from the area of the Circle to the meadow at the north end of Chestnut Avenue. Most of the relocated cottages were just shells—in their new location they usually became the main room of a house, but wings for sleeping quarters, kitchens, and bathrooms had to be added.

The net result of this cottage moving was to make the Tent Department—the Circle and the numbered avenues—healthier, more attractive, and safer from fire. Ironically, the first catastrophic fire in the Grove occurred only six months later, but not in the Tent Department; instead it was on lower Grove Avenue.

Dr. Huntley's cottage at 108 Grove Avenue burned to the ground; Superintendent B.S.Pendleton was there and filed this report:

"On the night of Dec. 15, 1907 about 11:40 I was notified by Joe Brake and Chester Knott that Dr. E.D.Huntley's cottage was on fire. My wife commenced at once to ring the bell. I ran to the fire, and found the fire was beyond control in Dr. Huntley's cottage. I went to work with the aid of others to save the nearby cottages. A man by the name of Miller was occupying the Huntley cottage and was there when the fire started. He told me that the fire took from a coal oil lamp. Dr. Huntley's cottage was totally destroyed by the fire. About $50. worth of [household] goods was saved. Mr. Williamson's cottage [110 Grove Ave, later "the Parsonage"] was saved from burning by hard fighting. However one side was badly scorched. Mr. Percy Foster's cottage [111 Grove] was blistered some. And the front door to Mrs. Merriams's cottage [107 Grove] was blistered."

The Williamson house still has charred wood

showing in its attic.

One year and one day later the Presiding Elder's cottage on Maple Avenue met the same fate, after catching from a brush fire. This time the fire occurred in daylight, but this time Pendleton had to fight it alone, and was unable to save anything of it or its contents.

An indication of how settled the Grove was at this time can be gleaned from the list of those whom Pendleton reported to have fought the Huntley fire in 1907—it includes eighteen men from twelve year-round households, including members of two contemporary families, the Teepes and Rynexes. The Teepes had remodeled a cottage at 105 Grove Avenue, near the fire; one of the firefighters was Mrs. Teepe's brother, Tommy Koontz, who had the cottage at #1 The Circle. Another was Frank R. Rynex, who had just built a year-round house at 202 Chestnut Avenue, on the west side of the Grove.

As the Chestnut Avenue side of the Grove began to develop, the question of easier access to Grove Avenue and the athletic field was raised again. Center Street had not yet been opened to the Laytonsville Road, and Switch (Hickory) Road came down from Railroad Street, but did not continue past Oak. The Association had lost its chance to put Oak through from Grove to Chestnut when H.B.Moulton refused to sell his side lot. Major Walker bought the cottage and lot from Moulton's widow and was not asked, or did not offer, to sell the lot. The only mid-block crossing was still on Lot 24 closer to the railroad, next to Mrs. Woods and across from the Woodward cottage. It had been reserved as a cross-avenue on the 1883 Cottage Department plan and was designated Oak Avenue on the 1886 Lang plat, but the reservation was dropped on the Maddox survey of

The men's clubhouse was moved from the Circle and placed in the athletic field near home plate.

1897, on which it became simply a numbered lot.

In 1905, Major Walker offered to purchase lots 23 and 24, apparently intending to build a house for his daughter Florine Walther and her husband. Some tension resulted at the annual meeting as Mrs. Woodward and others filed protests, hoping to keep the entire 50' lot open. After extensive discussion and several alternative motions, it was finally decided to reserve only the northerly ten feet of lot 24, and to seek another ten feet from Mrs. Woods's adjacent lot 25 to form a twenty foot right-of-passage. Eventually the Walther fence enclosed all of lot 24, but the ten foot section on lot 25 stayed open into the 1960's.

It was at about this time, 1905-1906, that Major Walker began to collect the series of double and triple lots on which several of his children would eventually have their summer houses. Over a period of a dozen years he built or improved houses at 401 Brown Street,

103 Chestnut Avenue, 102 Center Street, and 118 and 203 Grove Avenue, all of which housed family members, but he built others, too: 215 Laytonsville Road, 313 Brown Street (315 Brown was built for the Reverend Albert Osborn by the same contractor, at the same time), 410 Brown Street, 419 Oak Street, 120 Chestnut Avenue, and 16 Maple Avenue. He also built a house for his cook in Emory Grove; it is said to have been the only two-story house there for many years.

It was also at about this time that Walker began to be concerned about the relationship between home ownership and shares, and between shares and voting rights. While he had not yet volunteered to be a trustee (and no one had so far nominated him) his business sense was well known among the trustees, so when the Association bylaws were to be reviewed he was appointed to the committee. As with all things Major Walker took this task to heart and was soon elected Chairman. Walker called a meeting of the trustees in mid-year at which time several important changes were discussed. A package of revisions was presented at the annual meeting in May, 1906, which was adopted without modification.

These changes taken together represented the first significant modernization of the Association's structure—three specific provisions were important:

There were to be staggered three-year terms for trustees. This measure was designed to prevent sudden changes in the Grove's management philosophy and the disruptions that can be associated with them, such as those which had occurred during the Tracy- Gee period. When the Association was made up of like-minded people, continuity from one board to the next was

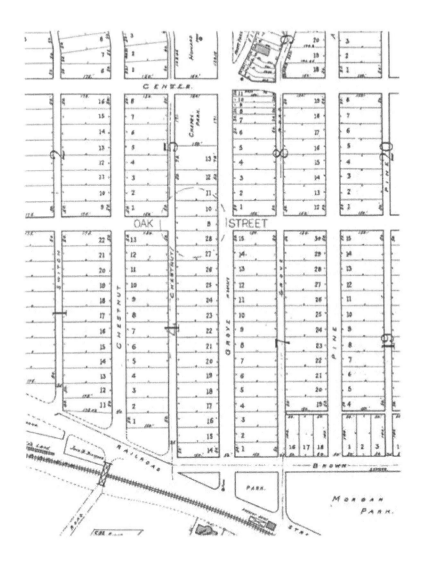

Oak Street was interrupted by one of President Moulton's lots. He refused to sell it back to the Association. Later, Major Walker left ten feet unfenced for use as a cross-through.

automatic. But when diversity of backgrounds and interests—and even of religion—came to the Grove, a more orderly system of making changes was needed.

All stock not located was to be located at once. If this could be accomplished it would remove the threat of argument—and litigation—over what constituted a vested interest in the Association. There would be a fixed relationship between ownership of stock and ownership of lots, so the argument over whether to issue leases or deeds would become easier to settle.

The words Camp Meeting were to be dropped from the Washington Grove Association of the District of Columbia and Maryland. This third provision was significant mostly in its implications: the camp meeting was no longer the Association's sole purpose, or even a separate purpose any more. Camp Meeting had been incorporated into the Chautauqua series and it was envisioned that it would continue only as a Chautauqua event—and last only so long as Chautauqua would last.

The changes were made in a spirit of harmony and progressiveness, and good business sense. Had the spirit carried through the Walker years and into the post-Walker era some of the issues raised later could have been settled more amicably. It is not likely that this would have saved the Association, for it was racing toward obsolescence, but it could have sustained the bright flame of the Chautauqua era and made the remaining twenty-five years more productive and harmonious. The immediate future, however, was bright, and Walker's personal stock was rising.

The Walker family continued to buy shares. By the end of 1907 they had accumulated 73 shares located on fourteen lots, including 10 lots near Service, one lot just off the Circle, and a group of three lots on Brown Street between Cherry Avenue and Maple Road. Brown Street at this time was a swamp at its low point—only in good weather could anyone expect to use it at all. In spite of attempts to stop them, the small farms out beyond Ridge Road continued to drive heavy wagons down it, which further undermined its base. Until Brown Street could be improved it would be impractical to build cottages there.

Major Walker put a proposition to the trustees: "We are expecting to form a syndicate of five persons to locate and improve Block 25, with five nearly fire-proof dwellings with permanent wire fencing and other necessary attractions, subject to the rules of the Association. We have five unlocated shares, and propose to purchase from you at par 40 shares more for $800, providing the Trustees will allow us $300 toward macadamizing the entire length of Brown Street 1420 feet from Ridge Road West. This will include 16 inch pipe under depression, filling, and grading, and macadamizing 12 feet wide in the center of Brown Street."

Walker went on to say, "A careful study of the Grove Plat will enable you to see that this is not a selfish scheme on our part, to make money, but a project to beautify and open up the most desirable land North of Brown Street and East of Pine Avenue. Before we go further, we desire a careful consideration by the Trustees, and definite answer." Though they objected to the idea of a syndicate and required Walker to have the shares all in his own name, the proposal was otherwise accepted by the trustees. Thirty-five shares were actually purchased from the Association and another 15 picked up in a private transaction; they were located on the balance of the nine lots which make up Block 25 and an additional lot in block 26, making a cluster of 13 lots in all at the end of Brown Street. The Walker family now controlled 113 of the Association's one thousand shares.

When the annual meeting came around in May of 1908 Major Walker was singled out for praise:

"We take great pleasure in recording our appreciation of the liberal expenditures and progressive ideas of our well-known citizen, Major S.H.Walker, and trust others will follow his leadership in the development of the unoccupied portions of our park." Major Walker was elected a trustee. With the new overlapping term arrangement there were both one- and three-year terms; Walker chose a one-year term. Later in the meeting he was elected Vice President of the Association behind Percy Foster, taking the seat recently vacated by the embittered H.L.Strang, the difficult John Davis, and the unfortunate Dr. Huntley.

The following year (1908-9) was a quiet year by official records: camp meeting had settled down into a ten-day routine, this year preceding the Chautauqua program and returning the Association half its $295. gross collections. Chautauqua began on July 27, later than usual, but it was well-attended and broke even, as usual. The Circle had been officially renamed the Plaza, and though it appears in print that way for a couple of years it is unlikely that the majority of people ever really called it the Plaza. By 1910 it was officially the Circle again.

Dr. Huntley, whose cottage had burned and who had only recently resigned as trustee, died over the winter of 1908-09. Carlton Hughes and H.L.Strang, the men who shared a poetic bent and had served so long together as Secretary and Treasurer, respectively, were both ill and retired from public life. President Foster was studying the idea of a telephone exchange for the Grove. A "Spotless Day" was held on the grounds for the first time, a community cleanup that became an annual event for several years. Major Walker paved Brown Street, bought 35 shares from the treasury at par (less $300), and arranged a mid-year meeting at the Grove, a "semi-religious social gathering" in his words, to promote development of lots on the east side of the Park.

At the next annual meeting Walker was re-elected to a three-year term as trustee. A previously unheralded Grove summer resident, L. Cabell Williamson, was elected president over Walker, but Williamson declined to serve. The Walker family now had accumulated 119 shares, and would have another 57 by the end of the year. Williamson had only ten shares, but his nomination and election was clearly in reaction to the threat of a Walker candidacy. After Williamson declined, two more ballots were taken, with the votes for president divided among John T. Meany, J. Walter Duvall, and Sam Walker. Finally Duvall and Meany dropped out and Walker was elected president.

What had been behind the obvious reluctance to elect him? Walker was easily the best-known Washingtonian at the Grove, and his stake in the Grove could hardly be ignored. He owned more shares than anyone else, he was apparently willing to invest in improvements, and he seemed to be in favor of the kind of constructive changes that other people were ready for. He had strong Methodist credentials and a reputation for philanthropy. But he also had a reputation for dominating whatever he undertook, for taking control. And with ownership of 20% of the stock—

easily a controlling interest in many public companies—
fear of his control was the issue.

THE WALKER PRESIDENCY

With Walker's election some kind of confrontation
became inevitable, and when the rift finally occurred it
was over a matter of principle, not of substance. The rift
healed over on the outside, and the Walker children
settled into various degrees of participation in Grove
life, but the strains of power kept the underlying wound
festering, where it would work at the very foundation of
the Grove. But the first year of the Walker presidency
began with progress on several fronts.

SUPERINTENDENTS

One of the problems promptly addressed by Walker
was the apparent inability of the Association to find and
hold a superintendent who could do the work he was
contracted to do, honestly and effectively. After
W.A.Scott left the job in the early '90's there followed a
succession of superintendents who for one reason or
another were unsatisfactory, and either quit or were
fired. An exception was George Bowie who hired on in
1897 and lasted almost five years, though not in perfect
harmony. Before the 1902 season was under way he quit
in a dispute over money, and was replaced by Thomas
Crown of Woodfield, Maryland. The following year
R.L.Pendleton was hired and remained two years, then
was replaced by his brother, B.S.Pendleton. The latter
Pendleton was ambitious for a larger role in the Grove,

and was subsequently granted the store concession as well, with the admonition that he should not let one job suffer in favor of the other. Apparently he did, for when he attempted to gain the hotel franchise too he was not only rebuffed in that effort but also discharged as superintendent.

In 1909, when Walker assumed the presidency, he installed an altogether new system. Instead of an outsider being hired to be the superintendent and do the work—in effect, be his own boss—Walker appointed one of the trustees, Frank R. Rynex, as superintendent, with authority to hire one or more helpers to do the work. The workers would report to Rynex, and Rynex would report to the Chairman of the Grounds Committee. In this way as many or as few men as actually needed would be hired, and kept only for the duration of their jobs. It was a splendid idea, and though it was not continued when Walker left, it did bring in a man who served the Grove long and well, and went on to become a full-time, long-term, though unusual, Grove resident—August H. Sorgenfrei.

Sorgenfrei began work in the Grove in 1910, and in 1911 moved into the superintendent's cottage, took over the barn and fields, and began operating the private livery stables along Grove Road behind the Assembly Hall. The job paid a modest sum, $20 a month during the summer, but it had other amenities. Besides the superintendent's cottage, a modest Grove-style cottage, were the grounds, composed of all of Block 3 and half of Block 6, which together could provide hay for feed and sale, feedlots for a modest number of hogs, steers, or milk cows, and even a chicken yard. Operating the stables netted a small sum of money each month for keeping and feeding other residents' and visitors' horses,

The 1909 Chautauqua program cover featured the Auditorium as seen by a center fielder on the ball diamond.

and allowed Sorgenfrei to keep a team for his own use and occasional rental.

Sorgenfrei became superintendent in the old style when Walker resigned. In 1914 he was provided with a new cottage, the old one having rotted out from the base. (The same fate had befallen the Auditorium sills, but the building was saved by the use of a recent invention, creosote, or "heavy carbon paint," in 1909.) He remained on the job until 1917, when he resigned as superintendent but offered to stay on, pay rent on the cottage, and keep the grounds for the Association over the winter. His offer was accepted, and in 1919 he bought the first of several lots at the north end of Block 3, and bought and moved a cottage from First Avenue to serve as his home. For the first time a superintendent had become a regular Grove resident, and Sorgenfrei, his wife Mary, and their daughters Bessie, Tessie, Gussie, and Mary participated fully and memorably in the Grove's religious and social activities.

THE LAKE

Food preservation became a problem for the Grove as soon as families began to stay for more than the two weeks of camp. When the Grove began to have year-round residents a regular supply of ice became a regular household need. The Grove had built a temporary ice house on lot 1A of Block 1 (where the Post Office is now), and ice cut from nearby ponds was stored there in straw. Major Walker saw an endless need for ice in the Grove, so he undertook the construction of an ice pond in the west woods below Maple Spring, from which he envisioned an endless supply.

There were insufficient funds for the project, and a

Maple Lake was build for ice production, but was soon a popular recreational feature of the Grove.

Gathering ice from Maple Lake. Though done for many years, it was never again profitable after the first boom years.

section of the Bylaws contained a $200 per year limit on such expenditures, so Walker advanced the money himself and proceeded with the project anyway, with the enthusiastic approval of the trustees. The Lake was designed to provide swimming and boating as well as a bountiful supply of ice. During the planning and survey it was discovered that Thomas Fulks had fenced in several hundred square feet of Grove land, and a suit was initiated to have the fence removed. Construction got underway in the summer of 1910 and by fall the shallow pond—named Maple Lake—was filling. Walker was handsomely rewarded that winter: in its first season the lake yielded over 300 tons of ice!

The Girl's Athletic Association clubhouse, built by Major Walker, sat north of the present tennis courts.

FIRST YEAR ENDS

Walker had undertaken a number of other activities with similar vitality. The trustees were not ready to grant a telephone franchise, but Walker got one line put through to the Rynex house for his use as superintendent, and another to the cottage of Reverend Sumwalt on the circle for his use as Chairman of the Religious Work committee and cosponsor with Reverend Osborn of the camp meeting services for the year.

The young women of the Grove had organized a Girls Club to pursue athletic and social endeavors— Major Walker advanced them $495 to build a fine clubhouse and tennis courts. Walker had new ditches built to carry stormwater from the circle to the west woods. The county had wanted the Association to declare the road from Laytonsville Road to the station a public road; Walker refused, and the county was forced to condemn the road and pay $225 for taking it. The Association used the money to grade and surface a new road, Railroad Street, which connected the station with Ridge Road, thus shunting the farmers and their heavy wagons away from Brown Street.

In his first annual report Walker proudly announced:

"We believe a NEW ERA has dawned upon the Grove, more residents than ever will continue with us the entire year and houses are being constructed and contracted for, to provide winter quarters, necessitating an extended system of sewerage, lighting, and heating. With this must come the regular Christian service every Sunday in the year and a continuous Sabbath School."

THE SECOND YEAR

Walker saw to it that regular services were held as promised. A congregation was officially formed and Reverend Osborn became its first regular supply pastor at the Grove, in the fall of 1910. His house was built at 315 Brown Street on a lot donated by Major Walker, who had the small cottage next door at 313 Brown built at the same time. Osborne's son Harold got the job of lighting the street lamps each evening, for which he was paid the sum of $12.50 a month. The main room of the Assembly Hall was fully decorated as a church, and the lower room was enlarged to house the Sunday School.

Improvements were made at the Lake that second year, and a wading pond was built at the fountainhead of Maple Spring. The Girls Club got its tennis courts, just north of the men's. The Preacher's Lodge, donated by the Ladies Guild and scheduled to become the Men's clubhouse, was finally moved to the park just behind the platted course of Pine Avenue in line with, but distant from, the Girls Clubhouse. The Major started a major new sewer project that year, too: the cottages on the west side of Grove Avenue had had a sewer, built in 1905, that ran under Chestnut Road, but the east side cottages had none.

The new system was designed by a professional engineer, one Professor Freeman, whom Walker cited as having laid out Garrett Park, and whose services were provided without cost by arrangement with Walker. Construction began in the spring on a sewer which would run all the way down Grove Road from Brown Street to the end of 6th Avenue, then turn and go back across the circle "through 200 feet of trap rock," eventually to spill out into a cesspool deep in the lake woods. Had this system worked as designed it would have provided the basis for the "extended system" Walker envisioned would allow the eventual settlement of the rest of the Grove.

There were some troubles with the county that

second year of the Walker presidency, but Walker took them up with the same enthusiasm which characterized most of his activities. First, the county discovered that the Association had enclosed part of the Laytonsville Road right-of-way within its west-side fence—over 300 feet of it in fact. In spite of Walker's attempts to forestall the action, the county ordered immediate removal of the fence. The county also chose to reassess the Grove that year; the property tax bill jumped from $75 to $265, nearly wiping out in a single year the $225 gained from the condemnation of Railroad Street. There were those among the trustees who thought that the increase was directly in retaliation for Walker's refusal the year before to open Railroad Street; given the politics of the times they were probably right. The Association protested the increase, its chief argument being that the Grove was a non-profit corporation, but a long battle ensued which the Association eventually lost.

A somewhat more chilling problem was presented in mid-summer by Dr. D.E.Wiber (who had been secretary while Strang was president, and who was now chairman of the Chautauqua committee): suddenly and for the first time the Chautauqua program was projected to show a deficit. Though it had always come out even or returned some profit to the treasury in all the years past, this year it would lose nearly $60. Dr. Wiber reported the expected loss and expressed the concern that "it may be that our people are tired of a Chautauqua Assembly, but prior to the advent of the assembly the Grove was a dismal failure. The Chautauqua with other modem ventures resuscitated the old camp ground." Clearly Dr. Wiber was referring to the Grove's function as a resort when he talked of failure, not its sense of community or its ambience, but this was a serious matter if the Grove was ever to be developed fully. After ten years of Chautauqua success, the leadership was suddenly shaken: its founder, W.H.H.Smith, resigned in disappointment and though Wiber remained on the committee, he became ill and died the following winter. Serious re- evaluation of the program would have to come before the next season could open.

THE THIRD YEAR

In spite of these difficulties, Walker's enthusiasm was unabated. His son-in-law, William B. Hardy, was elected a trustee. Walker continued to advance money for improvements, and continued to accumulate stock and build houses. In 1909 the family added 63 shares and in 1910, 75. They continued to buy and locate shares not only from the treasury at par value but from individual sellers at whatever the market would bear. Resentment of the Walker wealth or fear of its power, previously alluded to, began to resurface and some refused to sell their shares to Walker. It is said that W.H.H.Smith (lots 1-3 of block 8, or 201 Grove Avenue) refused to sell to Walker so the Major simply had someone else buy the shares and transfer them to him. By the end of 1910 the family owned over 25% of the outstanding stock. They controlled a majority of the lots in blocks 1,2, and 5 on the west side of the Grove and most of the lots fronting on or near the east end of Brown Street, about 50 lots in all.

It was at about this time that Major Walker started a new venture—operating a for-profit farm from within (or partly within) the Grove limits. It is not clear exactly how this began, but some of Walker's shares were located at the far limits of the Grove, out past McCauley

Brown Street after Major Walker's improvements. The drainage problem was never really solved.

Looking north on Grove Avenue in about 1900. The Foster cottage is in the right foreground.

Street and adjacent to Boundary Street. Neither Boundary nor any of the Avenues platted to run out to Boundary had yet been cleared, nor had any of the 10 blocks that make up the east woods today. Mrs. Walker bought four acres of farmland outside of the Grove but adjacent to Boundary Street. Through some machination a petition representing a majority of shareholders was presented to the trustees requesting that a fence be put up to enclose the unused Grove ground north of McCauley Street. Walker advised the trustees that the fence would cost $74. and in the next sentence he offered to rent the fenced-in area—all ten blocks—for "right of pasture for cattle, sheep, and hogs" for $25 per year. His request was granted unanimously.

One action was taken that year that never bore fruit. Four lots on Ridge Road at Center Street were reserved for a "rest home" for teachers, student nurses, and deaconesses of the Lucy Webb Hayes (widow of Rutherford B.) Training School "which includes Sibley Hospital, for the restoration of exhausted energies." Sibley Hospital had been the undertaking of some of the same Methodists who had founded the Grove. The rest home was never built, but the act of reserving the lots brought a little excitement when it was first thought that "exhausted energies" might mean tuberculosis! Later, one of the stockholders who had wanted to locate stock there decided to sue, but the matter must have been dropped, for there is no further mention of it in the minutes.

The expense of gas and the lamp-lighting were the subject of some concern that year—the treasurer L.F.Hunt moved at one meeting that no further money be paid on the lighting bill "until the value of light is demonstrated." Apparently the value of light was sufficiently demonstrated. In other activity, cement wings were added to the dike at the lake; the new Grove Road sewer was nearly completed. The cash position of the Association was at an all-time low because of Walker's many projects and the usual poor collection of assessments; Walker was now advancing money for operating expenses much earlier in the year. Almost all the expenditures of the Association came from Walker advances—and the cash income went almost exclusively to pay back the advances.

It was in this third year that the Association ran out of stock. There had been 1000 shares authorized, but 977 had been issued (nearly a third of it to the Walker family). The 23 remaining shares had all been subscribed to and partially paid-for in the past, but since the payments had not been completed, and the subscribers were difficult or impossible to find, the shares were finally declared forfeited. Major Walker bought ten of those immediately, young Irving Leroy McCathran bought 5, and Mrs. Walker took the remaining 8 shares early in 1913.

The lack of shares was a matter which would have to resolved for it left 300 or so unoccupied lots with no method consistent with the bylaws to get them occupied. It was a special concern to Major Walker, for he intended that the Grove continue developing.

THE FOURTH YEAR

Year four (1912-13) started out badly. Walker delivered his annual report in which he reported that the lake was finished, "with swimming, and two boats launched," and announced a vigorous new program to collect past due assessments. He alluded to a plan, soon to be unveiled, which would increase the shares of the Association.

But the meeting was tense and uneven. Walker spoke of continuing development, but there was another point of view, well-represented at the meeting but as yet unspoken; it was to come out shortly. After Walker's regular report Percy Foster resigned, both as officer and trustee, suddenly and without explanation. The president's son, Robert Walker, was nominated to fill the seat, but a protest was made and a roll call vote demanded. There were 374 shares present and voting, over 250 of them Walker family shares. Rob Walker was elected a trustee, then nominated and elected as Secretary. The meeting adjourned without further incident.

The Major worked over the summer on a plan to increase the available stock and presented it at a special meeting late in August. It was complex:

"That the trustees shall have the power to purchase at par, three-fifths of all outstanding stock, or so much thereof as they may deem necessary for the purposes of this Association, and to re-locate and reissue the same, allowing one share for 25 feet front or any fractional part thereof, on all lots outside of the tent department, and for said tent department they shall locate one share of stock for each 40 front feet or any fractional part thereof, a cash payment of $30 being made with each share of stock thus located, in either department."

In the simplest interpretation of the proposed statute, a tent department shareholder would not benefit in any way, since a typical tent lot was forty feet or less—if such a holder sold his share back for $20, he could repurchase it for $30, but it would still entitle him to just his original site. The typical cottage department shareholder, on the other hand, had five shares tied up in his lot—if he sold them all back for $100 he could buy five more for $150, and only two of the five would be required to locate his lot, leaving three to locate on another lot and a half. If 600 shares (three-fifths of the total outstanding) were repurchased and reissued in this way 240 would go into securing the lots they were originally located on, leaving 360 for new lots. Typical cottage area lots have 50 feet of frontage, so 180 new lots could be developed.

It had been the practice to extract an extra payment on newly developed lots—a shareholder might buy 5 shares at $20 each, then pay the Association an extra $300 to locate on a particular lot. There was no mention of this premium in the Walker plan.

It was immediately clear to some that this plan would be of benefit to anyone seeking to expand his holdings, and the more he held the greater the advantage, but that it would be of negative value to anyone who just wanted to own and occupy a house and enjoy the social and physical amenities of the Grove. But in the atmosphere of the August meeting it probably did not matter much how the motion read or how it was interpreted—the stockholders sensed that they were losing control, perhaps had already lost it, and they wanted to get it back. They may also have feared the establishment of a dynasty, now that three Walkers were trustees and two were officers.

The stockholders revolted, and refused even to consider the proposal, even though Walker quickly amended the plan to include a payment of cash for each lot, in addition to the shares required. The stockholders voted instead to refer the whole matter to a special committee composed of L.Cabell Williamson, Elmer

Cook, B. F. Brockway, Dan Garges, and A. H. Hiller. Most Grove business was put on hold pending the committee's report, which was to be delivered before February 1, 1913.

The committee called the stockholders back on the day before its deadline. Major Walker convened the meeting and then gave the chair to Vice President Meany, who called on the committee to report. First they delivered a strong rebuke to Rob Walker. As Secretary, he had been asked to supply the committee with data describing the fiscal condition of the Grove, including the number of shares outstanding, the names of the holders and lots on which they were located, details of unlocated stock, names of holders whose assessments were in arrears, statement of indebtedness giving the forms of evidence thereof, compilation of receipts to date and estimates of receipts for the balance of the year, the same for expenditures, the outstanding obligations for capital projects currently authorized, the amount of money in the hands of the treasurer, and a list of Grove property under lease for pasturage. He had not answered the committee's written requests at all, perhaps tom between a loyalty to his father and a loyalty to his position, or just doubting that the committee had been authorized to ask for so much. But he reluctantly relented in mid-January and agreed to release the information they wanted.

The Committee's first purpose had been to study and form an opinion on the 3/5 stock plan. Its report was a harsh and a direct repudiation of Major Walker's vision for the Grove:

"We are convinced that there is no necessity for passage of the resolution. We believe that by husbanding our resources...we will be able to pay our debts. . . and keep up the needed improvement in our property. We can do this without...throwing open the Grove to any colonization scheme. If further funds are necessary...we believe they can best be raised by a slight increase in our assessments."

The committee had also been asked to look into an offer to sell three and a half acres near Maple Spring.

"We are unalterably opposed to this sale or the sale of any land in fee."

Walker had seen the Grove as a good thing begun, and a good thing which needed to be finished. He had seen it as a good investment, had invested, and expected a good return on his investment. He had seen the lands to the east and north unused, unkempt, and had set out to clear them and put them to good use.

The committee had a different view. It saw the Grove as a home to its citizens and stockholders. Any improvements should improve the quality of life of the households now present, not the value of its stock. The report went on:

"While it might be asserted that our report should be limited to the subject matter of the two resolutions referred to us, we feel that we have a larger duty to the stockholders and with this in view, we make the following comments and recommendations."

There followed eight very specific proposals which had the effect of withdrawing all the land from pasturage, halting the harvest of trees, outlawing the keeping of livestock, moving the fences back out to the boundaries, and sharply limiting the powers of the president. As each proposal was read it was unanimously adopted by the stockholders. In conclusion the report read:

"The Committee would state that they think the policy of the Association should be...that the Grove is a place where the stockholders and their families, now residents, can enjoy the freedom of the land, the springs, woods and pastures without having to climb fences and be otherwise restricted in such enjoyment; we do not want to sell lots indiscriminately for the purpose of colonization, but to welcome as friends and neighbors such desirable persons as wish to join us; that we prefer to move along slowly but surely, and not be forced into debt by anyone interested in any speculation or money making scheme, so that it will be necessary to increase our taxes and assessments. We do not desire to dispose of any of our land in fee, as we could not then control the character of the persons with whom we must associate."

The meeting closed on a rising vote of thanks to the committee. With it the Walker era officially ended, and a long and bitter disengagement began.

The new form of stock certificate dropped the words 'camp meeting' and added a restrictive covenant.

PROFILES IV: PEOPLE

Frank Allen Rynex

Grandfather Samuel F. Rynex was an enthusiastically religious man, even from the 19th century point of view. He was a Presbyterian, and came to be the presiding elder of his Washington district. One didn't earn money as the presiding elder, however; Rynex operated a small department store in southeast Washington. Eventually he sold out, and clerked at Lansburgh's for the rest of his working life. His original share of stock in the Grove was purchased in 1890, and located in an eminent position on the circle.

He built a cottage there, and brought up two sons and two daughters in the Grove summers. In 1901, his son, Frank R. Rynex, bought the J.W.Wade cottage just across the circle to be his young family's summer home. His wife Gertrude was an accomplished landscape painter. They brought their firstborn, Paul, to the Grove, but he died in his second year. Later, Frank's sisters Byrd and Lucy owned and occupied their father's cottage. Lucy took a husband, but Byrd remained unmarried and cared for their other brother Caswell. Frank was as adventurous as his father was religious, and he had soon worked out a plan to make the Grove his year-round home. He bought five shares of stock and located it on Chestnut Avenue, which was just opening up to development, and still rather barren.

Frank R. Rynex built his house, possibly the first

structure in the Grove originally intended to serve the year round, at 202 Chestnut Avenue. Most of the other houses in the Grove were either on the circle (or just off), or on Grove Avenue, though a house had already been built on Oak Street, across from his lot. In 1904 he brought his wife Gertrude and their newborn son, Frank Allen, to live a good country life. He bought the four lots next to the house, and hired Zach Lewis, a black man, to live with them and act as as gardener, cook, and handyman.

Two and a half years later they had a daughter, Lucille; she and Frank Allen grew up there, among the first children of the Grove. The country life was a good one, and, though they were somewhat isolated, there were by then other pioneers in the Grove. Frank Rynex worked for the Department of Labor, commuting daily on the train. In 1911 Gertrude's mother, a widow just remarried, bought stock and had Sam Walker build her a house at 120 Chestnut Avenue, up the block from her daughter.

After a decade in the Grove, though, events began to foreshadow the end of this experiment in country living. There were other factors too, but in 1914 the first of three disasters took place in the house next door. The youngest daughter of the Welches, a family who was renting there, had apparently used gasoline to start the stove one morning—it exploded and she caught fire. She got outside, and her father managed to roll her up in a blanket, but she lived only a few days. Young Frank saw the drama from his bedroom window.

The next year, with another family in the house, a small girl stepped into a bucket of hot cleaning water and was badly injured falling down the stairs. But the last straw came in 1916 when a family with three girls had taken up residence there. All three girls came down with polio after swimming in a nearby pool. Though they all recovered, polio was not a disease one took lightly.

Rynex's reaction was swift—the family left immediately for Washington. Until they could get a place of their own they moved in with Frank's sister Lucy. Though they were through with year-round living in the Grove, Frank was Secretary to the Association at the time and continued in that office even after they moved back to the city. In 1917 his daughter Lucille became ill, and it was thought best that her mother take her out west for a cure. Young Frank, now 13 years old, and his father stayed on living in bachelor quarters. They continued to visit the Grove during the summers.

It was a day or two before the 4th of July, 1918, that Frank and another boy were on their way back from Gaithersburg, where they had purchased some fireworks for the coming celebration. Just outside of the Grove on the Laytonsville Road was a cherry tree, ready for picking. Frank climbed way up, leaned back to extend his reach, and his head made contact with the high voltage supply line. He was knocked out of the tree, but broke no bones. A doctor took him to his grandmother's house on Chestnut Avenue, but after several days the burned side of his head did not seem to be healing.

He was moved to Emergency Hospital in Washington where it was determined that the flesh on the wound was dead; when they removed it, they found that the bone underneath was charred. There being no skin grafting at that time, the only course was to stretch the skin from the surrounding area. After several weeks this procedure was successful and

Frank could leave the hospital.

At about this time Frank's father finagled a trip to Seattle in connection with his work for the immigration service. On the way he dropped Frank in southern California to visit his mother. It was an agreeable place, and Frank was happy to be reunited with his mother, so he stayed on, finished school, and became an electrician. His father returned to Washington, but not to the Grove—he sold his stock and house to the Deland family, and resigned as a member of the board of Trustees on May 9, 1919.

An electrician in Hollywood in the 1920's and 30's had many opportunities. Frank worked in lighting for the movies for awhile, got interested in ham radio, and worked in a shop assembling radios. While there, he was sent to install an antenna and receiving set for Douglas Fairbanks and Mary Pickford. In the 30's he had his own place, The Hollywood Day and Night Radio and Electric Shop.

In 1940, back in the Grove, Frank's grandmother died, and his mother stood to inherit the house. First she, and then Frank, came back to the Grove. They lived in her mother's house for a time, but were not comfortable in it. Soon after, they bought the house at 118 Chestnut Avenue, which had been the summer house of Henry Milans and was made up of two cottages which had been moved from the vicinity of the Circle. They totally remodeled it until hardly a board remained from the original. Frank met his wife Bessie May in the Grove in 1944. She had been working in Bethesda as a bookkeeper, and Frank, having one of the rare automobiles in the Grove, had driven by her several times on the streetcorner waiting for the bus which would take her to Gaithersburg, from which she would have to walk home. After several offers she finally accepted his offer of a ride. They married and brought up three girls, May, Phyllis, and Sylvia during the nineteen-forties and -fifties.

Mildred Couch Myers

The Couch family lived on the other end of Brown Street from the Rynex's. They were active and involved in many aspects of Grove life in the period from 1908 on. Mildred wrote this brief memoir of her time in the Grove:

"In the year 1908, when I was twelve years old, my father, mother, and I moved to Washington from Bridgeport, Connecticut. That summer we visited my aunt, Mrs. T. Tweedale, who had a cottage on First Avenue in Washington Grove. The next summer we rented a cottage next to hers, across from hers, across from the Assembly Hall.

"At Camp Meeting time , I remember people coming in their horse and buggies and tying them to the trees in back of our cottage. Up the street from us was an open air Tabernacle where their services were held. They liked the Grove so much that their two days of camp meeting were not long enough, so they built cottages to replace the tents. Six avenues went out from the Circle and many of the original cottages still remain. As they stayed longer the cottages were added onto. Finally they came out to the Grove as soon as the schools were out and they left the day after Labor Day. As the Grove grew many things developed—a men's athletic association, tennis courts, a full track for sporting events, an unbeatable baseball team (my father was the manager), a good band under Roy McCathran, a minstrel show, Chautauqua, and always the ten days of camp meeting. A woman's athletic association was also formed.

"A large Assembly Hall was built where all meetings, including Church services, were held.

"Before the past fifty years, the town was not incorporated. Stock was bought in the Association, and located on certain ground. This entitled one to so many votes in the Association meetings. The Annual Meeting on May 30th was always a very big event.

"As I have said, the Church services were held in the Assembly Hall. My Father played the piano for all services, was Librarian in the Sunday School. My Mother taught a Sunday School class and I played the organ and helped in the Primary Department.

"Later on a large auditorium was built where the Camp Meetings and other large events were held. Camp Meetings were held for ten days, which included two Sundays. My Father played the piano for all services and also for the Minstrel Show held there.

"Later Samuel Walker built for my family an all year round "bungalow" on upper Brown Street. The house is now owned by the Jenne family, I believe. I remember that on the day we moved from our cottage to the Brown Street house deep snow was on the ground and how thankful we were to be in a house that had a furnace! We still had outhouses and when we heard a horse and wagon and a man was coming to empty them we were always quick to determine which way the wind was blowing. My Father had a large pump on the back porch and every night he would pump water to fill the large tank in the basement in order to have running water inside of the house. I remember studying by the light of an oil lamp, how smelly they were at times and a chore to keep clean. It was a very happy day when we got electricity.

"We lived there all the year round for only a few years but during that time my Father helped Dr. Osborn to establish a year round church.

"There was a wonderful group of Teenagers who had so much fun together, playing together, going on picnics and hayrides and always an all day trip to Seneca on the river. In the Evenings, about fifteen or twenty would meet at someone's cottage to play games.

When I think what goes on today I give thanks for the good friends that we grew up with. There was never any trouble with any of them. We were a group of happy young people enjoying each other.

"At the end of World War I there was a dance at the Grove Hotel one Saturday night and 2nd. Lieut. Charles M. Myers asked me for a dance and later for a date. We were married in Washington by Dr. Albert Osborn on March 5, 1921. The past March 5th we celebrated our 66th Wedding Anniversary. We have had many wonderful years together.

"Dr. Osborn christened our son Charles Frank (then two years old) when we returned from duty in Panama in 1924.

"Two and a half years later our daughter Mildred Isabel was born at Fort Monroe, Va.

"Now Charlie will be 92 years old on May 6th and I will be 90 years old. We both look back with many happy thoughts of when we lived at the Grove and shall always give thanks for having been brought up in such a wonderful environment.

M.C.M."

THE ASSOCIATION

8

Disengagement

A TRUSTEES MEETING WAS HELD three weeks after the confrontational January stockholder's meeting. Walker was still in the Chair, so only routine business was conducted, including approval of the transfer of 45 shares from various sources to Walker and his wife. There was no mention of the events of the previous meeting, nor any movement toward taking action on the stockholders' demands. By the time the trustees met again a month later, a petition from impatient stockholders had been received. It demanded another special stockholder's meeting be called for the purpose of "ascertaining what action had been taken to carry out the recommendations adopted by the stockholders on January 31, 1913."

President Walker was aware of the petition and came prepared to resign; he began the meeting by reading the text of what would have been his annual report, three months before it was due to be presented at the May 30 annual meeting. His report listed the accomplishments of his administration, which were lengthy and impressive. He then made plain his view that the Association was apportioning more of the tax burden to unimproved property (of which he was the largest holder) than was its share. In the same vein he proposed that the Association begin paying a dividend on its stock, with funds obtained by renting the pastureland for profit.

His report went on to recommend that a program of timber management, including cutting and replanting, be instituted. He urged that the "property yard" south of Railroad Street and west of the bridge was "a valuable asset and should never be sold." He decried the system in which the owners of ten shares of stock could call a stockholder's meeting, 20 made a quorum, and 14 of the twenty shares could make or change the bylaws. He proposed that other Christian churches be invited to camp meeting and that each of those interested be invited to direct a day's services. He scolded the signers of the petition who had brought him to this point: "so many...are in arrears [on their assessments]." He denied the rumors that he had accepted stock in return for his services, noting the only exception being that of the $375 stock discount he was eventually allowed for having paved Brown Street. He reported that he had now voluntarily surrendered all the pastureland, for which he was paid-up to the end of the year, except block 30 and parts of blocks 13 and 15, which were still under cultivation. He followed his report with a brief letter of resignation, to be effective immediately.

Walker stepped down from the Presidency, but did not resign as a trustee—he had just been elected the previous May for a 3-year term. Walker's ally, J.W.Duvall, was elected to succeed him, but Duvall declined to serve, giving ill health as the reason. Finally the Vice President, John T. Meany, was elevated to the presidency, and Bert H. Brockway was elected vice-president. The Walker presidency was over, but not the

Walker presence.

The Williamson Era

The disengagement that began with Walker's resignation took its second step eight weeks later at the 1913 annual meeting. Opposing slates were offered for the three board openings, Walker nominating Robert Cook and Herb Davis for two of them, but Cissel nominated L. Cabell Williamson, Frank Rynex, and Mrs. Amelia Huntley. Williamson was a successful Washington attorney, a fiscal conservative, and the owner of the second-largest block of Grove stock. Mrs. Huntley, the widow of the former trustee, was an active Methodist missionary. The full Cissel slate was elected, and with it Mrs. Huntley became the first woman to serve on the Board of Trustees. Williamson was elected President, and John Meany was returned as Vice President. Rob Walker remained as Secretary and L.F.Hunt as Treasurer.

Walker's personal stock at the meeting was low, but it dropped even lower when his two biggest projects, the Lake and the Grove Road sewer, were both publicly called into question. It was revealed that because of weather conditions the Lake had not produced enough ice over the previous winter to justify expenses (no fault of the Major's, of course) and the empty ice house across from the property yard had been rented to Walker for storage. Furthermore, an ice manufacturing plant had been established at Rockville, and one was under construction in Gaithersburg, all of which made the Lake seem a questionable expense. Then Cissel called the stockholders' attention to some deficiencies in the new sewer. They were deemed serious enough problems that, pending the report of a special study, the stockholders voted to limit the sewer to "gray water" (wash water) only. The meeting ended on this sour note.

A thorough sewer study was undertaken during the summer, and on the first of August the stockholders were called to hear the results. The devastating report drove another wedge between Walker and his neighbors—the sewer was defective in every way. Above ground, the manholes had not been properly elevated, and silt was allowed to wash in. Below ground, the pipe joints were not properly sealed, so dirt could seep in and sewage could seep out. Furthermore, the slope of the pipe was uneven, so that at one low point the pipe was already half filled with sediment. The entire length of the sewer would have to be taken up and rebuilt.

At the same meeting a committee studying the forest reserves issued its report. With the help of a State Forester they submitted a plan that called for managing the forests for firewood production, a plan which supported Walker's claim that 30 cords or more could be taken a year while improving the forests at the same time. The report was accepted, but because it was in direct conflict with the conservationist mood and the action taken at the January 31 meeting, it was put aside. The meeting had degenerated into an unbalanced contest: the entire Association vs. Major Walker.

It is evident from the minutes, which were kept almost verbatim by Walker's son, Rob, that tension rose as the meeting went on. President Williamson tried to steer the meeting away from a personal confrontation with Major Walker, but prior to the meeting Walker had published and distributed a twenty-one page pamphlet, primarily an explanation and defense of his involvement with the Boundary Street fence. The Association had requested that he rebuild it at his own expense, but Walker argued in the pamphlet that the fence had been removed at the request of the Association, so why should he as an individual have to replace it. The issue would have been easily resolved under ordinary conditions, but in the acrimonious atmosphere of this meeting compromise was impossible.

There were those who tried to open the meeting to the issues raised by Walker. The air was electric when, near the end of the meeting, Dr. Ritter "rose to a point of personal privilege" on behalf of Major Walker. A parliamentary scuffle ensued in which Ritter was denied the floor three times, finally on the technicality that a point of personal privilege had to be taken on one's own behalf, not another's. This point was then debated, Ritter declaring that he would make it a point of personal privilege of his own, but then he was interrupted by a motion to adjourn, which by Robert's Rules of Order takes precedence over all other motions. The adjournment motion was seconded and carried by 47 to 15, and the divisive evening ended.

A grumbling dissatisfaction with Walker's personal vision for the Grove had grown into a distrust of his motives, and that led to fear of his power. Rumors fed on themselves and soon Walker was defending himself against "near-truths and half statements of fact that evilly disposed persons have poured in your ears," in the words of a pamphlet he printed and distributed later in the summer. Walker had brought this controversy on himself, but not by lust for power or evil purpose. He did have a fundamental and growing disagreement with some of his neighbors over the direction the Grove should take, but it was his insensitivity to the tension that his wealth and position created in people that brought the controversy to such a bitter end.

When this meeting was over the breach between Major Walker and the Association was complete and irreversible, but the disengagement had only begun. Walker was still a trustee and still had a legitimate ownership interest in a third of the Grove, and the unresolved conflict would flare up again and again. But in the years immediately following his resignation there were increasing distractions, as the technology of the cities began to stretch out to the Grove.

THE TIDE OF TECHNOLOGY

Electricity

Sparks had flown during the Walker confrontations, but another kind of electricity was coming to the Grove, and this development was welcomed by everyone. Street lighting by kerosene had always been considered too dim, and gasoline lights cost too much to operate. Acetylene gas was used in the Auditorium, but it was expensive, too, and awkward— it took 300 pounds of carbide to generate enough gas for an average summer season. Kerosene was a dangerous fuel to use in the cottages, and candles were considered primitive, and dangerous besides.

Water had to be pumped by hand in the Grove, except at the hotel which had a noxious gasoline-powered pump which was always breaking down. Though by this time electric motors were doing much of the work in the cities, and even on farms, all the heavy work in the Grove was still done by hand. The Grove was ready for electricity.

DISENGAGEMENT

President Walker had been working on getting electricity into the Grove during his last years in office. Finally the Potomac Electric Power Company, a newly-formed conglomerate of the area's small power companies, presented the Association with a contract. This was the Grove's first franchise, so the trustees considered and reconsidered it very carefully through several revisions. In its final form the contract gave PEPCO the perpetual right to set and maintain poles and wires along the streets and roads of the Grove, specifically excluding any poles on the walkways except to hold streetlights. Rates were to be renegotiated annually, but were not to exceed ten cents per kilowatt hour (even today rates for most customers are well under five cents a kilowatt hour). There was to be a minimum billing of one dollar per month for each connected building, though the Association insisted on a clause that buildings could be selectively disconnected upon a month's notice, thus saving itself and the summer residents a great deal of money during the winter months.

Pepco began clearing and installing poles in April of 1914, without waiting for the stockholders' final approval of the contract. The official community flagpole, which had stood at the comer of Grove Road and Oak Street for years, was in the way of the wires, so it was moved to what was then the far end of center field, about 400 feet from home plate, where it stands today. Sorgenfrei got permission to cut and sell the timber from along the right-of-way. The new superintendent welcomed the work, for it had not been a profitable year. He was normally expected to derive a substantial part of his income from the sale of ice and firewood, but the Walker controversy had put a hold on woodcutting, and the mild winter had denied him a crop of ice.

When the power was first turned on in July there were fifty-one customers, the Association included. But there was little actual lighting, since the cottages were just beginning to be wired, and there were too few available electricians to wire so many houses at once. In the course of the summer both the Assembly Hall and the Auditorium were wired with 33 forty watt lamps in the Hall and 86 in the Auditorium. In the fall, twenty-six iron poles were placed on the walkways and lamps wired in. The external wiring was similar to the present technology, but the interior wiring was very different. Two insulated wires—a hot lead and a ground return—were brought into a building through separate ceramic insulators. Once inside they were routed along studs and rafters with a 3" separation between them, and stretched between sets of ceramic insulators screwed or nailed to the wood.

The electricity that flowed in them had a pressure of about 110 volts, and alternated at 25 cycles per second. The lamps had clear glass envelopes, and the filaments glowed brightly, but not too brightly to be looked into. There was a visible pulsing in the emitted light because of the low frequency used; the human eye can detect frequencies of up to nearly 60 cycles per second. The following spring a 1 horsepower motor was purchased for $100 to power the hotel's water pump, though it was not until 1915 that the hotel was wired for lights.

All the outmoded lighting methods gave way to electricity. The coal oil chandelier from the Assembly Hall was offered at public sale. The community of Emory Grove bought the gas-driven street lights which had sat on short wooden poles along the avenues;

presumably they were used on the streets there until electricity was extended once more. The acetylene plant was sold for $50. The immediate fate of the Auditorium's gas lamps is not known, but subsequently they were discarded; several fittings and jets were later found in an old trash pit behind the Auditorium site.

The Telephone

Another civilizing utility that reached the Grove in this period was the telephone. Bell had invented the device shortly after the Grove's founding, and by 1878 there was a public telephone exchange in the District. Private lines had crossed the Association's grounds as early as 1894, but there was no general service available to Grove residents. A Gaithersburg line was run to the hotel in 1905, and a line was brought in to Dr. Sumwalt's cottage on the circle in 1909 for his use while serving on the camp meeting committee. Another line was run to Frank Rynex's house on at Oak and Chestnut while he acted as superintendent. After Walker's resignation Rynex purchased the instrument for $25, and became the first Grove resident to have a telephone for private purposes.

The Chesapeake and Potomac Telephone Company of Baltimore offered to wire the Grove in 1909, and outgoing president Percy Foster recommended in favor of it, but the trustees declined. Perhaps other private lines were put in, and in 1916 the trustees allowed a line to cross under Railroad Street to bring service to the Day Collapsible Box Company building on the Grove's old property yard. Finally in April of 1920 they granted a franchise to C&P which allowed the wholesale installation of telephones, "provided all telephone poles be put in alleys, and that no trees be cut."

Chautauqua in the Grove had by this time diminished to a bright but short season of entertainment. A Chautauqua longer than two weeks would not show a profit, and though profits were hardly the Grove's motive, the Association could not afford to entertain itself and its neighbors at a loss. When electricity came it opened up the possibility of a whole new world of entertainment—moving pictures.

Moving Pictures

The Auditorium had been wired in the summer of 1913. In the spring of 1914 several residents approached the trustees with the idea of buying a motion picture machine. The trustees backed the idea: if the residents were willing to put up the money, the trustees would allow them to charge admission to recoup their investment. Ten residents, headed by B.H.Brockway, rented a machine from the Webster Electric Company in Washington. With the projector came a fireproof booth to surround it and the operator—this was required because the pictures were then printed on a film of cellulose nitrate, a highly flammable material, which moved past a very hot carbon arc lamp as the film was being shown. The whole kit sold for $200. They rented it for the first season, but the idea quickly proved to be a big success, so they decided to buy it instead. Ten subscribers paid one dollar a month, and with a credit they got on the rental they had paid all but the last $50 by the beginning of the second season.

Friday and Saturday night movies fast became a tradition in the Grove. The popular films of the first few seasons included D.W.Griffith's classics, "Birth of a

Nation" (1915) and "Intolerance" (1916), Mack Sennett comedies like "Barney Oldfield's Race for Life" (1914) and "Teddy at the Throttle" (1917), and early Chaplin films like "The Tramp" (1915) and "The Immigrant" (1917). Talking movies were first produced in the late 20's, and by the early 30's they too were being shown in the Auditorium. The favorites talkies among the young people of the time were "Our Gang" comedies and Tom Mix westerns, and by then the shows at the Grove often included a cartoon and a newsreel, too. The tradition of showing movies in the Auditorium that began in this era continued long after Camp Meeting and Chautauqua were memories.

BLIGHT!

Advances in communication and transportation were bringing the continents closer together, expanding the markets for American products abroad and bringing goods to America from all over the world. But the same technology that was enriching American lives was to bring ruin to the nation's noblest tree—the American Chestnut.

Chestnuts and chinquapins were large shade trees of the beech family (which includes oaks as well) and were found in abundance in the mixed hardwood forests of the eastern United States. A fungus accidently imported from the Orient was introduced into New York City in 1904, from which it spread rapidly north, west, and south. By the mid 1920's the entire U.S. population of chestnuts was affected, and today no large examples of the species survive.

The Grove counted a large number of chestnuts in its forest inventory, and their proportions were initially increasing. Chestnuts were usually spared the axe out of respect for their beauty and the value their fruit; the nut itself has a unique and delicious taste, and is eaten both raw and roasted. Some of the Grove's summer residents would come back in the fall for a day of gathering chestnuts. In those days one could fill a gunny sack with chestnuts in a very short time.

The blight struck quickly. Caryl Walker Winter remembered a visit to the Grove shortly after her marriage in 1912. She was walking down Grove Avenue toward her father's cottage and remembered remarking to her husband that the leaves on Percy Foster's grand chestnut were already brown, but that it was only August. In August of 1913 the trustees were informed of a dead chestnut tree in Page Milburn's yard, and later, after a survey, it was reported that a number of chestnuts and gums were dead of the disease. In the fall of 1918, all the chestnuts were found to have been infected— they were ordered to be cut and sold en masse for their timber value.

Another favorite American shade tree, the elm, was also present in the Grove, but in smaller numbers. The elms are susceptible to another virus, introduced in the 1930's, which acts more slowly than chestnut blight to kill the tree, and which can be controlled somewhat by pruning. Ironically, a forester's report written in the 1920's suggested that the Grove's chestnuts be replaced by elms, and dozens were planted along the walkways. Today, however, no native or planted examples of the species survive in the Grove.

CONFRONTATION IN THE CORN

Major Walker continued to have his own ideas about

how things should be done in the Grove, and continued to try to do them his own way despite the trustees' desires to the contrary. When Walker rented the grounds north of McCauley Street and combined them with Mrs. Walker's land outside the Grove for planting, he had the fence along Boundary Street removed by the superintendent, with the permission of the trustees. When the agreement was rescinded in 1913 Walker was requested to put back the fence. In his view however, since as president he had ordered it removed for a legitimate purpose, he should not be required as a private citizen to put it back. Furthermore, he had a crop of com that was already knee-high.

Major Walker with helpers at haying time. Walker considered fallow ground to be a waste of the Lord's resources.

The first request to rebuild the fence was delivered to Walker in June. In late June the nervous trustees observed that he had erected some posts, but no wire. When there was still no fence in July a motion was made to complete the fence at Association expense and send the bill to Walker. Brockway suggested they hold the order until Walker had a chance to harvest his crop, but Frank Rynex argued that Walker had been notified before the crop was ever put in, so did not deserve the courtesy of additional time. In the end, Walker did win a delay until his crop could be brought in, but the fence was then hastily erected.

The following year Mrs. Walker's land was planted in rye. In late July, Sorgenfrei noticed that someone had apparently cut through the new Boundary Street fence at the end of 6th Avenue. He repaired the damage that day, but the next day Mrs. Huntley observed a team had driven through a fresh cut. Sorgenfrei drove to the site and observed "Mr. S.H.Walker and Mr. Charlie Myers, Jr. at said inlet, Charlie Myers having an iron bar and a wire cutter in his hand." Mr. Mills and his son, from the farm at the end of Railroad Street, were loading rye onto a wagon. Sorgenfrei placed his wagon across the cut. Sorgenfrei later reported to the trustees:

"Mills, on completing loading the wagon drove up to said inlet of boundary fence and asked me to give order to remove my wagon so he could drive out which I refused to do, he then asked of S.H.Walker whether he would stand the expense of suit for damages to horse and wagon which question said S.H.Walker answered with 'yes I will stand the expenses' thereupon I placed myself in the middle of the inlet saying that he would have to drive over me first, said Mills again asked of

S.H.Walker would he stand the expense of driving over man, horse, wagon, and all, said S.H.Walker answered again 'I stand the expense.' After some parleying S.H.Walker beckoned to the Mills and Charlie Myers, after some consulting three of them walked across adjoining property at which place the fence was cut thereby obtaining an outlet to the pike, I there upon stretched another piece of wire across 6th Avenue."

Walker was requested to present and explain himself at a special meeting of the board the following Saturday in the lower room of the Hall. When he failed to appear the board adjourned to visit the scene of the cut. Incensed by what they saw, they immediately referred the matter to the magistrate at Rockville. The following month Mrs. Huntley reported that the fence had been cut again. This time the trustees ordered Sorgenfrei to put in posts, which seems to have settled the matter.

Then the focus of Walker's actions shifted to another battlefield, near the comer of Oak and Ridge Road. Walker had built a cottage on lot one of block 32, 419 Oak Street, which he rented to a man named Worden. On September 14, Walker was accused of cutting five trees in excess of 5" in diameter—strictly against Grove covenants—and "killing by fire 18 small and 7 large oak, chestnut, and gum trees on lots 12 and 13 of block 31, the property of the Association." A committee of the board studying the matter recommended criminal prosecution. Walker, as had become his fashion, did not respond to the charges.

At this time Oak Street was not officially open to Ridge Road, and there were remnants of the fence which had enclosed the entire grounds still in place here and there. Ridge Road farmer W.H.Brake, neighbor and friend of the year-round residents of the Grove, protested the winter closing of Oak Street as it was customarily used as a shortcut by teams from his farm and others on the ridge. Walker joined the argument in February of 1915, asserting that his tenant had threatened to vacate if he could not have access to Ridge Road. The board argued that since Center Street was open to Ridge, and the gate there was left unlocked, Walker's tenant could take his wagon down Cherry Road, a platted but uncleared lane, to Center, and get out that way.

Sorgenfrei had added two large posts, ten feet apart, at the end of Oak Street, and placed a small post between them to prevent wagons from getting through. He reported that "I fully expected that the small post would be cut out by some parties, but great was my surprise when on my usual daily round on Tuesday I found not alone the small post cut, but one of the large posts as well."

Mrs. Benson, of 418 Oak Street, gave the following account:

"On the first day of February 1915 there had been erected across Oak Street a barrier of posts planted in the ground which said barrier prohibited the ingress or egress of teams at this point; that on the first day of February one of the said barrier posts was cut giving access by wagons at said Oak Street; that the following day Robert Walker came out and cut down two more posts."

Sorgenfrei had been instructed to clear the alley, but the Bensons had planted some fruit trees in it, and had a clothesline attached to another of the trees on it. The next day he came back and began to clear the alley. Mrs. Benson asked him not to cut her line, but he did, anyway. The following day he planted new posts, and was putting up wire "when Mr. Robert Walker came over and started to cut the wire; Mr. Sorgenfrei tried to stop him with no seeming result, Mr. Walker completing the cutting until the wire was all down."

Two weeks later Sorgenfrei notified the Bensons that their trees would have to be removed. They replied that they would do so in the Spring, but the ground was frozen, so they could not do it now. Sorgenfrei went on a rampage the next day, driving his team and wagon over the Benson's wood pile and several of their seven to eight foot fruit trees, twisting and skinning them. A complete investigation was conducted by the board in March, with testimony from all concerned. The conflict was never really settled, but when Walker's term as trustee expired that May he was not re-elected; the matter of the fruit trees was permitted to drop.

THE DEED CONTROVERSY

In the meantime, the war between the Walkers and the Association was being waged on yet another front: in the courts. Robert Walker had filed two suits, one on his mother's behalf, and one on his own behalf, to test the authority of the Association. The object was to obtain fee simple deeds, which the Walkers hoped would give them independence from the Association in matters dealing with their property. In July of 1913, Sallie Walker formally requested such a deed for her lots on Grove Avenue. In May of 1914, Robert Walker requested a lease for his property on block 26, in hopes of then invoking a Maryland law that said leases were redeemable for fee simple deeds.

But the Association was not giving leases anymore, it was conveying title instead by a form of deed which was closely tied to the Association bylaws. Walker argued that the bylaws allowed both deeds and leases; but the trustees refused to issue either the old lease form or a fee simple deed. In July 1914 suits were filed on both issues in circuit court in Rockville, and Judge Peters elected to hear the cases together.

The following June Peters decided against the Sallie Walker suit, but his decision in July was that the Association should grant Robert Walker a deed with certain enumerated restrictions. In August appeals of both suits were entered, and by October the Association was feeling pinched by the great expense of pursuing them. But finally, in March of 1916, to the great joy of the trustees, both appeals were decided in favor of the Association, with costs to be assessed against the Walkers. With the decision came relief from another thorn in the side of the board—Dr. Ritter had also long insisted on his right to a fee simple deed, and had recently refused to pay his assessments. Action to collect costs from the Walkers and assessments from Ritter was taken immediately.

THE DEEP FREEZE

Since Walker controlled a third of the Association shares directly, and had other supporters among the stockholders, it would have taken a relative handful of absent or apathetic voters to allow his plans to continue, despite a clear majority of individuals opposed to them. But in 1913 Williamson's solid block of 65 shares had been enough to tip the balance, and Walker admitted defeat by resigning. Williamson represented the voice of reason, which preached a policy of fiscal restraint. After he took office he openly expressed his anger at the poor financial condition the Grove was in, and took steps to remedy it.

But the court victory elevated Williamson to the status of a hero. Walker had tested the will of Williamson and the other trustees in the fields and in the courts, and lost every battle. But there was no truce, only an undeclared cease-fire. To prevent the power balance from slipping away, the trustees invoked a section of the bylaws that allowed them to refuse sale of stock to persons of bad character (specifically, to those who were not 'proper persons'), and thereafter refused to sell or transfer any more shares to anyone in the Walker family.

Under this interdict the Walkers could still buy shares on the open market, but the Association would not transfer them; in effect the shares would be retired, since neither the original nor the new holder could vote the shares. Even under this restriction, though, the Walker block could still take control if they could retire enough shares from among the group that was opposed to them. The Association waged an open and active campaign to discourage selling to the Walkers, and few did.

Williamson had served through these first three difficult years, often—like Walker before him—having to advance funds to keep the Association solvent. In his report to the annual meeting in May, 1916 he seemed weary, but expressed confidence in the future as he stated that "the stockholders can now feel assured that no legal question can be raised in respect to his holding of lots and improvements thereon, by virtue of locations under the stock and the certificate issued as provided in the By-laws." He asked that "each one for himself shall carefully consider what he can and ought to do to help beautify and maintain the Grove as an ideal place to enjoy himself with good water, fresh air, friendly Christian feeling and with every look a pleasant vision."

* * *

Williamson had helped the majority of stockholders repudiate a policy they did not support. Among that majority the strongest and most active element were those many families—most of whom owned only the minimum shares required to locate on their lots—who had forsaken the city for year-round country living in the Grove. The proportion of year-rounders continued to grow, and Williamson continued in the office for another five years, long enough to see the development of new factions and finally the election of a President whose full-time home was in the Grove.

9

Confronting the Modern Age

J|, CABELL WILLIAMSON WAS PRESIDENT for •
eight years—the same length of time Thomas P. Morgan
had served in the same capacity in the 1880's. But the
world of Williamson's time was very different. His
predecessor, Sam Walker, had started the work of
bringing the Grove into the twentieth century and, in
most respects, Williamson finished it. When he retired
in 1922 the Grove had electric lights, telephones, and a
year-round supply of manufactured ice for its iceboxes.
The automobile had arrived: some of the Grove men
were going into the automobile business, and garages
had begun to replace the horse barns along streets that
were newly paved with cinders for rubber- tired traffic.
Deeds had replaced 99-year leases, and a large number
of families lived in their houses all year

The Grove had fifty years' accumulation of
institutions and traditions, and social units to practice
them: the Anti-Saloon League, the preacher's meetings,
YMCA activities, Chautauqua, and the camp meeting
itself. But these early social units were based on ideas

and tied to organizations that originated outside the Grove; only when the residents began to form social units based within the Grove could it be said that the Grove was on its way to becoming a town.

THE CLUBS

No sooner is a middle-class distilled out of society than a fraternal organization is formed within it. In fact it may be reasonable to say that the existence of such organizations are part of the definition of a middle class. In this country, organized fraternal and sorority groups first emigrated from England, where they had evolved from upper class private clubs, and diffused into the middle class. In America they were linked with religion and their membership was culled from church congregations, overwhelmingly Protestant but interdenominational: their constituted purpose was to serve the greater community in a socio-religious manner.

Early in the 19th century the clubs were predominantly male, but many had auxiliary ladies' organizations. The first Oddfellows Lodge in Washington was formed, for example, in 1819, and its female auxiliary, the Rebeccas, was formed in 1853. The explosion of leisure time that came with the industrial revolution brought clubs within the reach of a large and growing middle class; by 1900 it was not uncommon for a middle-class adult man or woman to belong to several clubs.

The men of the Grove usually belonged to clubs in Washington, and sometimes they held meetings in the Grove. But before 1905 the closest thing to a Grove club was the exclusively male Board of Trustees—a "stag party," as Lucretia Walker Hardy would later call it. The first official men's club seems to have been the Men's Athletic Association, formed in 1905 to promote competitive sports in the Grove. Woodward Park and the lots between it and Grove Road had just been reserved as parkland and dedicated to athletic purposes, and the men already had two tennis courts and a ball diamond set up in it. In the park's early years a baseball team was established, and the club sponsored field and track events on the 4th of July and Labor Day. The competitive tennis and baseball teams were limited to serious young men, but everyone participated in the field day games.

After the disastrous Huntley fire in 1907 the men formed an auxiliary to the Athletic Club, the Fire Committee, which raised funds to purchase pumps and fire extinguishers for distribution around the Grove.

The Men's Athletic Association fielded a serious baseball team.

That same fire led to efforts to get distance between the crowded Circle-area cottages, and many cottages were moved, combined, or removed soon thereafter. The Preacher's Lodge on 6th Avenue was donated to the men's club, and they moved it into the park for a clubhouse, where it sat for many years at the south end of the field just under the canopy of trees.

Another men's service and social group that shared members, and the clubhouse, with the Athletic Association was the Washington Grove Band, formed in 1912 under the leadership of Roy McCathran. Snappy in their blue and white uniforms with garrison caps and brass eagle insignia, they played not only at Grove functions but all over the county, and sometimes in the city. The band thrived until the camp meeting and Chautauqua era came to an end, and it was finally disbanded in 1928. None of these clubs were made up exclusively of Grove residents; they often included members from Oakmont, east Gaithersburg, and the small farms on the periphery of the Grove.

In time, the national men's clubs formed local units in Washington Grove or Gaithersburg. An Oddfellows lodge was formed in about 1912, and a unit of the Rebeccas in 1913. The men met regularly in the Assembly Hall, and rented the Auditorium for entertainments. In 1919, the Oddfellows bought the Property Lot at the corner of Railroad Street and Switch (Hickory) Road (which Major Walker had admonished the trustees "should never be sold" in 1913) for the sum of six hundred dollars, and built a large hall for their meetings and socials. The building serves today as the Grove's Post Office. By 1920 there were enough high degree Masons to form a unit of the Level Club, which met on various occasions in the Assembly Hall, in the

Auditorium, and at the men's clubhouse in the park.

The women's organizations were actively engaged in Grove work much earlier than the men's. A Ladies Guild of some kind or other existed in most church congregations in the nineteenth century, and the Washington Conference of Methodists itself had a Ladies Guild, made up of members from the churches in the conference. The Guild took an active interest in the annual camp meeting, and provided one furnished cottage on the circle for the Presiding Elder's use, and another one on 6th Avenue for the succession of invited preachers who served each camp season.

In 1905 the Guild beautified the Grove's "front entrance", the area at the end of Grove Avenue in Morgan Park, establishing thereby a tradition that was later taken up by other women's groups. For several years they sponsored prayer meetings in the Auditorium during the summer, apparently designed to be attended by girls and women only. They selected and paid for the Assembly Hall furnishings when it was built in 1902, and made considerable additional improvements there in 1909. Though the Ladies Guild was not a home-grown Grove organization, it considered the camp meeting to be one of its prime areas of responsibility.

The first women's group in and of the Grove was, like the men's, an athletic club. The loosely organized and unnamed group was first formed in the summer of 1908 by a cadre of active and energetic young women. They were given use of the Presiding Elder's cottage, which the Ladies Guild had just moved to Maple Avenue. On request, the Trustees granted the young women the use of the men's tennis courts "when the men weren't using them." Their meetingplace was lost to fire that December, but their enthusiasm was unabated. In

August of 1909, they re-organized formally as the Girls Athletic Association and later called themselves the G.A.A. for short. They wrote a constitution and bylaws admitting all women between the ages of fifteen and thirty. The trustees allowed them to cut four trees next to the men's tennis courts where they could build two courts of their own; they contracted with the superintendent to undertake the task that fall.

Major Walker had just been elected President, and four Walker daughters were in the club: Florine, Janet, Caryl, and Rosalie. The club sent a delegation to the Major, who agreed to build them a clubhouse on lot 18 of block 8 in Woodward Park, just north of, and facing, the tennis courts. He advanced them the $495 cost of the building; it was very substantial with wide porches on

The Girl's Club organized picnics and other outings in addition to its athletic and volunteer endeavors.

three sides, and generally more attractive than the men's clubhouse. It was dedicated in August of 1910 with a show—a Japanese Drill—by the girls, to the music of Stuart Walker's phonograph.

In 1913 the clubhouse was furnished with wicker chairs and canvas hammocks, curtains on the windows, and two dozen Japanese lanterns on the porches. It was wired for electricity in 1917. The young women paid Walker back with interest within two years, mostly with money earned from selling refreshments at Grove happenings. There was intense competition for the privilege of selling ice cream and sandwiches at athletic events in the Grove, and the G.A.A. had obtained the exclusive franchise for Labor Day meets. Other women's groups used the same fundraising technique at other events.

The Girls' main athletic focus was on tennis and track. They competed throughout the county and in Washington, and hosted meets in the Grove. The club's constitution read that it was "for the purpose of physical culture and amusement," and eventually most of the Grove's young women joined, even if they were not athletic by nature. In the decade or so of its existence, the club embraced wider interests, and opened it clubhouse to other activities, including meetings of the Women's Club. During camp meetings it operated a "Mother's Rest," a sort of ladies lounge and baby-sitting service.

In its later years the club served more a social than an athletic purpose, especially in the summers. For the younger girls it was the focus for many a summer day's activities. A favorite daytime event was the 'strawride,' in which a team of horses pulled a wagonload of hay and teenagers out to Seneca Creek for a day of boating and picnicking. In the evenings there was lounging on the porches and making music. Dancing had become very popular among young people, but it was still generally forbidden for the children of pious Methodists; in fact it was proscribed in the Grove's public places. Dancing did take place in the Grove, however, though at first it was confined to private homes. In 1918 the Girls boldly discussed holding a public dance at the Grove for soldiers recuperating at Walter Reed Hospital, but they failed to get the blessing of the Trustees. The ban on dancing was finally broken in 1920, when the girls simply went ahead without permission and staged a small dance in their clubhouse.

The following summer was the club's last. Perhaps the dancing lost them the support of the Trustees, or perhaps there was some falling-out among the members that drained the club's energy; no cause is recorded. It may be just that one particularly empathic group of people converged at one time and formed a social unit that would take them through the metamorphosis from youth to adult, and having accomplished that, outgrew the device that brought them together. Whatever the case, the G.A.A. held its close of season meeting at the end of August, 1921, and never met again. The club house was maintained by the Trustees for several years, during which time it got little use, and it was finally turned over to the present Woman's Club in 1927.

The Ladies Guild was a creature of Washington, D.C. that did good work in the Grove during the summers. The Girls club, on the other hand, was a creature of the Grove, but many of its members returned to Washington in the winter, and its winter meetings were usually held in the city. But the original Woman's Club was the first women's organization that was exclusively a creature of and for the Grove's full-time residents. Through a succession of forms it would also prove to be the most enduring.

The Woman's Club (or Women's Club—the documents conflict on the correct form) began with great modesty and few members on October 20, 1910. It first met at the home of Mrs. Osborn, the wife of the first appointed minister of the Washington Grove Church. They first called themselves the Women's Society, and they were not a traditional Ladies Guild of the church. Their stated purpose was to be of service to others, but also to study and keep up with current events as well. They pledged to omit all gossip, and decided definitely not to serve refreshments. At first Mrs. Agnes Couch was the only member who also belonged to the Girls club, but in time there was a larger cross-membership. They opened each meeting with a bible reading.

For their literary pursuits they read fiction to each other, reviewed articles from the newspapers and, over a series of meetings, they studied the women of the bible. At one meeting they had readings and a discussion of Mormonism, while at another a nurse discussed preventative measures against tuberculosis. They did modest good works, making bandages and caps for Sibley Hospital. They sewed aprons to sell, and if an impoverished area family came to their attention they collected and distributed food and clothing to it. They also discussed gardening and child training, and made an earnest study of the measures that could be taken to prevent an epidemic of disease in the Grove.

Their entertainments and expenditures were modest, too. They held a reception for the first birthday of the Grove church in 1911. They made robes for the

Oddfellows (among whom were probably many of their husbands) and held a joint reception with the men's group in 1912. They held a porch picnic at the Rynex's to celebrate their second anniversary. They bought cups and saucers for the club in 1911 and discussed the purchase of a coffee urn for two more years, appropriating the money at last in 1913.

Like the Girls club, the Woman's Club meetings suddenly ceased without comment, in May, 1913. But its members were found in two other women's groups the very next year: the Rebeccas, the women's auxiliary of the Oddfellows, and a new group, the Woman's Guild of Washington Grove. It seems likely that most of the original group (with perhaps the coffee cups and urn) went into, or became, the Rebeccas, and the Woman's Guild was established by the others to continue doing Grove work. The new guild attracted a wider membership than had its predecessor, and included both part- and full-time Grove residents. The nature of their work was consistent with their identity as a woman's group of the period. While they did provide curtains for the Assembly Hall, for example, their efforts were not all wicker and chintz; they also contributed substantially to the treasury of the Association.

In 1914 they paid for part of the rebuilding of the Superintendent's cottage, in 1916 they made grand horticultural improvements to the entrance at Grove Avenue and Railroad Street, and in 1921 they paid for a new roof for the Auditorium. (They specified that the new "patent" shingles be used, but the cost was too high and they had to settle for cedar shakes dipped in stain instead.) They raised money in the traditional ways, selling ice cream to baseball crowds and giving lawn parties. In the early 1920's they helped keep up the clubhouse that had been orphaned by the Girls, and financed a new kitchen in the hotel.

By this time attendance of the camp meeting and Chautauqua-like programs had waned substantially, which contributed to a decline in the summer population. The summer residents were aging, and their children were marrying and moving away. Fewer new families were attracted to the Grove and a gradual reformation was underway. These changes were reflected in the Grove's clubs; the G.A.A. ceased operating in 1921, and the Women's Guild activities tapered off until no mention was made of it after 1924. There was a similar decline in the vitality of the Men's Athletic Association, with a similar period of latency in the mid-20's.

But while outside interest and participation in the Grove had declined, the dedication of its growing number of full-time residents only increased. Later in the decade a new women's group would form and take up the work of its predecessors, to nurse the Association through its twilight years, and the Town through its infancy.

THE GREAT WAR

World War I had little direct effect on the Grove, and no Grove resident is reported to have been killed or seriously injured in the war effort. Among those who are known to have gone off to war were Charles Myers of the singing Myers family, Page Milburn, who later wrote the first history of the Grove, Harold 'Dutch' Osborn, the son of the Grove church's first pastor, and John Meany, the son of the Association's long-serving Vice President.

The war did produce a patriotic fervor, accompanied by food and materials shortages throughout the United States. In the Grove, meetings were often opened with the Pledge of Allegiance and a song—usually 'America' or 'America The Beautiful'— in addition to the usual prayer. The high prices being paid for wood on the open market caused the trustees (as it would again in World War II) to modify their forest management policy. In 1917, they authorized 500 to 600 cords of wood to be cut, noting with regret that not much work would be done at the Grove that year, but pledging "as loyal citizens, to cheerfully make all sacrifices in giving support of the President of our Nation in his tasks of coordinating the resources of this Nation to bring to a successful termination the greatest and most significant war of all ages."

The national food shortage inspired Maple Avenue resident George Hendricks to seek permission to plant the area behind the Auditorium, near his cottage, with staple crops. The Board gave permission, and went on to declare large areas of the Grove's parks (though certainly not the ball diamond itself!) available for cultivation.

The Girls' Club and the Woman's Guild were both active in the war effort. The Girls staged entertainments at the Grove and at Walter Reed Hospital, an amputees' center. They wanted to offer their clubhouse for overnight visits by convalescing soldiers, but the trustees considered this an indelicate idea. Eventually many soldiers did stay over in the men's clubhouse. The women made bandages and volunteered at local hospitals. The Grove Band was very busy during 1917 and 1918, too, attending patriotic demonstrations and playing for each new company of young men as it

The Men's clubhouse was home to convalescing soldiers in 1918.

The Grove Band c. 1918.
Organizer Roy McCathran is at far left.

boarded the train at Rockville bound for training camp.

But the biggest effect of the war on the Grove was the least noticeable at first: it accelerated the separation of the community of Washington Grove from the city of Washington. The Grove had already ceased being a a mere summer extension of a Washington religious and social unit and had established a separate and unique identity, but it was still bridged to Washington through the interests of its year-round commuters and its part-time summer residents. Washington at the end of the war suddenly found itself the capital city of a major world power. Washington Grove was already an anachronism, still holding camp meetings when their effectiveness had diminished and their appeal had largely passed. Many of the young people, at least figuratively, had seen Paree: what would keep them back at the Grove after that?

Nor did the Grove any longer hold any excitement as a speculative investment. There was no more treasury stock for sale, and the stockholders had voted not to create any more. There was no longer an open market for the existing shares—the few shares that became available were taken up quickly by the Walkers or those opposing them. Fewer city people seeking summer homes were attracted to the Grove; the automobile had opened the entire county to development, and there was competition from a dozen other communities. Even the resort towns on the Chesapeake Bay and the Atlantic coast were now accessible by car.

The reduced activity in the Grove did, however, seem to make it more attractive to families looking for a real home. The camp meetings, though still being held, were confined to the Auditorium and its environs, and the Chautauqua-like entertainments were now of local origin, the creation of Grove residents and their close neighbors.

August Sorgenfrei, the superintendent hired by Walker, and his family provide an example of the sort of changes that were taking place at that time. In 1910 he was just the hired man, living in what amounted to tenant's lodgings on a subsistence farm that was made up of the six acres in Block 3 and 6. But unlike previous superintendents he and his family had worked into the fabric of Grove life. By 1918 he had become a stockholder and resigned as superintendent and, though he still contracted services to the Grove (as did other residents) the Sorgenfreis had become equal members of the community. In 1921 he purchased two cottages from the circle area and moved them (one intact and one in sections) to lots he had purchased on Chestnut Avenue, where he reassembled them into a permanent residence that stood into the 1960's.

The changes that were making the Grove more of a community than a corporation prompted a new look at how an old problem should be handled, and set the stage for a temporary but blunt solution to the Walker controversy.

THE LOEFFLER RESOLUTION

Carl A. Loeffler was one of the last of the well-connected and high-ranking Washingtonians who made the Grove their summer home. He built the unusual house at 108 Grove Avenue, next to President Williamson's, on the site of the Huntley cottage that had burned in 1907. He was a Republican staff member in the Senate who served in several capacities from 1910 until the 1940's and his Grove house is rumored to have hosted such dignitaries as Senator Warren G. Harding. He served as a trustee of the Association for several years and was the author of several Senate-quality resolutions during his tenure.

The Walkers' challenge for control of the Association did not end with the 1916 court decision against them, but it did take a different turn. There was a certain amount of stock that became available from time to time from the usual turnover of real estate. Walker began to purchase such stock through surrogates, who would then sign the shares over to him. As the result of an earlier decision the board would not transfer the shares to Walker, denying him the right to vote them, but each share thus purchased reduced the overall pool of shares that could be voted. If this continued, Walker would gain control when the pool was reduced by about fifteen percent, since he and his family owned or influenced about 35% of the shares by then.

When this tactic was discovered in 1918 there were angry protests at the annual meeting. The trustees first attempted to overcome the problem by refusing not only to transfer the shares into Walker's name, but also refusing to acknowledge that they had been sold. This allowed a seller to continue to vote shares even though he had taken money for them, and thus raised a serious legal problem. Finally Loeffler, after a patriotic introductory speech, proposed a resolution that he said would protect against "an autocratic despotism in the management of our civil rights and property interests, equaled only by the Prussian system, which all lovers of liberty unite in denouncing and destroying." His resolution would simply modify the bylaws to limit any stockholder to 20% of the capital stock, and enjoin the trustees from transferring stock that would cause that limit to be exceeded.

The resolution passed easily, and though it did not remove the threat of control passing to a few, it did legalize the ad hoc action that had previously been taken by the board of trustees to limit stock ownership. More significantly, a clear majority of shares and of shareholders both had voted to pass it. The policy that had been directed at a single stockholder had been clarified and made to apply democratically to all. Though it once again frustrated the Major, its toughness and relative fairness helped lead to a temporary reconciliation between the Walkers and the Association, before the final legal test.

THE ELECTION OF 1922

As President, Williamson's manner was calm and his management style was firm. He was trusted and competent, and was returned to office year after year. But another man, as ebullient as Williamson was austere, was about to inherit his job. Where Williamson inspired confidence, this man spread laughter; where Williamson was respected, this man was loved. The other man was called a "born leader," and "the ultimate emcee:" his name was Roy McCathran.

The McCathrans had deep roots in the Grove. McCathrans had first visited the Grove at about the same time the first Walkers did, but they became stockholders much earlier, and had a presence and an impact on the Grove before the turn of the century. The first McCathrans in the Grove were Stillman J. and James K., first cousins, who each took a cottage: S.J.'s on 4th Avenue and J.K.'s on 6th.

Preservation of the trees among the tent sites and

cottage plots had become official Grove policy very early, but the avenues had been designed to be broad and sweeping. In 1889, when Grove Avenue was about to be cleared across its entire fifty foot width, it was James McCathran's motion that led to an extension of the tree-saving policy to include those on the avenues. Thereafter only enough trees could be removed from any walkway to make a straight path. James McCathran was an ardent defender of the Grove's early traditions, and led a successful fight in 1904 to keep Sunday papers from being sold in the Grove.

In 1906 he sought and received permission to move his cottage to Maple Avenue where he became one of the first to settle in the area east of Woodward park. Shortly afterward his family took up year-round residence there. James's son, Irving LeRoy McCathran, was born in 1888, and must have had the Grove in his earliest memories.

Roy McCathran studied law at National University and emerged as a patent attorney—his father had been a patent draftsman—in 1912. He married Sarah Osborn, daughter of the Grove church's first pastor, in July of 1913. She had graduated from Goucher College in Baltimore and would go on to teach Gaithersburg's high school students. In 1916 he began the house at 111 Maple Avenue (one Walker-owned lot removed from his father's house) and took up year-round residency. In 1923 the Reverend Osborn, plagued by years of drainage problems at his Brown Street house, built a new one at 109 Maple Avenue, next door to his daughter and son-in-law.

Roy was an extraordinary young man. An accomplished comet player, a singer and dancer, he was also a first-class organizer. He founded the Washington

Grove Band in 1912 and led it for 16 years. He was several times music director for the camp meeting. He was active in men's athletics and organized field day events. He brought men's wrestling to the Grove, though some of the old-timers were scandalized because the wrestlers wore rather revealing tights.

He was first nominated as a trustee in 1916 at the age of 28, but he declined election. In 1919 he accepted the nomination and was elected, replacing the departing Frank Rynex. He took an active role on the board, and was well aware that there were two major issues confronting the Association as its annual meeting and election approached. One issue involved things and required blunt and direct action—the sewer system had deteriorated and was now as bad as it had ever been. Worse yet, the Grove's wells were beginning to show some contamination; some had already been condemned.

The other issue involved people, and called for some delicacy and finesse. President Williamson had seemed tired at the previous annual meeting in 1921, and had asked then to be retired from the presidency. He was elected over his protests and stayed in office, but became seriously ill during the year and was increasingly unable to attend meetings, so little progress toward a solution of the sewer problem had been made during the year. When the annual meeting came he was too sick to attend it, but a powerful faction wanted to keep him in office anyway.

The first hurdle they encountered at the meeting was Williamson's re-election as a trustee, since his latest term was expiring. Williamson, Edwin Swingle, and Francis Hiller—the President, Treasurer, and Secretary—were all nominated to be returned to their

IRVING L. MCCATHRAN
Roy McCathran as a young patent attorney.

posts as trustees. There were several speeches of support of the trio, then Swingle himself rose to speak against the nomination of any others because, he said, "it could result in the failure to re-elect the President." But Clarence Welch rose and nominated Maurice Browning, whom he said had "been requested by a considerable body of respected stockholders to accept such a nomination," and spoke against Swingle's plea to close the nominations, implying that Swingle might be in fear of losing his own seat, not the President's.

It was then announced that Williamson expected to return to the Grove soon, and was expecting to be re-elected. Dr. Elmon Cook moved that Williamson be elected first, then the other two seats determined by separate ballot. Mrs. Hardy, parliamentarian of the Daughters of the American Revolution, objected that the procedure was contrary to the Grove's bylaws. Needham Turnage suggested that since Browning was a prominent Republican and the county was overwhelmingly Democratic, that it might be better for the sake of relations with the county not to elect him. Browning himself rose to say, "we should be thanking Williamson, not re-electing him to burdens he can no longer bear." Loeffler took exception, accusing Browning and his supporters as having a "cut and dried plan to run over the opposition."

Roy McCathran moved that Williamson be unanimously re-elected a trustee which led to "much cheering," but no action. Osborn took the floor and described Williamson's present medical condition, and added that "it would be unwise to burden him now".

Loeffler then produced a surprise letter signed by Williamson saying that he still wanted to be President. Roy McCathran demanded to know the source of the letter; it was S.C.Cissel who delivered it, but no one would say who wrote it. Loeffler argued that it did not matter who wrote it as long as Williamson signed it, but after much pressure was applied Loeffler confessed to having penned it himself. This led to more arguing about the genuineness of Williamson's signature on the letter, but finally the election was called and the long voting procedure began.

For the three openings for trustee, the voting went 674 for Browning, 601 for Hiller, 530 for Williamson, and only 301 for Swingle. Apparently within the established Williamson majority there had been two factions, one for Swingle and one for Browning. The election of Browning had been assured ahead of time by the Browning faction's uniting with the Walker's minority block. The election of officers was the next order of business, and Browning nominated McCathran for President. Swingle nominated Williamson. Roy McCathran took the floor and accepted the nomination, taking pains to assure everyone present that neither he nor anyone backing him had any malice toward Williamson. When the vote came it was 670 for McCathran and 271 for Williamson. McCathran accepted the gavel, and as his first action nominated Williamson to the office of President Emeritus. The motion was carried by unanimous vote. (Thirty-five years later McCathran would become the first Mayor Emeritus.)

With the election of McCathran a long period of transition had come to an end. Control of the Association had passed to its full-time residents, who accepted this gift from the City of Washington and set out to rebuild it in the State of Maryland. It would take a long time.

WHEN OUR COUNTY HEROES COME HOME

To the tune of "When the Fighting Irish Come Home"

Dedicated to the boys of Montgomery County, Md. who went ACROSS.

1.

Jack get out your ball and bat
And Tom go get your glove,
Let's have a game or two,
There'l be lots to do.
Girls you get some things to eat,
Some pies and bread and meat.
We'll have the town all jollied up
Just like a County Seat;
For this county must get ready in
advance
To welcome back our Fighting Lads
from France.

CHORUS :

Twill be the greatest day we ever planned,
when our county heroes come home,
And you'll hear them sing My Maryland,
and they won't just sing it alone,
For you'll be there and I'll be there, and
the Grove Band, if they dare to come.
Twill be a sight to see old Mont-gomery
when our county heroes come home.

2

Such a welcome they will get,
We have'nt seen in years,
And there'll be some tears
mingled with the cheers.
We'll have with us all the folks
Who sent them off to France.
And all the girls will want to kiss them
If they get a chance.
The Band will give us all a Jazzoree,
To welcome back our boys from
Germany.

By I. L, (Roy) McCathran.

With his poetry, Roy McCathran often celebrated life in the Grove, but he also wrote rousing lyrics as in this example.

THE ASSOCIATION

PROFILES V: PEOPLE

Edna Reber

Edna Reber has lived in Washington Grove almost all her adult life. She has been a prolific writer; in her letters, poems, and descriptive prose she celebrates the life around her. In spite of adversity she has an abiding faith in the Lord, and it has given her the strength to continue and the serenity to express herself. But her gift, and her ability to share it with us, is uniquely her own, and a significant contribution to our Washington Grove heritage. She writes:

"One summer day away back in 1913 my girlfriend invited me to her family reunion. She told me about her cousin and how handsome he was. I wanted to look my best so I wore my middie blouse with the sailor collar, a red Windsor tie, black stockings and patent leather shoes, skirt to my ankles and my hair high up on my head (a Psyche knot we called it). A real old fashioned girl.

"We met her cousin on the train that carried us into the country. He had come from Washington Grove to my home town in Phoenixville, Pennsylvania, near Valley Forge. We were met by a team of horses at the station and drove out to the farm. I was in heaven for I loved the country in the summer with its fragrant smell of new mown hay, honeysuckle, wild flowers, meadows, orchards, tall trees, clear streams and the sound of birds.

"And now here was a young man so different from the country fellows I'd known. I think I lost my heart that day.

"Picnic tables had been set up on the lawn and delicious food was served. The young people sat on the ground and talked, then we went to a ball game and George (for that was my girlfriend's cousin's name) played. After the evening meal we sang around the piano. Those old songs told a story and we loved them. Soon someone came in and said, 'There's a full moon, come on out.' George and I walked down to the gate and soon found ourselves alone. It was a lovely night, one I'll always remember. We stood listening to the water in a little stream nearby and night birds called. (The moon and I have always had a love affair.) We did not linger long for the country folk retire early and soon we heard George's dad call that it was time for bed. We walked hand in hand not talking much. When we reached the porch we found the house very quiet. We climbed the stairs together stopping midway when he kissed me goodnight.

"Mary was waiting for me wanting to know what I thought of her cousin. I thanked her for inviting me to the reunion and we talked on and on. I could hear the little stream singing along outside our window. In the morning we had to leave for home while George and his Dad stayed on.

"After living in Pennsylvania for twenty years, my family moved to Maryland in July. I've heard it said that real marriages were made in heaven and now I believe it.

"George and I were just sixty miles apart and soon

he began driving to Baltimore to visit me. My family liked him. For a time all went well, then came a misunderstanding and I saw him no more for nearly three years. Then one day he sent me a valentine. I opened and read it and tossed it in the air. Mother picked it up and said, 'Why not answer; he's a nice young man.' I read the card again and, as I remember, it said something about walking down a line to see the lovely flowers there and it also said, 'I want the flowers to see you.' In May George came back to me and we were married the following Christmas day in 1916.

"I remember the evenings he'd play his violin and I played the piano and we made beautiful music.

"That's how I met George Reber. For almost forty-nine years I have loved his memory."

George and Edna Reber spent the first year or so of their married life in Washington, D.C. In the Grove they first lived in the cottage that Judge Harlan had occupied on Chestnut Avenue. Then a year or two later they rented the house at 419 Oak Street from Major Walker. Mrs. Reber remembers the Major tapping his cane on the back steps when he came to call for his $18 a month rent. In 1920 they were able to buy the house. George made his living mostly as a builder working with his father George, Sr., who lived in Oakmont, across the tracks.

George also did home improvement work in and around the Grove. Many of the old cottages were being remodeled for modem year-round living. He perfected what he called a colonnade, a sort of indoor columned portico which served as a room divider, and installed many of them in the Grove. He was active in the government of the Grove for several years, serving as acting Superintendent, deputy sheriff, and as a member of the board of trustees in the mid-twenties.

A local epidemic of typhoid broke out in 1931 brought on by infected milk. George Reber and his sister Katie, who had been living across the walkway at 418 Oak Street, were stricken and died in September. Others, including his younger son, Robert, were hospitalized, but survived. Penicillin had been discovered in 1929, but its application was not practical yet.

Richard (Dick) Garrott Walker

Dick Walker is the third son of Robert H. Walker and a grandson of Major Walker. He and his brothers grew up in Washington during the winters and in Washington Grove during the summers. The many Walker cousins went to school together, played together, and went to church together. Dick first remembers staying in their cottage on the Circle, then at the house they built at 409 Brown Street. When he was five years old, his father built the new house at 103 Chestnut Avenue (in an era before official house numbers, his father called it "No. 1 Brown Street"), and they began to spend their summers there.

When Dick was still little he contracted typhoid fever, reportedly from swimming in Little Seneca Creek. Doctor's orders were to stay quiet all summer—it was completely antithetical to Grove boyhood, but he did it. In subsequent summers his activities were more typical of those of other Grove boys; baseball, tennis, keeping up with older brothers. The boys helped their father build one of the premier private tennis courts in their back yard. The Lake was by then a swamp, and they and others built numerous treehouses on its periphery.

In the twenties and early thirties the Grove was still well-served by deliverymen of all kinds, who brought groceries, furniture, coal, coal oil, and the like; Dick particularly remembers Rodney White, who lived on Brown Street and huckstered everything from fresh vegetables to ice from his wagon with its set of scales affixed to the back. Dick and some of the other boys delivered fresh bread and cakes that the Wadsworth sisters baked in their cottage at 112 Grove Avenue.

As the depression deepened across the nation it was also felt in the Walker family, where sometimes two salaries had to be divided among three families, and there was doubling up in some of the Walker bedrooms in town. The year Dick finished junior high school the Robert Walker family moved out to the Grove year-round. The boys went to Rockville High School, though there was by then a twelve-grade school in Gaithersburg. From his perch atop the Central Avenue bridge he remembers the hobos yelling "top of the hill!" and jumping off the train at the Grove, because from then on the train would begin speeding up. The hobos would walk all over town offering, "Two hours work for a meal?," and often getting it.

Dick got his first automobile at the age of fourteen, a '23 Chevy open touring car with the engine frozen up, which he earned by thinning six acres of corn on a Ridge Road farm. He got the car going and drove all over the immediate vicinity without such amenities as a roof, a muffler, or a driver's license. He delivered the Times-Herald, Washington's last morning alternative to the Post, by driving his car, still sans muffler, up and down the walkways.

Dick graduated from Rockville High School in 1938;

the next year the school burned down and was replaced by Richard Montgomery High School. Dick's father, Robert Walker, died later the same year, and not long thereafter the family sold the house on Brown Street and moved to Kensington. When World War II came the boys all went into service; Sam Walker the Third into the Navy, younger brother Bob into the Marines, and Dick, when he was old enough, into the Army.

10

Building a New Consensus

ROY MCCATHRAN'S ELECTION AS president in 1922 brought the Association under the control of the year-round residents. It was accomplished with a minimum of rancor and left no bitter feelings in its wake. Herbert S. DeLand was nominated for vice president (Loeffler challenged the slate by nominating J.T.Meany to continue in his position as VP, but Meany declined), and Francis L.L.Hiller was offered for the positions of both Secretary and Treasurer. One person filling both positions was a new concept, but after considerable discussion it was deemed acceptable and Meany and Hiller were unanimously elected.

The new officers were solid Grove citizens, though only McCathran was a full-time resident. DeLand and his family had first rented the house at 128 Chestnut Avenue, and then bought the Rynex house and gardens when the Rynexes left the Grove. A substantial stockholder with 25 shares, DeLand would be an officer in the Grove for ten years, until he sold his interest during the depression.

Francis L.L.Hiller , an old-school religious man, first came to the Grove with his mother, Laura Hiller, in about 1902, and purchased stock of his own in 1911. He was first elected in 1922 and held office on and off for the next 15 years. With his combination of wry humor and personal humility he provided the continuity that maintained the Grove's fiscal integrity through its most troubled years.

Each of these men was to make valuable contributions, but they were not destined to operate for long as a team. They had no sooner assumed their positions at the annual meeting than they walked into a bee's nest: young people had been observed playing tennis on Sundays, and it was high time that something was done about it.

Francis Hiller, at left, apparently being presented with something by Roy McCathran, who was later to become the first Mayor of the new Town.

SUNDAY TENNIS I

The 1922 annual meeting, which had already been through the wrenching experience of replacing Williamson as president, was then forced to confront another emotional subject. Sabbath-breaking was going on, and a solution would have to be found. Dr. Osborn put it in the form of a motion: "We believe this practice to be a serious infraction of our time-honored observance of Sunday as a Day of rest and worship," and resolved that the trustees take "all necessary measures" to prevent the recurrence thereof. Mr. Hiller and Mrs. Huntley spoke strongly against sports on Sunday, and the motion carried.

The practice was apparently well-entrenched however, for in the weeks that followed, the admonitions of the trustees went unheeded. By August they had exhausted the remedies they thought the resolution allowed, and McCathran called a special stockholders meeting "to reconsider, redraw, or amplify the resolution" with respect to tennis and other sports. At the meeting in late August there were widely diverse opinions. DeLand wanted the trustees empowered to take legal action against the players, but others expressed the view that it had become something of a tradition, especially at the McCauley Street court, to play tennis on Sundays. It was mentioned that such action did not seem either immoral or criminal. Hiller spoke in favor of strong regulations, calling upon the history and purpose of the Grove, saying that Sunday should be observed "to Methodist standards." Time. Loeffler read a speech on intolerance, and Hiller rose again to say that if this meeting should nullify the action of the annual meeting, he would resign. The question

was

The tennis courts at tournament time.

called and Mrs. Hardy's motion stood: playing on Sundays would not be permitted, but violators would not be criminally prosecuted.

Hiller, always a man of his word, immediately resigned as an officer and trustee, reserving only his right to explain his action. He resigned, he said, for two reasons: first, "as a protest against lawlessness," that the Association was not protecting the legal rights of the stockholders, and second, because "to my mind the action taken on August 26 marks the end in fact, if not in form, of the Grove Association as a religious institution." Those words would take on a deeper significance a decade later.

Perhaps the Association was never a religious organization at all, but only a capital stock company with a religious purpose—the camp meeting. The words "Camp Meeting" had been dropped from its name in

1906, and the camp meeting itself had been moved to the Auditorium and isolated from the Grove's daily life since 1905. But Hiller had a point: the tennis players had gone against one of the underlying tenets of Methodism—keeping the Sabbath holy, a crime for which perpetrators had been arrested and fined in earlier times—and the Association upon vote of the shareholders had failed to enforce it.

In most places, playing sports on Sunday was no longer a serious enough matter for people to take a stand upon, and over the next few years the Association would abdicate its remaining religious duties both in fact and in form. But in the Grove the principle was still in effect, and the tennis controversy was sure to surface again. It did, but with surprising results.

CAMP MEETINGS END!!!

This might have been worthy of a headline in the county papers except that camp meetings in the Grove, like so much else in history, did not come suddenly and decisively to an end, but rather lurched and stalled their way into oblivion over many years' time. The Grove had started as a camp, become a summer resort, and was well on its way to becoming a small town, but through it all the ten-day to two-week camp meeting had been its centerpiece.

Originally the Grove was overwhelmingly Methodist, but over the years the near totality had dropped to a majority, and then diminished to a mere plurality. Since the formation of a Methodist congregation at the Grove in 1910 took Sunday worship off its hands, the Association's only active religious role was to arrange for and support the camp meeting. It gave its ongoing moral support to the new church but avoided alliances that might seem to favor one church over another. The Association had begun to see itself as State, and the Washington Grove M.E. Church as Church, with a careful division to be maintained between the two. The division was far from complete, however.

The camp meeting was still on the permanent agenda of the Committee on Religious Services, a subdivision of the Board of Trustees, and for a decade the committee had been headed by Dr. Osborn, who was also pastor of the church. But during the waning years of Williamson's presidency the camp meetings were faltering; there was less support from the surrounding area, and fewer Grove people were attending. In 1922 came the first open discussion of ending the camps altogether.

The camps of 1920 and 1921 had been led by Dr. John E. Fort of Elderbrooke Methodist Church on River Road near the District of Columbia. His post-camp reports called for building up a better musical service and either expanding the camp's Chautauqua aspects or bringing in a "big evangelist" to appeal more to the countryside. In 1922 another modest camp was held, staffed entirely by local preachers and under the direction of Dr. Osborn, who had that year announced his retirement from the Grove Church. For the 50th Anniversary camp meeting in 1923 a special committee of President McCathran, Dr. Elmon Cook, the new head of Religious Services, and two others, had hired a Dr. Dorsey Miller of Hillsdale, Pennsylvania to try to get more life into the program.

In the fall, Dr. Cook was able to report that the camp was "the most successful...in lo these many years," with collections at $882. and a surplus of $48. But by January of 1924 the trustees had independently concluded that Miller "was too expensive for the Washington Grove Community," and furthermore, that his services "were not entirely satisfactory to all stockholders." They discussed hiring Evangelist William B. Waters of Montgomery County to do the next camp, and finally the board made him an offer without consulting the Religious Services Committee.

The Committee was upset that Waters had been hired and incensed that they had been left to work out the details. They balked at hiring him, arguing that Waters "was not a satisfactory person to hold this meeting for various reasons, none of which, however, reflected on his personal character." Their specific objections were not put into writing, but it was, they said, a question of the "methods he pursued in conducting his services." The Committee met in special session in May, but voted to stand behind the trustee's decision. Dr. Osborn broke with the committee and made a personal appeal at the annual meeting, but the contract had been finalized the week before; it was to be Waters in 1924.

Waters's camp, though well-attended, grossed only $542 and broke even only by virtue of $125 it received in private donations. Following camp a special stockholders meeting was called to hear Osborn's objections to the procedure, but no resolution was put forward which would satisfy the Association, the Committee, and the Church all at once. Cook, now chairman of the Committee, called no further meetings during the year, and pressed his resignation upon the President the following January. It was followed, for other reasons, by the resignations of Browning and

Welch.

For many, the results of the 1924 special meeting signaled the end of the camp meetings, and with the three resignations in January 1925 it seemed unlikely that they could continue. In fact, Rosalie Shantz's book, "Grove Gatherings," flatly states that the last camp meeting was in 1924, and Dr. Page Milburn's Reminiscence in 1927 speaks of the camp meeting days as a thing of the past. But Roy McCathran had not sought re-election in 1924 and Edwin Swingle had replaced him—and the new president was not going to allow the camp meeting to die in his term. He appointed Reverend Corkran, the new pastor of the Grove Church, and two of its ardent members, August Sorgenfrei and George Reber, to fill the vacancies.

Some conflict must have arisen over the course of the summer between the new committee and the old guard. On May 4, 1925 the Committee reported that a "program for summer" had been organized and that Camp Meeting will begin about July 23 and continue 10 days." There was also to be a vacation bible school. But on August 5, immediately after the camp closed, Swingle replaced the entire committee with a slate of former activists including Osborn, Hiller, Mrs. Huntley, and the new pastor, Rev James Milburn.

The next annual meeting, in 1926, did not explain the sudden change, but it was reported that the "1925 Camp Meeting was well attended and proved to be a success." The camp broke even with $613. collected. The Milburn committee did not convene for nearly ten months, almost too late for a 1926 camp. But a camp was then hastily organized and led by Milburn himself. If its gross revenue is an indicator of the attendance, it was not a well-attended meeting—only $266. was collected and $284 expended, the balance made up by "a friend."

The same committee was reappointed by Swingle, but it made a new plan for 1927: the Washington Grove Camp Meeting Institute was to be formed as a cooperative effort of the Grove Church with the Gaithersburg Methodist churches, Grace Methodist (South), and Epworth (North). In 1927 the camp ran 12 days and included a vacation bible school and community sings in the evenings. Its flyer boasts "Miss These Treats at Your Loss," and "Better Come!" Total collections were a miserly $120. The Milans subtracted $4. from their printing bill to make things come out even.

The 1928 meeting, again under the Institute, had apparently lost the support of the Gaithersburg churches, and seemed to have degenerated into a forum for the Maryland Chapters of the Lord's Day Alliance and the Anti-Saloon League, both of which though religious in origin were political in action, serving as lobby organizations for their respective causes.

What had been sensed by many in 1924—that the camps had lost their meaning—was obvious to all by the end of 1928: the camps had even lost their drawing power. A resolution to end them forever was widely circulated before the annual meeting of 1929. The final wording of the motion that resulted was a knife in the heart of the camp, and its unanimous adoption, without discussion, was the final nail in its coffin: "Recognizing the changed conditions that have come with the years, and believing that the summer religious meetings, whether called a Camp Meeting or a Camp- Institute, no longer function in such a way as to serve the best interests of the community, but are instead a source of embarrassment both to the Association and the local church. .." The motion went on to turn over all responsibility for religious services of any kind to the Board of Trustees of the Washington Grove Church.

There had been attempts throughout the country to continue camp meetings and tent revivals by grafting

Washington Grove Camp Institute
July 22nd to August 1st (inclusive)
THE AUDITORIUM

Preaching Services---Sundays---July 22nd and 29th

July 22nd, Morning 11 A. M. Visiting Minister, The Rev. W. W. Davis, Secretary Lord's Day Alliance of Maryland

Lord's Day Observance Rallies

The Lord's Day Alliance of Maryland will hold its Annual Montgomery County Lord's Day Meeting

Afternoon 3 P. M. The Rev. Forrestt J. Prettyman, Minister of Wilson Memorial M. E. South Church of Baltimore

Evening 8 P. M. Dr. W. W. Davis, General Secretary of the Lord's Day Alliance of Maryland, will speak.

July 29th, Morning 11 A. M. Minister, The Rev. A. T. Perkins.

Law Enforcement Rallies

Afternoon 3 P. M. Dr. George W. Crabbe, Supt. of the Anti-Saloon League of Maryland

Evening 8 P. M. The Rev. B. Franklin Auld, Asst. Supt. of the Anti-Saloon League of Maryland

Week Night Services, July 23rd to August 1st

Bible Lecture Course

Monday, Wednesday and Friday, July 23rd, 25th and 27th---8 P. M.
Monday and Wednesday, July 30th and August 1st---8 P. M.

"EVENINGS WITH THE PROPHETS"

Instructor, The Rev. Alpheus W. Mowbray, of Washington, D. C.
Formerly Bible Instructor in the Lucy Webb Hayes Training School
Real Vacation Opportunities to Learn God's Word

Evenings of Song and Drama

Tuesday, July 24th, 8 P. M. Mr. A. H. Heil, Leader
Thursday, July 26th, 8 P. M. Mr. A. H. Heil, Leader
Tuesday, July 31st, 8 P. M. Mr. A. H. Heil, Leader

Happy Evenings with the Old Hymns and Bible Dramatization

Vacation Bible School
July 23rd to August 3rd

Every Morning (except Saturday) 9:15 A. M. to 11:30 A. M.

BIBLE STUDY   GAMES   RECREATION
Profitable Hours for the Children

Miss These Treats at Your Loss   *Better Come!*

The end of the Grove's oldest tradition, the camp meeting, came in 1928 when the Camp Institute, a pale imitation of the camp meeting, closed forever.

them onto other socio-religious forms, such as the Chautauqua or the Bible School, but their long decline and ultimate end was foreseeable everywhere. In the Grove the decline and cessation of its primary tradition took place against the backdrop of a growing and increasingly formal organized church.

WASHINGTON GROVE CHURCH, Incorporated

The first year-round congregation was established at the Grove by Dr. Osborn, with the enthusiastic support of Major Walker, in 1910. Dr. Osborn continued as its pastor for about twelve years and saw the church grow from sixteen members in 1910 to over a hundred in 1922. Osborn was a prominent organizer of the camp meeting, too, and remained an officer and member of the Religious Services Committee for seventeen years, by his count.

During Osborn's years it became a de facto tradition that the pastor of the church was also a member of the Religious Services Committee, and was also in charge of the camps. During the Williamson presidency, even though the committee continued to have a separate existence from the church, its personnel and their tasks became intermingled. For a time it seemed that the church and the camp were two responsibilities of the same body. But with the election of 1922 there were changes coming that would permanently divide the duties of the church and the Association.

Difficulties were foreshadowed by Dr. Osborn's retirement from the pulpit. Though he remained active in the church, upon his retirement he also resigned from the Religious Services Committee. His son-in-law, Roy

McCathran, had just been elected president and was taking an active part as president, for a change, in the selection of a camp meeting director. It was as a group effort that the trustees and the committee hired Dr. Miller of Pennsylvania for the 50th camp meeting. Osborn's retirement also meant a new pastor for the Grove congregation.

The new minister, Rev. Charles H. Corkran, would need housing. One of the first strains between the Association and the church occurred when the church contracted to rent the vacant superintendent's cottage from the trustees for that purpose. The rent was to be $25. a month and the trustees spent $200 making improvements, but the church put off moving Dr. Corkran in for several months. In the meantime Dr. Osborn, who had contracted Grove builder George Reber to build him a new house on Maple Avenue, next to the future Mayor and his son-in-law, Roy McCathran, offered his Brown Street property to Dr. Corkran. Corkran finally purchased it in November of that year, ending the immediate need for a parsonage, but angering the trustees who had put out money for improvements to the superintendent's lodge that they had no use for. The church refused to pay for the improvements or pay rent for the time the building stood empty.

It was the Miller camp meeting that brought the two bodies into direct confrontation the following year. Miller had been hired in a cooperative effort, but when the Miller camp was declared a failure, the trustees went from a merely active role to a pre-emptive one. In mid-winter they hired the camp meeting leader directly, and left the details of camp to be worked out by the committee. Both the church and the committee were deeply offended, and Dr. Osborn led in challenging the rights of the trustees to interfere with the work of the Religious Services Committee. The battle raged all spring, and Osborn hurled a final legal challenge at the annual meeting. The stockholders decided that the camp should go on as planned, but called a special committee to interpret sections 19 and 20 of the bylaws, which established the Religious Services Committee and defined its work.

The committee's six-page report, read at a special stockholder meeting called in August, was a thorough legal examination and opinion of the statutes involved. It drew the conclusion that the trustees retained the absolute power over the religious life of the community, and therefore over any related committees, especially with respect to the salaries and expenses of operating the camp meeting. The report was accepted as read. That winter president Swingle attempted to assuage the church by appointing three church trustees to the Rel. Ser. Committee. But it was increasingly apparent that the church would serve in an advisory capacity only, and would never be able to wrest religious control from the Association.

The church, unable to participate to its satisfaction, chose to separate itself from the Association. It had already made one request in favor of independence—in May of 1925 it attempted to purchase the Assembly Hall for its exclusive purposes. The trustees rebuffed the request on the grounds that the Association was multi-denominational, and could not therefore favor one group of Christians over another. Soon after, the church moved to set up its legal independence. Unbeknownst to the trustees it drafted a corporate charter and filed it at the county courthouse on Jan 13,1926. It had also

Reverend Osborn and wife Phebe. Aside from being an inspiring pastor, Osborn was also a prolific writer of both religious and secular, even comical, material.

purchased or had been given Mrs. Huntley's property, Lot 4 of Block 27, on Maple Avenue behind the Auditorium, and filed for a fee simple deed at the same time.

The story leaked out to the trustees, who demanded to know what was going on. On April 1st Charles Becker, an officer of the church and respected neighbor just outside the Grove, wrote to confirm the facts and state that it was the Church's intention to build a parsonage on the Huntley property.

At its next meeting the trustees voted to acknowledge the letter without comment, but quickly consulted with their attorney in Rockville about the legal aspects of the church's activities. For one thing, the transfer of a deed without the permission of the trustees was illegal under the bylaws, as had been attested by the court of appeals. In addition, the implications of an independent corporation operating within the Grove were wholly unknown. When the facts that a corporate charter had been granted to the church, and that a fee simple deed had been issued for the lot were verified at the courthouse, a terse letter was sent to the new corporation inquiring as to its intentions, especially with regard to the Assembly Hall. Their reply stated that they "intend to conduct religious services within the corporate limits of the property of the Association [but] only so long as such conduct is satisfactory to all concerned."

President Swingle reported on the matter to the stockholders at the annual meeting in May. After the usual elections were held a surprise petition was presented by the church: over a hundred signatures requested the trustees to "set apart permanently 200' front by the depth thereof of land of Grove Avenue on or adjoining the Assembly Hall for Church and Parsonage purposes." A separate motion was already on the floor that would give the church authority to use the Hall rent-free for ten years, the church to make such improvements it deemed necessary, all operating expenses to be paid by the church. Swingle suggested that action on neither motion be taken immediately, but that the trustees be directed to work out an accommodation with the church and present it to the stockholders at the next meeting.

Roy McCathran then offered a compromise in which the key elements were: 1. that the church amend its charter to disclaim encroachment of Association rights, and 2. that the church return the property deeded it in fee simple and have it transferred again with the proper form of deed. If that were done, he said, he would then propose the sale of the hotel and its site to the church, with a right-of-way to be established from the site, across blocks 3 and 6, to the Laytonsville Road. Having offered this alternative, he then expressed his anger at the church's activities, terming them "a foolish financial venture."

A delegation of three from the church met over the winter with a delegation of 3 from the trustees. Among them they worked out a limited agreement to be presented in unanimity at the May, 1927 annual meeting. The elements of the agreement were:

1. that the Maple Avenue lot was to be re-deeded to Mrs. Huntley,

2. that the church's articles of incorporation were to be amended so that the church would be subject to the Association bylaws and regulations so long as it operated within the Grove's legal

boundaries, and

3. that the lot was to be re-conveyed to the church under the usual form of deed, and that its use was to be the construction of a parsonage.

But even this limited compromise failed at the meeting when Dr. Osborn, one the church's delegates, balked at the interpretation of item 2 as it was explained to the stockholders. The trustees refused to reconsider the wording, and the matter was laid on the table.

Discussions continued over the fall and winter months of 1927, however, and during that time the Huntley property was deeded back to Mrs. Huntley; the church had decided instead to buy the Williamson property on Grove Avenue (#110) and use the house already there for its parson's home. The ten shares of stock were transferred from Mary Williamson on the 1st of December, 1928. The church continued to meet in the Assembly Hall, which is what it really wanted anyway, and in the absence of a camp meeting the church seemed to be meeting the religious needs of the residents, which is what the Association wanted. Furthermore the church's charter as worded seemed to be presenting no problems for the Association. It remained only to find a legal way to accommodate the church.

In May of 1929 the stockholders were presented with the following resolution:

"That...those stockholders who are also members of the board of trustees of the Washington Grove Methodist Episcopal Church be constituted the Committee on Religious Services, and that the nature and extent of the religious services to be held each year be left to their discretion..., that the committee shall be

An Osborn and McCathran family portrait in the early 1920's. The house in the background is Osborn's at 109 Maple Avenue. Roy McCathran is at right rear.

authorized to raise and expend whatever monies may be required for such purpose without accounting to the Washington Grove Association..." The resolution was adopted unanimously and without discussion, and in a single action the stockholders had ended the camp meeting tradition and abdicated their role in the religious life of the community. The Association, if it ever had been, now ceased to be a religious body.

* * *

The end of the camp meeting tradition and the establishment of an independent church were parallel features of the end of the Association's religious era. Another feature of the time, the penultimate civilizing influence in the Grove, occurred during the same period—and it brought the wonder of indoor plumbing.

THE SEWERS

Before the turn of the century, when the cooking and wash water was dumped in the woods, night soil was picked up by the honey wagon, and the outhouses were set over lime-and-fill trenches in the gazebo park, the Grove did not really have a sewage problem. But once families began to linger into the fall, and then stay the year around, some kind of buried sewer system was inevitable. Several systems had been installed to handle the several degrees of liquid waste from storm water to gray water to raw sewage, routing it to various cesspools and septic boxes. None of these systems ever worked for long, including the extensive Grove Road system designed by professionals and put in during Major Walker's time.

The Grove continued to have to rely on the scavenger service of J.H.Nugent and his successors. The Walker sewer initiative had been the result of a complaint from Thomas I. Fulks and the finding of a state inspector that the Grove Hotel's cesspool in the west woods was polluting the Whetstone Branch, which fed Fulks's fishery. But the engineering problems with the Walker sewer were evident from the first, and were compounded by the increasing number of year-round residents. By 1922, despite Williamson's efforts to save it, the sewer was a certified failure. With the population over a hundred, and with many still relying on Nugent's scavenger services, the trustees sought the help of the state's health department.

An engineer surveyed the Grove and presented a plan by which the Grove, in concert with the towns of Gaithersburg and Rockville, could build a complete water and sewer system. Its operating costs were estimated to fall under $21 per household per year, and its capital costs could be amortized by bonds guaranteed by the two municipal corporations and the Association. Another possible solution lay with the City Suburban Sanitary Commission (later the WSSC), which had been created in 1918 by joints acts of the District of Columbia and the State of Maryland to coordinate sewer and water services in Washington and the suburban areas of Montgomery and Prince Georges counties.

The annual meeting of 1923 endorsed the concept of a joint venture with Rockville and Gaithersburg, and President McCathran, Robert Milans, and Ed Swingle were appointed a committee to enter into negotiations. Over the next twelve months they met with all the officials concerned, and returned to the annual meeting of 1924 with an agreement for a joint project of

Gaithersburg and Washington Grove only. The design, construction, and financing was to be the responsibility of the Sanitary Commission, and construction, it was announced, would begin the next Spring.

McCathran pronounced that the plan "undoubtedly is the most progressive step which has ever been taken at any time during the history of Washington Grove." It was certainly the largest construction project ever contemplated in the Grove. The WSSC engineers set up offices halfway between the two communities and studied the area's topography, soil patterns, and water sources for several months, and finally announced the details of a plan whereby water would be taken from Maple Lake and/or wells in its vicinity to supply the water service for both communities. The sewer service would involve a sewage pumping station, also in the Grove's west woods, with a treatment plant in Gaithersburg. Construction, it was thought, could begin as early as July.

An important feature of the plan was a fire hydrant system to be installed throughout the Grove. With the coming of sewer and water the trustees were looking forward to a period of "extended growth" in the Grove, and ordered the clearing of the remaining avenues and roads to accommodate the newcomers. All of the undeveloped land south of McCauley Street was to be included. But things have a way of taking longer than expected, and it was fully a year before construction really began.

The WSSC sewer system differed from earlier attempts in a number of ways. In the Grove, all the previous sewers had been run under the streets and alleys, taking the path of the honey wagon. The new system had both sewer and water mains run under the much wider Avenues. Heavy excavation equipment was brought in, whereas previous efforts had used manual labor exclusively. Excavations began on Grove Avenue, and the work went smoothly enough, but as they approached the circle they encountered bedrock. The period of construction, and therefore its expenses, were much greater than had been anticipated. In addition, the springs in the west woods proved to be inadequate for the water supply, so additional piping had to be laid from Gaithersburg.

All the mains had been laid and the trenches closed by the following April. The pumping station was built in May, and applications for hookups were accepted as of the first of June, 1927—four years and a day from the stockholders' vote. The full-time residents embraced the improvement and by winter most had installed indoor plumbing and made connections to the system. The Association was eagerly anticipating the cessation of the scavenger service, and announced that it would end on June 1, 1928.

One of the paramount values of the new system was brought dramatically to everyone's attention in late winter. The Jones cottage at 113 Chestnut Avenue caught fire, and though it was totally destroyed, the cottages around it were saved by the availability of water from the hydrants close by, and with the assistance of the Rockville and Kensington volunteer fire departments. In 1934 there was another potentially disastrous fire on crowded upper Grove Avenue, and again the cottages all around it were saved.

Meanwhile the summer residents and absentee cottage-owners had not acted as quickly as the residents to connect to the sewer and water. One problem was a lack of motivation—during the summer it was not such a hardship to draw water from a pump, or even to use the outhouse—but another was the question of money. Plumbing fixtures were expensive and skilled plumbers were required to cut and thread the water pipes, and to pack and seal the drains with hot lead. In addition a deep trench had to be dug out to the appropriate avenue to lay the pipes. And though the annual rates were modest—20 cents per front foot of property along the line—the WSSC charged a whopping $79 connection fee. The entire job could easily cost $200, or ten times what a typical cottage owner paid in annual taxes.

The cost of maintaining a summer house in the Grove was no longer trivial, and the average summer resident was no longer a well-connected and affluent Washingtonian, either; the demographic cross-section of the Grove was broader and included aging widows of modest means, heirs who kept their lots only for the small rental income they would fetch, and others who had lost interest in the Grove but could not sell their property at an advantage because there was such a small market for it.

The Association helped out by extending the scavenger service until January 1, 1929, but the agreement with the sanitary commission was that all public and private waste systems in the Grove would be abandoned. The trustees were required to notify the WSSC of any case of improper waste disposal. An extension to April 1, 1930 was offered but the Association began to audit the sewer connections made and to compile a list of those remaining to be connected. The WSSC had severed the old sewers during construction and left them discontinuous. By the end of February a number of cottages were found to still be using them, however, with the effluent simply going into the ground.

A month after the deadline four known cottages—all on Grove Avenue—were still using the old sewers. In June the owners were reported to the authorities for action; by July the offenders were reduced to two, but those two continued to hold out. Over the next eighteen months investigation revealed that several others were not connected, including the Walker cottage. By this time the great depression had spread throughout the country, and any quick resolution of the problem was impossible. Walker summed up the situation in his 1931 reply to the trustees' complaint: "I am unable, under the present conditions, to comply with the notice."

The completion of the Grove's biggest, if not its most glamorous, undertaking was completed with a flourish of success just when it could do the least toward accomplishing its main aim—to get the Grove more fully inhabited.

ENVIRONMENT FOR CHANGE

Obviously the new sewer and water system was a needed and welcome improvement irrespective of the direction the Grove might take in the future. But it was also a step in a deliberate and planned effort to get the Grove more fully occupied; and by this time few people doubted that with growth would come a change in the Grove's government.

The growth plan was ironically like Major Walker's scheme of fifteen years earlier: make some attractive improvements and you will be able to sell off the rest of the lots, improve the tax base, and maybe even bring the stock value back up to what you paid for it. Several residents, Roy McCathran among them, organized the

Montgomery Building Association in the early twenties to encourage development in the Grove.

The big difference between these two movements was in the type of community they projected—Walker was promoting the Grove's resort-like atmosphere for a summer community, while the McCathran group was hoping to develop a neighborhood of year-round residents. The Grove was very clearly moving in the latter direction.

THE HOTEL

A symbol of the difference between those directions was in the fate of the hotel. It had been operated from the first as a convenience for those stockholders who were without cottages, and as a draw for those who might, after being exposed to the Grove, become stockholders. It also returned a small sum to the treasury each year. But it needed constant maintenance and, as modem conveniences came to be expected, constant improvements. A kitchen had been added, a water tower built, gas generator installed, electric pump fitted, and electric wiring strung; in later years these improvements began to cost more than the hotel could ever return. As the camp meetings wound down there was less patronage, too. Finally the "poor season" reported for 1923 prompted the appointment of a committee to study the hotel's future.

Their report came a year later, following a season in which repair costs had again outstripped revenues. The building was found by the committee to have a fundamental flaw in its foundation, and though it had been shimmed and cabled, major repairs were needed. They recommended that its furnishings be sold and that the building be razed.

Taking those actions was set aside in the hope of finding another way out, but the following summer no lessee was found and the hotel remained empty. The final decision to raze it was made that August, and a sale of the furnishings at auction was set for Labor Day. It was a sad day for the Grove, but a great sale! Hundreds of items—beds, chairs, lamps, washstands, dining room furniture, porcelain, even the electric pump—were sold to a crowd that rivaled that of a camp meeting Sunday. The Association netted over $300 on the day.

The building itself was offered by bid, but no bids surfaced over the winter, and by spring of 1927 it was boarded up with barricades on the porches and cellar door and warning signs posted all around. There still being no offers from outside, the revitalized Woman's Club asked for and received permission to have it removed at their expense. When the ladies advertised their intent, it was local builder George Reber and his father who submitted the best bid—they would remove the building without cost, for its lumber value. The building was removed, the cellar filled in, and the ground graded and seeded by fall.

THE NEW WOMAN'S CLUB

No records have been found to describe the transition from the Woman's Guild of 1924 to the Woman's Club of 1926, but it seems to have been re-formed among the year-round residents' common interests in both athletics and community service. The group requested permission to use the Girls' Clubhouse for meetings and the Auditorium for basketball in fall of

1926. The following season the women asked for exclusive use of the Clubhouse (the Girl's Club had owned the building but not the land) but they ran into some unexpected resistance. Loeffler had just been elected president of the Association, and took the lofty position that giving exclusive use would be tantamount to giving away the stockholders property, a thing he felt that as president he could not do. He proposed a compromise in which the women would pay a modest rent, but that met with a stony silence.

Another compromise that would make the Woman's Club the official custodians of the building failed, too. During the deadlock the president and his treasurer, Robert Milans, both offered their resignations, but action was postponed and the meeting was abruptly adjourned. The board met three days later in the clubhouse, where several more motions attempting to clear the impasse failed to gain seconds. Finally the club was offered exclusive use of the building "at all times except when authority to use is given to other organizations, upon application." Everyone accepted this compromise, and the resignations were withdrawn.

The club set to work on having the hotel removed, and later installed a miniature golf course on its site, to everyone's delight. It also set out to establish a permanent and equipped playground for the smaller children, near the clubhouse, with slides, sand pits, seesaws, and swings. This plan was not met with universal approval, however; located just behind their house at 207 Grove Avenue the Alonzo Tweedales saw it as a personal intrusion and a denial of their full property rights, and fought bitterly to have it located somewhere else. After nearly a year of arguments and threats their complaint was abruptly dismissed and the playground was put in.

The Woman's Club in this form, under the leadership of (Mrs. Roy) Sarah (Osborn) McCathran, and (Mrs. George) Sara (Couch) Seaton, became an active and lasting institution, surviving the great depression, the incorporation, fire, war, and the gray flannel suit era, all the while contributing substantially to the welfare and pleasant environment of Grove life.

THE LAKE

The lake enjoyed a brief renaissance during this period. Unused for ice since the 'teens and largely ignored for recreation (the exposure of flesh that water sports encouraged was heavily discouraged by the Methodists), the water had become choked with weeds. Its extinction had been threatened by the WSSC, but it was spared by its very inadequacy as a water supply.

But the Hiller boys and their friends took an interest in it, and in the summer of 1927 it was revitalized for the purposes of boating, its bottom cleaned and its spillways repaired. The new interest was fleeting, however, and over the next decade the lake settled back into the forest floor and its bed became only a wide course for the spring and a source of fresh watercress for resourceful housewives.

THE FINAL WALKER CHALLENGE

The differences with the Walkers over stock ownership and transfer rights was a sore that would not heal until common interests could overcome the enmity.

A significant effort was made in 1925 by Walker's daughter, Mrs. Hardy, to put things right between the Major and the Association. Major Walker had become unapproachable on those subjects, but his eldest daughter and her sister Janet Smith paid a call on the board of trustees to offer to attempt a settlement between the board and their father. The meeting got underway on a bad note, Mrs. Hardy referring to the board as a "stag party," and continued anything but cordial until Mrs. Hardy left without any conclusion being reached. Apparently a seed had been planted, however, because the following January Walker, without further solicitation, sent a check for $365 to cover, he said, everything he owed. The trustees, wary of another legal offensive, refused the check (though they needed the money) as it was not exactly what the Major owed, but the Major wrote back that he would submit the exact amount if they would but advise him of the amount.

No action was taken, but concern over another Walker challenge was heightened when in the spring of 1926 Robert Walker offered a stock certificate, which he had purchased from a Mr. Krick, for transfer to himself. Under the Loeffler resolution of 1918 the trustees were still refusing to transfer shares into the Walker family, and thus returned the certificate stating that the shares were not fully paid up. Walker paid the back assessments and presented the certificate again; this time they refused on the grounds that it was improperly endorsed. The endorsement was corrected, but each time the transfer was requested again the matter was postponed.

Mrs. Hardy ran for office as a trustee that May. Her competence and personal appeal were sufficient to win her the office as, in spite of her family connections, the stockholders elected a woman trustee for only the second time in its history. When her brother presented the Krick stock again in September the trustees simply voted to deny the transfer, but for the first time, with Mrs. Hardy voting, the denial was not unanimous.

Walker came back to the board again, late in 1926, this time with a complete legal argument running to 17 pages, and using the language of the appeals court verdict of 1915 (which had gone against the Walkers) to demonstrate that the trustees no longer had the grounds to deny such stock transfers. The paper combined the clear voice of reason and a compelling legal argument, and implied that if the trustees failed to take favorable action he would take the matter directly to the stockholders where he expected, he said, to win. The election of 1922 had, after all, broken a solid anti-Walker majority and the election of 1926 had put a Walker back on the board of trustees.

Apparently the board was persuaded when it saw the letter Walker was prepared to send to the stockholders. At a board meeting in January, 1927, an historic compromise was worked out wherein the Krick stock would be transferred to Walker. Though it was only two shares, the transfer was the first increase in legal Walker stock allowed since the board first acted to freeze their holdings in 1914. Even more significant in the compromise was the appointment of a committee:

"Whereas, certain stockholders are dissatisfied with the conditions of titles and government now prevailing at Washington Grove, Maryland: and

Whereas it is the desire of this Board of Trustees of the Washington Grove Association that entire harmony shall prevail between the several stockholders of this

Association;

"Now Therefore, Be It Resolved, that the President of this Association be and is hereby authorized, empowered and directed to appoint a committee, consisting of five persons, who shall be stockholders of the Washington Grove Association, to look into the matter of titles to land in, and the government of the community known as Washington Grove, Maryland, and to report back to this Board with their recommendations as soon as practicable."

Trustees Cook and Hiller had voted against the Krick transfer, but there was no dissension on the appointment of a committee—it was unanimous. President Loeffler appointed the five members immediately, and included Walker as one of them. Fifty-four years after incorporation, a quiet revolution was in the air, and a harmonious—apparently—steering committee was going to direct it.

11

Reorganization—Failure

THE GROVE'S LAST DECADE as a private corporation began the very day the sewers were finished—May 31, 1927. But it was not that bold improvement which ended the Association's corporate life. In fact, the new utilities gave the Grove new hope of staying private for a long time.

But just what form of government the Grove would have was never more undecided. A panel had been appointed in January to study the mixed matters of stockholders' rights and the form of government itself. The members represented a range of views; if they could agree on a plan, the Grove would move quickly into a new era.

THE FIRST AND SECOND REORGANIZATION COMMITTEES

Five well-respected Grove residents had been appointed to the committee, including Robert Walker, Roy McCathran, Paul Cromelin, Dan Garges, and Needham Turnage. Before the committee could meet each member had to be qualified as a certified stockholder. But Robert Walker had transferred all his stock to his mother during the power struggle of 1913, so he owned only the two Krick shares that the board had recently agreed to transfer to him.

However, when Walker presented the shares for transfer he added a new demand: that the shares be issued to him in the original form of certificate, without the imprinted covenant that the stock was "held subject to the conditions imposed by the Charter, Amendments thereto, and By-Laws of the Washington Grove Association." Henry Milans, the Secretary-Treasurer, passed the request on to the president, who called a special meeting. Walker made his request again at the meeting and stated, according to the minutes, "that he had, in his pocket, signatures to a petition for the purpose of calling a special stockholders meeting, and...that he intended [to do so]." He was informed that the board had no power to issue him a certificate in any form other than that prescribed in the bylaws. Walker excused himself and left.

Since Walker continued to be unqualified as a stockholder, the committee could not be officially informed to begin meeting. When the next few weeks brought no end to the impasse, and since the annual meeting was fast approaching, the trustees voted to withdraw the name of Walker and substitute another. But there was too little time and the 1927 annual meeting came around before the committee had a chance to meet.

It was a significant meeting for several reasons. Politically, President Loeffler, increasingly engaged in the business of the U.S. Senate, announced his retirement from Grove affairs. Reverend Hiller, who had returned to office after six years absence, was elected the new president. Sadly, Charles Myers, whose fine tenor voice, in Loeffler's words, "thrilled us with pleasure and afforded consolation to the sorrowing, rests with his kindly nature in the Temple of Memory." Page Milburn, who had been present at the Fourth of July picnic in 1873, and who had written the first history of the Grove, had also died that year. Practically, after fifty years, indoor plumbing had come to the Grove. But at this meeting the main topic on the mind of everyone present was an item of new business—nothing less than the future of the Association.

The topic was of as much concern to resident non--stockholders as it was to non-resident stockholders, and the entire Grove community was represented at the meeting, though only stockholders could vote. In his opening remarks Loeffler admonished the stockholders: "We should not discard what we have until we are reasonably assured of the wisdom of the substitute. To find the substitute—to work it out—that is the problem."

Robert Walker came to the meeting with his legal argument in one hand, his moral argument in the other hand, and a signed petition in his pocket. He was technically not a stockholder, but was allowed to vote the Krick shares as proxy. As soon as the routine business was out of the way, Walker rose to offer a ten paragraph resolution the effect of which was to declare the Loeffler resolution of 1918 "repealed and annulled." Walker's sister, Mrs. Hardy, seconded the motion and discussion followed, but then Maurice Browning offered a substitute motion, also prepared in advance, which would dissolve the existing reorganization committee (which had not met) and replace it with a new one made up of five members, of whom three would be lawyers.

The committee would have as its charter duty to formulate a plan of government which would guarantee "standard values" for the property of stockholders "equal to that of other property in neighboring towns." Finally, according to his motion, the new committee would report its finding by August 3rd.

On the strength of Browning's motion Walker withdrew his own, but the new motion failed to obtain a second. Then, upon the plea of the retiring president, minor modifications to the motion were allowed and the way was cleared for a second committee. President Hiller announced the makeup of the new group: the three original members were to remain—McCathran, Turnage, and Garges—and Mrs. Hardy and William Hallam were to be added.

The committee worked through June and July in apparent harmony, and delivered its report at a special meeting on August 3. Its recommendations were simple and direct:

1. that each property owner was to be issued a fee simple deed,

2. that the government was to change to that of a municipal corporation, with the details to be arranged by a new committee, and

3. that the Association was to be dissolved and the assets distributed among the stockholders

Detailed resolutions were presented to support each of the recommendations. The fee simple deed form for lots was to include only three covenants: (1) that any house constructed thereon would conform to building setback lines, and cost not less than $1000, (2) that no use for mercantile, manufacturing, or mechanical purposes would be allowed, and (3) "That for the purposes of sanitation and health neither the party..., his heirs, or assigns shall or will sell, rent, lease, or otherwise dispose of said land or any improvements thereon to anyone of a race whose death rate is of a higher percentage than that of the white or Caucasian race." The covenants were intended to take the place of the Association's present tight control over the use of Grove property.

(These covenants were eventually adopted and remained on the deeds well into the 1950's; the third one was actively used to discourage blacks, Jews, Orientals, or native Americans, for that matter, from seeking to settle in the Grove. The exclusivity of the Grove as envisioned by its founders, at least in their promotional literature, was intended to support the utopian ideal of a homogeneous community of persons with common beliefs. The third covenant reduced that lofty notion to the language of bigotry, and left little doubt as to its contemporary purpose.)

There were several procedural skirmishes at the meeting over the committee's recommendations, but when the voting came support for the plan was nearly unanimous: 865 shares for, 48 against. Within a few days the board had item 1 of its recommendations ready for implementation by establishing a set of rules for issuance of deeds. Each deed was to require a ten dollar fee which was to be deposited in a separate bank account labeled "Reorganization Fund of the Washington Grove Association." Items two and three were to take a little longer.

This committee stayed intact and made progress over the winter of 1928-29 toward planning the new government, though in the spring it lost Roy McCathran to the pressures of his business. By May 29 it had narrowed its study to two possibilities: the Grove could become a municipal corporation or a Special Taxing Area. The municipality had been a very popular form for community organization in Montgomery County at the end of the last century: the only municipality in the county prior to 1888 had been Rockville, but nine new towns and one city (Takoma Park) were chartered between 1888 and 1906. But between 1906 and the onset of the depression all ten new communities had elected to be special taxing areas. The chief difference between the two forms was that Towns were separate political entities while special taxing areas were administrative subdivisions of a county. Towns provided and administered their own services (though they could elect to contract with the county or another town to share resources), but the tax areas had services provided by the county and only the administration of services was handled by their locally elected officials.

One way to gain a municipal form of government was to merge with an existing town. Dan Garges represented the reorganization committee in talks with Dr. Bates Etchison, Mayor of Gaithersburg, on the possibility of an annexation or merger. A major concern of the committee was the cost of any new government, and Gaithersburg's low tax rate, only fifty cents per hundred dollars assessed value, was comparable to the effective Grove rate. Etchison replied that he had "talked with a good many of the people here and everyone seems to think it would be a good thing for both places, if it can be worked in some way."

At the annual meeting of 1929 the committee reported its findings, but made no recommendation as to the merger. It did clearly convey the fact, however, that no merger, annexation, or new corporation could be accomplished until the Maryland legislature next met, and that was almost two years away. The stockholders renewed the committee's charter, President Hiller taking McCathran's place, and asked it to come up with a firm recommendation. But a year later it had broadened, rather than narrowed, the choices. At the 1930 annual meeting it listed the following options: (1) the indefinite continuation of the Association with its elected board of trustees, (2) re-incorporation without the religious features, "along the lines of a country club, private business, or social corporation," or (3) the formation of a municipality to be known as '"Washington Grove."'

On two points the committee was definite:

"It is our opinion that the question or idea of annexation with the present town of Gaithersburg...is not wise or feasible, as thereby we would lose our identity and the name 'Washington Grove', so dear to our hearts, so rich in fond memories, so prized at present, and so full of future hopes and ideals noble in their purport." On this point there was no dissension and the stockholders promptly agreed that there should be no annexation with Gaithersburg.

The other matter on which the committee was agreed was that it was not "sufficiently advised" to undertake the formulation of a new charter, and wished to be relieved of that burden. A series of motions was was offered which would authorize the committee to have "something" drawn up, but this was premature since it had not yet been decided what form the new corporation would take. The confusion on the floor was compounded by a motion Roy McCathran introduced to democratize the proceedings by suspending voting by stock, to allow all residents to participate in deciding their community's future. Then Elizabeth Reiss, a leading opponent of reorganization, demanded to know more about what was being proposed. She got no answer; instead McCathran interjected a quick motion that the committee simply "continue," and that the meeting adjourn. Abruptly, it did.

Now there was only six months before the legislature would meet, and there was still no firm plan. The committee picked up McCathran as a member again, but lost Hiller, who had declined re-election. Finally, in March of 1931, with the session in Annapolis half over, the draft of a new charter was brought to the stockholders for review.

It is clear in retrospect from the records that the drive toward municipal status had been losing momentum for some time, even among its enthusiastic supporters; but apparently no one was aware that there was widespread discomfort with the plan among the stockholders at large. When the stockholders reconvened on August 7 no one was willing to take a strong position.

Chairman William Hallam reviewed the committee's history and recommendations, but then spoke of his perception that there was an apparent misunderstanding by many concerning the 1928 resolution of the stockholders to seek incorporation into municipal status. If they did not want it after all, he said, they should rescind the 1928 resolution. Roy McCathran also backed away from the proposed charter, admitting that it needed several changes before it was acceptable to him, and adding (rather curiously) that he had no special interest in seeing it adopted. Hallam and Garges both rose to emphasize that the committee was only presenting the draft, not recommending its adoption.

In the face of all this equivocation, Robert Walker rose to remind the assembly that the 1928 vote had been 845 to 48 and "that a more nearly unanimous action on a question nobody could hope to secure." But president Robert Milans spoke of "severe criticisms" he had heard, and said that many stockholders were "very positive" that they had not voted to incorporate. Then the support collapsed entirely: Dan Garges took the floor to say that the change would be a "costly mistake"; then Dr. Elmon Cook said that he had voted for incorporation but "claimed the privilege of changing his mind." He moved that the action of 1928 be rescinded. There was no second.

The sense of the meeting was clear by now, but Robert Walker rose again to argue the matter, citing the flaws in the present system with respect to individual rights and the lack of appropriate and usual municipal services under the present system. But no minds were changed. Hallam interjected a motion which would relieve and discharge his committee from any further service. After a recess, the motion was seconded and passed; with it, the second committee passed into history. Robert Walker then moved that the stockholders rescind, by unanimous consent, the act of 1928 which had created the movement toward incorporation. They did so, and the matter was seemingly put to rest.

What had caused the plot to take such a twist at this late hour? The stage had been set in 1928: it had not changed, and the same players were on it. But a cold wind had blown in that was slowing things down all over the world. The period from 1928 to 1931 witnessed a series of events external to the Grove that were bringing on a new ice age in financial matters. At first they brought caution in the capital markets, then fear, and finally frozen terror. Eventually it would be called the Great Depression, and the Grove was among the first to know about it.

THE GREAT DEPRESSION

The capital stock of the Grove had been in a depression for years. The last treasury stock had been sold during the stockholder wars of 1913-1914. Most of the value of the stock after that was in its connection with a lot or lots; there was virtually no market for unlocated stock. Changing tastes had diminished the Grove's appeal as a religious and cultural center, and the automobile had brought finer resorts into traveling range. What remained at the Grove was its tall trees, good air, tranquil atmosphere, and its easy access to Washington. With the coming of the water and sewer system the trustees saw an end to the Grove's depression, and they began clearing wide avenues and cross streets deep into the east woods in anticipation of a new population boom. It never came. Once again, as in the 1870's, external economic conditions would lay a heavy hand on the Grove's ambitions.

Looking backward at the Great Depression of the 30's it is easy to think of it as having begun on Black Thursday—October 24, 1929—and ended the day Hitler's army marched into Poland. But for many Americans the depression began earlier, and for others it never began at all. In the late 20's interest rates were high, and capital was being created to finance increases in output without increases in productivity. On the stock market share values were up, but personal income was slowing down.

Sages had predicted a crash years before it came, but

when it came not even the sages could predict how long it would last. There were rallies of buying over the next several months, but they were only the punctuation for periods of deeper selling. It took two years for the market to settle into its murky bottom, two years in which capital vanished from the banks and almost everyone—individuals and businesses alike—simply stopped spending. What was a panic at first turned into a recession; by the election of 1932 almost everyone was calling it what it was—a depression. The Association, as a corporate body, spent the rest of its life under the influence of that depression.

In the general euphoria that followed the 1928 resolution to incorporate, and in their desire to obtain the new fee simple deeds, the Walker family settled up all its old debts with the Association. By the end of the fiscal year, and on the eve of the stock market crash, the Association had more cash than it was accustomed to.

All but $200 of its remaining debt was paid off, and the estimated budget of $2850 for 1929-1930 was projected to break even. The following May, in spite of the fiscal crisis in the stock market, Hiller could report that it had been "an uneventful year," and that a small surplus of funds would remain at year end. But the flow of money was slowing; within a few months into the new fiscal year the Association was facing a cash shortage, and a $500 deficit had been projected for fiscal year 1931.

By winter the Association was behind in its electric lighting bill, and did not have sufficient funds to pay the Superintendent up to date. Hiller fired off a letter to his fellow board members in which he quoted Grover Cleveland—"It is a condition and not a theory that confronts us"—and Boss Tweed—"What are you going to do about it?"—to get the point across that he was out of money. In February the trustees voted to borrow $500 to meet immediate cash needs, and the Women's Club donated $100 from its treasury to the general fund.

By the end of fiscal 1932 the Association's debt had risen again to close to $2000, partly because of improvements made on the Superintendent's cottage. In another letter Hiller blasted the "Cheerful Cherubs of big business" for "assuring us for more than a year over the radio that returning prosperity was just around the comer and soon we should all be singing 'Happy Days Are Come Again'." Even the more prosperous Grove residents were feeling the pinch; Roy McCathran resigned as a trustee, citing the "troublous business times" that kept him in town long into the evenings. Trustee William Teepe resigned for the same reason. Even Major Walker had to curtail expenses; he wrote the board that "in the present circumstances" he could not connect his cottage to the sewer and water service. Rosalie Hardy Shantz, Walker's granddaughter, opened a tea room in her mother's home at 102 Center Street, from which the Association received a $15 annual boarding house fee.

In the fall of 1933 the Superintendent was discharged, partly out of dissatisfaction with his services, but also to save money—and no one was hired to replace him. The expense of his telephone, electricity and water service was also thus saved. He rented back the cottage for $15 a month, though later he was often unable to pay it.

Several Grove residents were in similar straits. The Grove helped by allowing those in need to cut designated trees for firewood, provided that for each tree cut for themselves, a tree would be cut for the

Association. In the direst circumstances the trustees gave residents firewood. The county established an Unemployment Committee which apparently provided labor for public works projects, and paid modest wages and/or food to unemployed persons in exchange for day labor. The Grove took advantage of this for help in cleaning up the lake woods, which had become an unauthorized but well-used dump for everything from daily garbage to derelict vehicles.

In 1933 the Association attempted to reduce the street lighting either by lighting fewer hours or fewer lamps, but the original contract with Pepco was still in force, and its terms so favorable that very little could be saved by writing a new one with up-to-date prices. The Woman's Club donated $50 toward the electric bill at a difficult time during the winter. The same year the insurance on the Auditorium and Assembly Hall was cut back for a savings of $29.11.

Many of the Grove's summer residents could not afford to operate two houses and turned to their Grove cottages for rental income, bringing in an odd mix of tenants, some of whom were the subjects of serious complaints. Others simply abandoned their property for taxes, and some cottages were left empty and vandalized. When the first properties were to be sold at tax auction, Hiller commented that "Anybody can buy any Grove house sold for taxes, and get title, probably [in spite of the covenants] even a Negro." The Association purchased some properties itself, but in July of 1934, McCathran commented that the Grove seemed to be the only one bidding in the real estate market, and that it could not afford to load itself up with lots on which it would have to pay taxes to the county.

One cottage on the circle was used as a party house

by a relative of the absentee owner. In February of 1933 it was reported that "a large party came out— fourteen couples in all—and had a 'whoopee' party until way beyond midnight, dancing and yelling in the Circle." The young man was arrested and a considerable quantity of hard cider and stronger liquor was confiscated.

By fiscal 1934 the annual budget was under control and in balance, though still bearing a heavy debt load. The feat had been accomplished by a combination of curtailed services and added fees, including the ten dollar charge collected for each fee simple deed. The depression was keeping things a little shabbier than they had been, and holding off important improvements, but it had not bankrupted the Association. And life in the Grove, with the great depression as a backdrop, continued in both its lighter and darker moments.

SUNDAY TENNIS II

One of the more significant incidents that arose after the Association's shift away from a primarily religious institution was a renewed push toward allowing Sunday sports. A decade after the Sunday tennis controversy, an active Tennis Club was still holding matches during the summer with tournaments on Labor Day. In 1932 the trustees expended ten dollars on a trophy—a silver cup—to be presented each year to the winning team at the Labor Day tournament, and the team could keep it if they won it three times running. Unfortunately, the following month the boys were observed playing tennis and speedball on a Sunday. The matter was taken to the trustees, and after considerable discussion it was decided to hold firm on the previous policy prohibiting such play. The president, Robert Milans, was appointed to take the boys aside in an informal setting to try to get their cooperation.

TENNIS DATES SET

Washington Grove Tourney to Be Held September 2, 3 and 4.

The Washington Grove singles tennis championships will be played September 2, 3, and 4, at Washington Grove, Md., it has been announced. This is the second year of competition for the trophy donated by the Washington Grove Association. Pat Deck of Washington won the cup last year. Three wins insure permanent possession.

The championships are open to any amateur player in Washington and suburbs.

Entries must be in the mail by 6 o'clock, August 30, and should be addressed to George L. Seaton, Washington Grove, Md. Blanks may be obtained at the Tennis Shop, Fairway and Tennis Racquet Shop or may be procured by phoning Seaton at Gaithersburg 158-W. The fee of $1.25 must accompany each blank.

The notice in the Washington Star that rekindled the Sunday tennis controversy.

The meeting worked, apparently, but a month later Sam Walker, Robert Walker's oldest son and president of the Tennis Club, met with the trustees to request that once per year—on the day before Labor Day—that games be allowed on a Sunday. Otherwise, he argued, the tournament matches would be spread out over two weekends, diminishing enthusiasm and making it impossible for some players to enter. He implied that the club would be willing to help enforce the rule on all other Sundays, but the trustees replied that it was not in their power to change the rule; they would have to deny the request.

The boys acquiesced, and the 1933 season passed quietly until late in August, when the *Evening Star* carried the customary announcement of the Grove's Labor Day tournament. Unfortunately, it contained the uncustomary information that the tournament would be held on September 2, 3, and 4; Saturday, Sunday, and Monday. The trustees' reaction was anything but quiet, and they took the organizers to task over the announcement, but in the end it was put down to a misunderstanding, with appropriate apologies all around.

This led the trustees into further discussion about Sunday tennis. It was brought out that some players were apparently making their own Sunday rules: they would arrive at the court in late morning and wait, equipment in hand, until the precise moment that services were concluded, then begin play. Finally it was decided to employ Mr. Phoebus, who also collected the trash, to remove the nets each Saturday night and put them up again on Monday morning. This very effective method seemed to satisfy almost everyone, and the season was about over, anyway.

But in the spring of 1934 the Maryland legislature got into the act. While modifying some State 'blue laws' they legalized sports activities on Sundays after 2 p.m., on state-owned facilities. The trustees were put under some pressure to follow suit, but at a meeting in April they decided that this was still a matter for the stockholders to decide.

They took up the topic at the May 30 annual meeting. After the preliminaries were disposed of, former president Ed Swingle moved that the Association allow Sunday sports with the same restrictions as to hours that the State had set. A "chorus of seconds" followed the motion, according to the minutes. Swingle, Robert Walker, and others spoke in favor of the proposition; Elizabeth Reiss, Elmon Cook, and Walter Hoofnagle spoke against it.

Then Francis Hiller rose and asked "for a bit longer time than he usually occupied in addressing the stockholders,...in view of the fact that he had been a sort of storm center of the question" in the past. When he had opposed allowing Sunday sports in 1922, he said, he had hoped for five years, but he had gotten 12. He said that it was "too late to re-make a mid-Victorian Sunday," and that they should allow tennis on Sunday, and not even try to curtail the hours, since it would lead to more controversy. Browning followed Hiller and spoke strongly against allowing it, but when the respected Reverend Osborn stood and endorsed the idea, so long as it was done after church, the matter was decided. The vote was 31 to 5 in favor, with restrictions only as to the hours, and all sports except baseball were to be allowed.

This decision changed Grove athletics forever, though other changes had been taking place. The regular baseball program had long since been discontinued, and the grandstand had been condemned and dismantled in 1929. The Men's Athletic Association had drifted apart and its clubhouse was being used by the boy scouts. But it was in poor condition and the Women's Club had asked that it be dismantled in favor of an addition to the old Girl's Clubhouse, in which they were meeting. In

1934 it was taken down and the lumber from it was used to build a kitchen addition.

THE LONG ROAD TO PAVED STREETS

For the Grove no modernizing feature would ever be as welcome as the indoor toilet. But years after the last honey wagon had rolled through its alleys, the Grove still lacked its ultimate civilizing improvement— the paved road. In its early history the Association's greatest recurring concern was over the integrity of the walkways, as each summer hundreds of thousands of footfalls churned whatever topping had been laid into splinters, dust, or muck. That problem had finally been solved by a combination of compaction and attrition; the many toppings had been packed to a hard mass, and the summer visitors had dwindled to a few.

The earliest problems with the roads occurred when area farm wagons or local delivery vehicles, driven over wet tracks, caused deep rutting which was unpleasant to cross but otherwise of little concern to most Grove residents. Later when a few families kept carriages, and others were staying year round, the condition of the roads became a more practical matter. By the mid-1920's the grounds committee, the superintendent, and the Board of Trustees itself found themselves increasingly preoccupied with the condition of the streets and alleys.

Many of the roads had a good base, built up over the years, of packed earth and cinders. Cinders were the fire-hardened kernels of unburnt coal that accumulated in the fireboxes of steam locomotives, and which the B&O would donate by the carload to anyone who wanted them. But all the Grove's mile or so of roadways and alleys were susceptible to rutting in wet weather, and some would break up entirely in the freeze-and-thaw cycles of late Fall and early Spring.

In 1927 a Committee on Roads was appointed to look into a permanent solution, and the sum of $2000 was appropriated to pay for it. The committee hired an expert who surveyed the roads and eventually recommended a bituminous road system over a stone base, with an estimated cost of $6500-7000 per mile. This was too far out of budget for serious consideration, so the committee recommended instead to lay down a six to eight inch base of cinders (heretofore the cinders had only been a topping), pack it down over the winter, and add oil during the summer months to act as a binder and cut down on dust.

Six carloads of cinders were brought out by the B&O and, after county road scrapers prepared the beds, were hauled and spread a wagon load at a time by local farmer Ora Mills. The work was complete in July of 1928, and a speed limit of 15 mph was posted throughout the Grove. The low speed limit was designed to protect the Grove's roads at the same time it protected its citizens.

By this time all the major roads in the vicinity of the Grove were paved, including the Gaithersburg-Laytonsville Road. But the main road into the Grove from Rockville and beyond was still Central Avenue (then Washington Grove Road), and it was still unpaved. Oakmont Avenue was still a private farm lane. In the Winter of 1929 the trustees wrote to the county requesting Central Avenue be paved. Fortunately, in the atmosphere of dwindling optimism that characterized the first months after the stock market crash, the county acquiesced, and laid down a hard surface on Central

Avenue and Deer Park Drive.

The oil and cinders proved fairly durable and for a couple of years the only maintenance required was filling potholes and re-oiling. In 1931, to save money, the Association sprayed old crankcase oil, which it obtained free for the hauling, on the roads and alleys. While the savings was surely appreciated, the smell of used crankcase oil in the hot summer months apparently was not, and the practice was discontinued.

In 1932 the streets needed a scraping to get them level again, and once again the county was enlisted to help. The scraping improved matters only slightly, however, and soon the complaints began to dominate the trustees business meetings. The Women's Club was particularly adamant about the poor condition of the roads and prodded the trustees' to get some better system, and in 1933 Major Walker broke several years of silence to add his own formal request for road improvements.

That summer a new tactic was tested: the potholes were filled with cinders and a fresh coat of oil was applied, then the county's steamroller was enlisted to compress the mass into a hard surface. For two days the giant roller rolled over the streets exerting pressures ten times that of ordinary vehicles. This last measure was much more successful and, with repairs, managed to serve for the balance of the Association's existence.

As traffic began to increase in the waning years of the depression there was increasing agitation for fully paved streets. The Association's inability to raise the money for this improvement was one of the frustrations that kept reorganization in the backs of Grove minds. The residents needed paved roads so they could be assured of passage in winter and spring, and the non-residents wanted paved roads to make their properties more accessible and therefore more salable. Without full power to tax and collect the taxes, though, the Association would never be able to accomplish this final civilizing influence.

Reorganization might be the only way.

THE ASSOCIATION

12

Reorganization—Success

THE ONSET OF THE DEPRESSION had brought the collapse of the first reorganization effort. In July of 1931 the second committee's recommendations were rejected and the committee was disbanded by action of balky stockholders. But within the Board of Trustees most knew that something would eventually have to be done, so the following November they appointed a new committee of seven, which included Roy McCathran, Robert Walker, Herb Davis, and Francis Hiller, to study the possibilities. Walker was still not officially a stockholder, but was allowed to vote the Krick shares as proxy, so his presence on the new committee was accepted.

They met very little over the next six months, and issued a modest report to the 1932 annual meeting, perhaps because they were wary of stirring up the foes of reorganization. The slow pace was partly due to the repeated absences of Chairman Davis, who was Insurance Commissioner for the District of Columbia and traveled widely and often in that capacity. He missed the annual meeting, and had just been sent to Europe when a special stockholders meeting was scheduled to meet that September. Robert Walker was disapproving of the slow progress, and said so;

President Milans replied that things were moving well enough. But when nothing had been decided in the Spring, and it was revealed that Davis was again to miss the annual meeting, Walker approached the Board on May 29 and demanded that a new committee be appointed. After he left the room there was heavy discussion, and finally Roy McCathran pointed out that Walker was in a position to make a lot of trouble, and furthermore that he was right about the inaction. He moved that Walker be allowed to vote another 25 shares as proxy (he had recently purchased the DeLand's Grove holdings) and that the trustees support the creation of a new committee. It was carried.

The morning session of the annual meeting was devoted to reorganization. Walker praised the makeup of the present group but pointed out that "the interests of the Grove community have suffered because of several years of procrastination." Then he made a motion to abolish the present committee. Apparently the stockholders were ready to consider reorganization again, and endorsed Walker's concept of a smaller committee; Milans was already prepared with his choices, and promptly selected Walker himself, McCathran, and Mrs. Hynson for the new committee.

Robert Walker was increasingly a successor to the role his father, the Major, had played twenty years before. Though he had not a single share of stock in his name, he was nonetheless in a visible and often controversial position on many Grove issues. His request that the DeLand shares be issued to him in the old form of certificate, much in the way he had earlier requested that his lease be issued in its old form, had been denied. At this same annual meeting he somewhat theatrically offered to sell the shares back to the

Association for $4 each, "the face value being $20 per share, and the price usually much above that." Later he dropped the price to $2 a share if the Association would spend the other $2 on improvements to the intersection of Brown and Chestnut Streets, on the corner of his lot. Later in the meeting he got into a shouting controversy with the chairman of the grounds committee.

Walker was apparently as much respected as feared, and having been appointed to the new committee, undertook its work with enthusiasm. They met several times during the summer and fall, and by November had secured a draft charter from the Association's Rockville attorney, Robert Prescott. Over the winter Roy McCathran was developing an alternate plan. The Maryland legislature was to reconvene in January 1935, and when the stockholders met in May, 1934, Walker was so certain that some form of charter resolution would be adopted in time for state action that he proposed eliminating the elections by just extending everyone's term for one year. This was rejected as it was in conflict with the bylaws, but in fact each trustee and officer was re-elected without challenge.

Walker presented the Prescott plan first, which would incorporate the Grove as a Special Taxing Area, and was based on the assumption that the least government would be the best. But another faction of stockholders (perhaps those who lived in the community year-round) favored a stronger form of government. McCathran then presented his plan in which the Grove would be incorporated as a Town. A Mayor and Council would collect the taxes, provide the services, and govern for the general welfare of the people, while the Association would continue to exist as the owner of the unsold lots and outlying grounds. The latter plan was discussed with generally favorable reaction, and finally a special meeting was called for July 2.

In the meantime the concept was put into print, along with a complete sample charter, and entitled "PLAN NO.3". It was widely circulated before the meeting. It had been designed to solve the problem of tax collection and administration without attempting to distribute the assets of the Association. It was hoped that this feature would gain it the wide acceptance that the 1931 plan failed to achieve. It did not.

Reverend Osborn opened the meeting with a plea for caution in consideration of the plan, and expressing his fears that the religious needs of the community would not be met by a purely secular government. He introduced a motion that nothing be done until all the details of the ownership and management of the Association's land and buildings be clarified. The potential sudden loss of the Assembly Hall as a church building must have been much on his mind. There was discussion by Walker, McCathran, and Hiller in favor of the plan, but the evening ended with another postponement to July 30.

Over the intervening four weeks considerable lobbying must have taken place, and when the meeting was reconvened McCathran knew there was insufficient support for his plan. He rose at the meeting and reiterated that the plan had been developed in response "to an insistent demand that something be done," but that "after months of consideration there appeared to be a general condition of apathy." He then moved that his own plan be tabled, an action that would effectively kill it. His motion was not only seconded, but then was amended to discharge the committee from further consideration of the matter! It passed, as amended, and

PLAN NO. 3

Submitted by the
Committee on Reorganization
Appointed May 30, 1933

Committee Consisting of Mrs. M. W. Hynson, Robert H. Walker,
and Irving L. McCathran.

This plan provides for the transfer of only the streets, alleys, roads, parks, and public buildings to the Town of Washington Grove, and provides for the giving of a deed to each property holder to place a uniform title in the hands of each owner.

All of the plotted lots not sold and all of the outlying property still in the hands of the Grove Association are still being held as the undivided assets of the Association. This property may be transferred in part or as a whole to the Town of Washington Grove if desired, or a new corporation may be organized to administer the assets of the corporation as the stockholders in their judgment may see fit, independent and separate from the town organization.

It is suggested that upon the passage of this Act, the Washington Grove Association of the District of Columbia and Maryland deed in fee simple all streets, alleys, roads, parks and public buildings to the Town of Washington Grove, in the County of Montgomery, and State of Maryland, and the said Washington Grove Association shall forthwith issue our present form of deed to each property owner who has not heretofore received such a deed, for the purpose of placing a uniform title in the hands of each property holder holding title under the grant or grants from the said Washington Grove Association.

It is further suggested that the Town of Washington Grove assume all debts of whatsoever character, including bills rendered for collection of trash, garbage, cleaning of the streets, lighting of the streets, and other expenses involved in the upkeep of the grounds of the said Washington Grove Association including any unpaid notes outstanding, and that the said Washington Grove Association assign to the said Town of Washington Grove all bills payable to the said Washington Grove Association and all claims of whatsoever nature as well as all cash in bank or cash on hand at the time of the passage of this Act.

It is also suggested that the stockholders designate, at the annual meeting, a specific date for the calling of a special meeting for the consideration of any amendments or suggestions offered with respect to the attached Bill, and it is further requested that any amendments which are to be offered to the proposed Act be submitted in writing

Plan No.3, written in 1933, was the basis for the eventual reorganization of the Association into a municipality.

another blue-ribbon committee—and three more years of work—had failed to persuade the stockholders. The trustees were forced to look for another way.

In the meantime there was more municipal-style work to be done in the Grove.

* * *

THE GAITHERSBURG-WASHINGTON GROVE VOLUNTEER FIRE DEPARTMENT

Gaithersburg had an active cadre of volunteer fire fighters as early as the 1880's, and by 1896 they had incorporated, bought some sophisticated equipment, and had begun work on a firehouse near the building on Diamond Avenue that was to be their headquarters for over seventy years. When the Grove and Oakmont had accumulated some year-round residents they naturally contributed to the base of volunteers. The 1907 Huntley fire made fire prevention and protection a high priority in the Grove, and the 1914 burning of community leader Ignatius Fulks's house had a similar effect in the Town of Gaithersburg.

Two disastrous fires in downtown Gaithersburg, in 1924 and 1926, got beyond the control of the small company and threatened the entire city. The need for a well-disciplined and well-financed department was evident to all. The Gaithersburg-Washington Grove Volunteer Fire Department was chartered in February of 1927 with great enthusiasm, but almost immediately internal problems arose and the original charter was abandoned. After reorganization in 1928, the department was re-chartered and re-incorporated, but without the word "Volunteer" in its title.

The department was chronically underfunded and had no access to public money; when the great depression dried up contributions altogether, they were forced to seek aid from the state government. Annapolis took Washington Grove by surprise late in 1933 during a special session when it passed legislation establishing full public funding by local taxation for the "Gaithersburg-Washington Grove Fire Department, Incorporated." The bill had been, according to the Grove, "engineered through the legislature without the knowledge of the Board of Trustees, or consultation with the people of this community." And what angered the trustees was that it gave the county power to tax the Grove's residents for services that covered a much wider area.

Robert Walker called this "a very bad practice, no matter how necessary the services of said Fire Department may be." The act specified that two members of the Department's seven-member board be appointed by the Grove, two by Gaithersburg, two from among the ranks of the department, and one from the area not included within the incorporated towns. With the prospect of increased taxes, the trustees voted to delay the appointments as long as possible. There may have been similar sentiment in Gaithersburg, for it was not until mid-1935 that its board members were named. Late in 1935 the governing commission was finally able to meet.

The charter of the corporation empowered it to operate a fire company within a designated area of the 9th election district of Montgomery County, but it did not specify whether the department should or could go beyond its charter area if it were needed, nor whether it could enter into cooperative arrangements with other fire companies. Some within the Grove argued that its activities should be strictly limited to fire and rescue operations within its district because (1) people inside the district were paying for it, and (2) because if it were responding to a call outside the district it would not be available for a call inside the district. Roy McCathran led the fight to allow it to serve all the area it could, a position that was finally adopted.

Once the unit became operational, the young men of the Grove participated eagerly. At the sound of the fire siren businessmen, grocers, barbers, teachers, carpenters, and high school boys suddenly deserted their posts and drove madly to the station house, or directly to the fire. Gaithersburg and Washington Grove had been socially separated by their highly different origins, and had accumulated little common history. But the camaraderie built up among the volunteers by mutual community service and shared danger had a significant bridging effect on the two communities.

The GWGVFD began one of its richest traditions on Labor Day, 1939. A massive parade, with floats, marching bands, and fire equipment from all over was organized to begin in the Grove and end at the Gaithersburg School. The equipment lined up in the Woodward Park ball diamond in marching order, all during the morning, and the parade began at one o'clock.

The volunteer system and the GWGVFD outlived the depression, World War II, and the cold war, but was eventually replaced by a paid force and survives today largely as a fraternal organization.

REORGANIZATION III

The annual meeting of 1935 adopted, for the first time, a house numbering system, designed by Roy McCathran's father, James K. McCathran. It also introduced a new set of ordinances—one that was based on the Town ordinances suggested by PLAN NO. 3—for consideration as "community order rules." The ordinances were read at the annual meeting, but a vote was put off until a special meeting could be held in August. The proposed ordinances were benign, and included prohibitions against such things as loose dogs or livestock, hunting without permission, disturbances of the peace, driving on the walkways, maintaining a privy, and casting dead animals upon the walkways.

But when the meeting came to order Robert Walker was anything but benign. He immediately called for a quorum count of stockholders, then he made formal objection to the meeting's continuing at all, citing the short notice given. After the ordinances were read, Walker again objected to the ordinances and questioned the right of the trustees to enforce them. Then he moved that the motion to enact them be tabled.

There followed an exchange between Walker and Roy McCathran in which Walker was sternly reminded that he had supported the same set of ordinances under the incorporation plan. Walker nonetheless continued his opposition, and then publicly announced that he no longer intended to pay any assessments "under present conditions." The Walker motion to table the ordinances was called and, surprisingly, succeeded. Once again the stockholders showed a great resistance to change, though this time it was under the threat of losing the assessments against the Walker properties. Ironically, changes more sweeping than those just rejected were to become a necessity.

The Grove's attorney in Rockville, Stedman Prescott, had rendered the verbal opinion in 1933 that, largely because of the diversity of titles issued to its residents, the Association was legally powerless to collect its assessments. He also recommended against bringing suit in equity to test that power, presumably in fear that if the suit failed, more would stop paying their fair share. The trustees reviewed their position in 1935, and decided to seek a second opinion on the subject from a tax expert. After a fruitless search for another attorney they returned to Prescott and asked this time for a written, annotated, opinion. The question, as they put it, was succinct: "it is possible [for the Grove] to collect delinquent assessments by a civil suit in a court of equity."

Prescott rendered his opinion in July. To be legal, he said, and in accordance with the charter and bylaws, assessments (1) must be annual, (2) must be uniform, and (3) must be assessed upon the stock OR upon the lots and improvements thereon. Since they were clearly not uniform, and were assessed against both the stock and the lots, they were not legally collectable. But McCathran pointed out that Prescott had not said whether the condition was a curable one, and moved that Prescott again be employed to expand on his opinion.

The reply received a month later was vague, and not encouraging. In the meantime another Rockville attorney, Thomas Anderson, had expressed himself willing to bring suit in a test case, "against a party of his own choosing." He cited a recent decision in which a party had been forced to pay assessments to a legally constituted community for street lighting and other services directly received. The trustees decided to press the suit through Anderson. The party selected was James P. Lynch, who held 20 shares located on the property at 405 Brown Street, and who had not paid his assessments for some time; the court, Anderson reported, would hear the case the following March (1936). But there were delays and in May the case had still not come to trial. Then the trustees were vexed to find that Lynch had hired Prescott to defend him! Prescott was a dangerous adversary under the circumstances, his having studied the Association's position so thoroughly and recently. But since the annual stockholders meeting was imminent, both lawyers held back to see what would develop. The case was destined never to come to court.

THE ANNUAL MEETING OF 1936

What was to be the Association's last regular annual meeting began in the usual way, with the reports of the President and standing committees. President Milans noted the deaths of two prominent Grove residents in the past year; Roy McCathran's father, James K. McCathran, and the first woman to have served on the Board of Trustees, Amelia Huntley. It was also reported that, as had happened once before, the Association had allowed its charter to lapse, but happily the situation had been saved by the timely filing of fresh papers. (Although there were stockholders and residents for whom the sudden and unexpected death of the Association would have been the happier event).

Roy McCathran announced his desire to retire from the board, once again because of the pressures of his business. In spite of many, including Robert Walker, who urged him to stay, he did retire and nominated Dr. Elmon Cook to replace him as a trustee. President Milans also elected to step down, and Cook was nominated and unanimously elected the new president as well. Cook was one of three sons of George Cook, one of the Grove's founders, and was widely respected throughout the Grove. After his election was announced, a committee of Robert Walker and Roy McCathran was appointed to escort him to the chair. Dr. Cook is reported to have been both a warm and humorous man, and immediately upon his taking office there was a change in the atmosphere of the meeting.

Cook had accepted the presidency (it had been arranged before the meeting) only on the condition that the Lynch suit be dropped. He stated that "the one indispensable thing for success is harmony and good feeling." Shortly after, a motion to dissolve the suit was passed, and then McCathran moved that a new committee on Revision and Reorganization be formed. This motion was also unanimously approved (apparently also having been brokered ahead of time), and, in the new aura of optimism, a second new committee was named to plan the renaissance that was expected to follow reorganization. This was to be known as the committee on Development of the Grove Community, and its charter was to look into the placement of a new hotel in the Grove, and to contact an experienced real estate development company to market the remaining unsold lots.

The reorganization committee met with the stockholders again on July 10 to review the options available. There was a formal presentation by Dr. Cook, and general discussion followed, but no action was taken. Over the winter the committee, working closely with the trustees, labored to formulate a plan that could be accepted by the stockholders in time for action by the legislature. Finally on March 12, 1937 it was ready with its report.

The railroads were apparently not running that Saturday, but it was important that a large majority of stockholders be present to vote. In his formal announcement of the meeting, Francis Hiller, as Secretary, appealed to the stockholders soliciting drivers to run carpools out to the Grove for the meeting. He also noted that daily bus service was available to the Grove from 9th Street and Constitution Avenue.

When the meeting finally got underway, with 603 shares represented, the topic was incorporation—the committee was recommending a municipality along the lines of "Plan No. 3", though with numerous minor revisions. On the floor of the meeting Roy McCathran argued that incorporation had become "practically a necessity," and "that the present setup neither preserves the ideals on which the Grove community was founded, nor secures what may be secured by incorporation."

He described a government administered by a Mayor and six councilmen, funded by a uniform tax rate, and elected by the votes of any property owner over 21. He noted that under the proposed charter "all matters must come before the qualified voters for decision." Some took the floor to suggest that the charter should follow more closely that of Gaithersburg, which was typical of the Town charters in Montgomery County; but McCathran contended "that this plan was better because it brought all important matters, especially all matters of taxation, before the voters."

At last three propositions were put before those

present:

1. That the Grove incorporate
2. That Plan No. 3 be the form of government; and
3. That the Association deed all its property to the Town.

A vote was taken on the first item: it was unanimous except for Elizabeth Reiss, holding nine shares, who said "it would only make a muddle." Under the bylaws this forced a stock vote on each of the three propositions, but when the count was tallied there were 594 votes in favor of each proposition and only nine against: the stockholders were at last united in favor of incorporation! The March 12 meeting ended with a unanimous resolution that, in spite of the passing of the Association, the Washington Grove Church would be allowed to continue with its present privileges. The committee on the Development of the Grove Community apparently never met.

The new charter was quickly and efficiently escorted through its required three readings in the Assembly at Annapolis by Stedman Prescott, and signed into law on May 18, 1937 by the governor. It was to become effective on May 30, and on that date the Association would cease to exit.

An orderly final stockholders meeting was held on May 29 at which the property of the Association was conveyed to the Town of Washington Grove. Dr. Osborn was the last person to address the stockholders, "urging that, while the Town of Washington Grove was the legal successor to the Association, we do not forget the spiritual heritage which has come down to us." The meeting—and the Association—was ended.

PROFILES VI: POSTMORTEM

The following remarks were made by Francis L.L.Hiller at a farewell dinner at the Tilden Gardens home of Dr. and Mrs. Elmon Cook in the summer of 1937:

"In the preamble of the charter of the Washington Grove Association it is set forth that about 1874 'certain ministers and laymen' of the Methodist Episcopal Church 'have associated themselves together' for certain purposes therein specified; with their powers relative to the temporal affairs of the camp-meeting association which they were forming rather carefully set forth. Just reading the Charter you would find it mostly given to temporal matters but we know that temporal matters were not the chief purpose back of this organization. Back of the organization here set up was a great purpose; a religious, moral and civic purpose: They wanted to advance the Kingdom of God among men; they wanted a camp-meeting where the salvation of God could be preached to needy men and women, and life as Christ envisioned it furthered. It is everlastingly true, as the Scriptures say, that 'without a vision the people perish.' These men and women had a vision, which was the Kingdom of God among men. They had some ideas about dancing, card playing, theater-going and the observance of the Sabbath day that we in our Superior wisdom think were hard, narrow, and bigoted. Perhaps they were needlessly severe, but when our present style of living produces men and women of more sterling character, and of more worth to God and to the community than these old pioneers, we shall be in a better position to criticize. Christ's words still stand— 'By their fruits ye shall know them.' The founders of Washington Grove belong to the generation that took seriously the pronouncement of Emerson—

So nigh is grandeur to our dust
So close is God to man
When Duty whispers low- 'Thou must'
The Youth replies- 'I can'

"Sublime words these. That thrilled a whole generation of American Youth.

"No fact of the present day spirit in America seems to me to be more sinister in its significance than is the failure of youth to-day to respond to great religious and moral ideas and ideals—to be thrilled by them— to believe their realization possible. The Pioneers of Washington Grove had ideals and were thrilled by them. They believed that Christ's Kingdom on earth was a possibility. They had intelligence enough to believe something and 'Intestinal Fortitude' enough to live out the convictions of their beliefs in spite of a ridiculing and gainsaying world. They could say and mean it: 'I believe in God, the Father Almighty, Creator of Heaven and Earth, and in Jesus Christ his only Son, Our Lord.' They also had convictions about certain moral and religious customs, and were not ashamed to order their lives by what they believed to be the desires of God. To my mind the thing most needed in the religious and moral life of America to-day is men and women who have convictions about God, and Life, and Salvation, and the courage to live them out.

"These Pioneers had a vision and saw some

realization of that vision on the Washington Grove grounds, where hundreds of men and women found a new center of their life's activities, and peace with God. To some of us the new spirit in America's life—of which the decadence and dissolution of the Washington Grove Association is only one of a myriad of evidences—does not bring much satisfaction. Modem life has a thousand conveniences and luxuries (all good in themselves) of which our fathers knew nothing. But are we better men and women for all of these things? Perhaps we can comfort ourselves with the thought that it was ever thus; that each new generation leaves the ideals and customs of its fathers like stranded and useless wrecks on a lee shore. About fifty years ago someone wrote:

When Washington was President
As cold as any icicle
He never on railroad went
And never rode a bicycle
He read by no electric lamp
Nor sat beside a gramophone
He never licked a postage stamp
And never saw a telephone.
'His trousers ended at the knees
By wire he could not send despatch
He filled his lamp with whale oil grease
And never had a match to scratch
But in these days it's come to pass
All things are with such rushing done
We've all these things—but then, Alas!'
'We seem to have no Washington.

"Let us hope that the future holds all the good things

that the advocates of this change prophesy. Let us face the future with courage and faith; but let us pause a moment to-night to honor the past and the Pioneers who made that past glorious. So I ask you all to stand with me in honor of the past and the men and women of the pioneer days of Washington Grove.

"I propose this toast:

'To the Founders and Pioneers of Washington Grove. We honor you to-day because we of to-day are better men and women as the result of your lives- Honor to your purposes Blessings to your memory Peace to your ashes.'

Francis L. L. Hiller"

EPILOGUE

When the Town succeeded the Association on May 30, 1937, the great weight of the Great Depression had begun to lift, and people were beginning to sense it. The Grove had become a community of homes, and a majority of them were now used year-round. The far-off rumblings of war in Europe were beginning to swell the bureaucracy in Washington, and the flight from Grove cottages, which had been caused by the one-two punch of water and sewer fees and the Depression, had ceased. The new town set off on a course that would make it into what it is today. That journey would take eight more years, and carry the town through the end of the depression, through a second World War, and into the postwar prosperity in which it has existed ever since.

* * *

After the act of incorporation had become law, and the final meeting of the Association was over, the practical reorganization could be begun. An organizational meeting was held on July 10, 1937 at 7:00 pm in the Assembly Hall. The purpose was to elect "a temporary chairman, a clerk, and three judges of election and proceed to hold election for Mayor and Council." Any property owner, or tenant for more than five years, who was also over twenty-one years of age, could vote.

The first Mayor and Council meeting was held on

July 12. Continuity was to be the order of the day. After the election of the remaining officers of the Town—Hiller became the first Clerk and George Felt the first Treasurer—it was voted to grant the Women's Club and the Athletic club the same privileges they had held with the Association. Andrew Heil and Alfred Christie were returned to the Fire Board, and Mr. Phoebus was to continue to collect the trash and garbage.

The new tax structure was complex, but uniform: all property was to be taxed at 10 cents per $100 of valuation, the value to be determined by the county tax assessor. In addition, each dwelling unit was to pay a flat tax of $11.00, and each lot located along a sewer line was to pay another ten cents for each running foot of frontage. The Council immediately moved to send tax bills reflecting the new rates and stating any amounts still owing from past Association levies.

With the power to collect taxes now in his hands, the Mayor sent his first annual list of delinquent taxpayers to the County Attorney. There were 33 properties listed, but with its new powers the Grove immediately collected on all but 4; those remaining were sold at auction the next spring. So effective were collections that the next year only three properties were listed, and only one was sold for taxes. The number went to 9 in 1939, but from 1940 the 1943 there were none.

The new tax rate schedule became a tradition of its own—the tax levy stayed the same for the next ten years. Other new traditions were begun, too. Sunday evening worship services in the auditorium became almost as popular as the movies being shown there on Friday nights.

Some practical matters were resolved in that first summer of the new town. A uniform speed limit of 25 miles per hour was set, and signs were posted throughout. All the public wells were now contaminated, so McCathran ordered the pumps removed and the wells filled in. This caused a minor fracas at the First Avenue well, where Mr. and Mrs. Cross made some threatening remarks—but the mayor had two policemen from Rockville standing by when the pump was pulled out. McCathran later quipped, "We pulled the pump and got Cross." The old wells were filled in with "oily cinders" that had been intended for the roads.

The Mayor's top agenda item, however, was the paving of the roads. A rough estimate of $8000 had been obtained, and McCathran figured that he could get about two thousand of that by selling the superintendent's cottage. He calculated that the remaining six thousand could be paid off in ten years at $800 a year, principal and interest included. It took a year to put the program together, but the following August he obtained authority to finance the project with road bonds. In the spring of 1939 the Grove got its first paved roads.

Nineteen thirty-nine was a year of incidents in the Grove. In the first week of August, Al Christie, Sr. was showing "Sh! The Octopus," an obscure Warner Brothers movie, to the regular crowd in the Auditorium when suddenly the screen seemed to catch fire. The shocked audience finally realized that it was the film, which had become stuck in the projector, had melted, and then had begun to bum, that was being projected on the screen. Fortunately they were no longer using the old tin booth, or Christie might have been badly burned.

In the second week of August, only 300 yards from the Auditorium, the Woman's Club's clubhouse caught fire late at night. It did not bum to the ground, but was thoroughly gutted and could not be repaired. Four months later the decision was made to build a new clubhouse on the site of the old hotel.

It was late in 1939 that the last significant change in the Grove's street patterns was made. The Wade Park area between 4th and 5th Avenues was one of the quietest and most attractive parts of the Grove. But the Maddox plan had not anticipated the automobile, so only narrow alleys gave access to the cottages there, and there was no place to park a car. The Mayor and Council purchased lot 6 of block 12 and took down the old Reiss cottage, then opened up a new road, called Acorn Lane, to connect Chestnut Road through to McCauley Street. Jackson Park nearly disappeared as a result, and Wade Park was halved. It was also in 1939 that the Auditorium finally got indoor plumbing.

The Circle, years after the tabernacle was gone and electricity was lighting the walkways.

In 1940 the Sunday tennis controversy erupted again when players were found on the courts during church. Reverend Osborn led an unsuccessful fight to enact an ordinance against it. America was not yet at war, but the buildup of troops had begun, and many of the Grove's young men enlisted in 1939 and 1940. So many had joined up by the time Pearl Harbor was bombed on December 7, 1941 that the tennis problem sort of solved itself. Reverend Osborn died in 1944, and was spared the complete breakdown in Sabbath- keeping that followed in the post-war era.

In 1941 the Oddfellows Hall and Walker's Store became the last victims of the depression and were seized by the First National Bank of Gaithersburg and sold at auction. The commercial comer was the subject of a referendum and town meeting called for the purpose of declaring the area a commercial zone, a use that was otherwise prohibited by the charter.

When America finally went to war the Grove went into a period of patient inactivity. Most athletic events were cancelled and most improvements were postponed. A close cadre of those who stayed home continued to give modest entertainments, and the newsletter "Grove Gatherings," which had been founded in 1934, kept the town posted on servicemen's whereabouts. An honor roll of those in service was posted in 1942, and the same year the Women's Club donated $50 for the purchase of equipment in case of "possible bombing activity by the enemy." In 1943 most of the open grounds in the Grove were made available for Victory Gardens.

Those who served in the armed forces included the three sons of Robert Walker- Sam III, Bob, and Dick; the two sons of Caryl Walker- Phil and Walker Winter; the Reber boys- Bill and Bob; Roy McCathran's son

The Woman's Club, at the clubhouse, at the conclusion of an entertainment. Miss Maxine Winter, granddaughter of Major Walker, had just completed a song.

EPILOGUE

Donald; brothers John and Donald Blood, and Bill and
Al Christie; Bill Teepe, Donald Magruder, and Harold
Marks; and neighbor Bill Becker. Most of those who
stayed behind served the war in other ways. Unofficially
the war ended on VJ Day, August 15, 1945, but the
military occupation of Germany and Japan was just
beginning, so the actual homecoming of soldiers was
spread out over a year or more. Dora Hendricks's
nephew, Charles Coleman, who had lived in the Grove
with her in the summers, did not come back at all.

Those who did, came back to finish the work of
building a Town. What emerged when the war was
finally history was the Washington Grove of today. In
1937 the town had risen from the ashes of the
Association, but it still held one of the Association's
earlier goals—to fill itself out. It had learned to hold
back some land for parks, but it was still toying with the
idea of selling lots in the east and west woods. Then the
war put everything on hold—everything, that is, but the
phenomenal growth of Washington, and the
establishment of a suburban landscape around it.

Near the end of the war, when housing was at its
scarcest, newcomers had to look further and further out
of the city for a place to live. Several new families
found the Grove convenient because of the railroad, and
charming, even if a little seedy. Many of its new
residents fell in love with the Grove, and though they
came to rent, they stayed to buy.

The new residents and returning servicemen and
women converged to bring a new and renewable energy
to the Grove, a synergistic association of fresh ideas and
strong backs combined with a knowledge of and respect
for the Grove's traditions. Together they reawakened the
Grove's physical beauty and, when they turned their

energy to the undeveloped areas to the east and west, treated them as assets to be preserved, not developed. Together they established the phenomenon of continuous revival that keeps the Grove, in the words of Roy McCathran, " a town within a forest, an oasis of tranquility, a rustic jewel in the diadem of the Great Free State of Maryland."

* * *

Except for the vanished chestnut trees, the words written by Carl Loeffler in 1915 could have been written today:

WASHINGTON GROVE

"Men gathered here in years gone by
To worship God beneath his sky.
And built these dwellings round his shrine,
Among the Chestnut, Oak and Pine.
A hallowed spot—a place of rest,
From city life and busy quest,
Your charms are great, alluring too—
With spring we yearn and turn to you.
The spell you cast o'er every one,
Who to this quiet grove has come,
Sinks deep into the very soul,
For here at last they find their goal;
Yea, here indeed, both hand in hand,
Do God and nature combined stand.
Each tiny bird each warbling thing,
Speaks but thy praise when loud they sing.
The peaceful starry nights serene,
Make joy of life almost supreme.
The gentle people living here,
Return with each recurring year,
To seek the pleasures that you hold,
And join once more the friends of old.
The fairest praise that we can speak,
Would seem but poor and even meek,
Compared with what we well might say,
Of your allurements of today.
Let no discordant note e'er gain,
A place within this fair domain,
That binds us all in unity,
Each one to all, and all to thee."

THE ASSOCIATION

NOTES ON SOURCES AND BIBLIOGRAPHY

I have attempted to use the best practical sources for the factual material. As to much of what happened in Washington Grove no source is better than the recorded minutes of the meetings of the various bodies, since they were written within a short time of the actual events, and in most cases their accuracy was later reviewed and endorsed by the people directly involved in the meeting. An obvious problem with minutes, however, is that they leave out much of the discussion that leads to the action being recorded, which sometimes leaves one to infer the reasons that things were done.

The newspapers are excellent secondary sources, though generally they report only on what their editors are interested in, and the inaccuracies in their stories, whether born of haste or of bias, are seldom corrected in subsequent editions.

As to the hard facts about people, the most solid sources are the brief biographies that were printed in commercial directories or the the obituaries that later appeared on their behalf in newsprint. But neither of these sources even hint that anyone had a personality, and both are eager to hide any mysteries or scandalous behavior.

It is difficult to draw any conclusions about the personalities of prominent Grovites of the last century except to infer from their writings and their few recorded oral statements whether they were 'strong' or 'weak', 'confidant' or 'wary', 'pious' or 'manipulative'. For many of this century's leaders there is more material available in the form of letters and other written documents, and there are also a few old-timers still around who remember these people well enough to render an opinion about them. Almost every Grovite born before 1935 has some opinion about Sam Walker, for example.

As for the few other Grove events that I chose to include in the Association's history, most are from newspaper reports, or from the records of various clubs and other organizations. There are a few sources of gossip, but I have not quoted them. The following sources are listed by category, and within the category in approximately the order of their usefulness:

ASSOCIATION RECORDS

Minute books, Board of Trustees Meetings
Minute books, Stockholders and Annual Meetings
Minute books, various committees
Stockholder record book, compiled version
Plats and maps
Treasurer's Records
Subject files

METHODIST CONFERENCE RECORDS (LOVELY LANE CHURCH MUSEUM)

Proceeding of the Baltimore Conference, 1872-86
The *Christian Advocate,* newsletter, 1872-1886

GROVE ORGANIZATIONS

Minutes, Girls Athletic Association
Minutes, Women's Club (1910-13)
Minutes, Woman's Club (1927-40)

NEWSPAPERS

The *Sentinel,* Rockville, Maryland, (1872-1938)
The *Evening Star,* Washington, D.C., (1872- 1890)
The *Republican,* Washington, D.C., (1873-1876)
The *Baltimore Methodist,* Baltimore, Maryland
(1872-1888)

PUBLISHED HISTORIES

Grove Gatherings, 1975, Rosalie Hardy Shantz,
published by The Woman's Club of Washington
Grove, Maryland

Reminiscences of Washington Grove, 1927, Page
Milburn, published by Major Samuel Hamilton
Walker, Washington, D.C.

Boyd's *History of Montgomery County,* Maryland,
1879, Thomas Hullings Stockton Boyd, published
by Regional Publishing Co., Clarkburg, Maryland

Castings From the Foundry Mold, 1968, Homer L.
Calkin, published by The Parthenon Press,

Nashville, Tennessee

Montgomery County, 1984, Jane C. Sween, published by Windsor Publications, Inc., Woodland Hills, California

Washington Past and Present, 1930, edited by John Clagett Proctor, published by Lewis Historical Publishing Co., Inc., New York, New York

Chautauqua, 1974, Theodore Morrison, published by The University of Chicago, Chicago, Illinois

Before the Mayflower, 1962, Lerone Bennett, Jr., Published by the Johnson Publishing Co., New York, New York

ILLUSTRATION CREDITS

Collection of Philip Winter: pages 83,123,131,143, 157, 173, 175, 182, 184, 186, 188-2, 190, 195, 199, 208, 210-2, 211, 245, 255

Collection of Donald McCathran: pages 81-1,169,265-1, 272, 284, 297, 301

Collection of the Columbia Historical Society: pages 3, 12, 191

Archives of the Town of Washington Grove: cover, inside binding, pages 38, 43, 49, 88, 102, 104, 125, 160, 193, 199, 201, 210-1, 216, 224, 258, 265-2, 286, 293, 341, 358,360

Collection of the Montgomery County Historical Society: pages 24, 70,78

Collection of the author: pages 27,32,65, 81-2, 82, 121, 188-1, 275, 329

ABOUT THE AUTHOR

Philip Knox Edwards III came to the Grove late in 1945*, shortly before his third birthday. Except for a twelve-month stay on the coast of northern California, he has lived there ever since. His education began at the age of five at the Washington Grove Elementary School in Oakmont. It was then a two-room frame schoolhouse without indoor plumbing. He attended Gaithersburg High School and later earned an engineering degree at the University of Maryland.

The author served briefly on the Washington Grove Planning Commission, and was subsequently appointed, then elected, Mayor, and served in that capacity during the years 1973 to 1977. Since then he has been the official town historian, a position which led naturally to the writing of this history.

(The author is not related to the Reverend Philip C. Edwards, who was pastor to the Grove's Methodist church from 1932 to 1936.)

*astounding correction—my sister Fritzi informs me we didn't move in until January of 1946!

THE ASSOCIATION

APPENDIX I: LIST OF OFFICERS

YEAR	PRESIDENT	VICE PRESIDENT	SECRETARY	TREASURER
1873	F. Howard	W.R.Woodward	E.F.Simpson	J.A.Ruff
1874	?	"	"	?
1875	?	"	"	?
1876	?	"	"	?
1877	?	"	"	?
1878	?	"	"	?
1879	T.P.Morgan	"	"	B.H.Stinemetz
1880	"	"	"	"
1881	"	"	"	
1882	"	"	"	J.T.Mitchell
1883	"	"	"	"
1884	"	"	"	R.Cohen
1885	"	"	"	J.W.Wade
1886	"	"	"	"
1887	W.R.Woodward	R.Cohen	"	"
1888	G.T.Woodward	H.B.Moulton	"	"
1889	H.B.Moulton	L.W.Northington	W.Choate	R.Cohen
1890	G.T.Woodward	F.A.Gee	"	R.W.Dunn
1891	"	"	"	"
		(resigned-J.R.Mickle)		
1892	"	"	"	"
1893	A.T.Tracy	M.D.Peck	C.Hughes	H.L.Strang
1894	F.A.Gee	"	"	"
1895	M.D.Peck	W.Choate	"	"
1896	"	"	"	"
1897	"	"	"	"
1898	"	"	"	"
1899	"	"	"	"
1900	"	"	"	"
1901	H.L.Strang	"	D.E.Wiber	R.L.Bains
1902	"	J.W.Bovee	"	R.Cohen
1903	"	R.Cohen	"	R.L.Bains
1904	"	P.Foster	"	"
1905	"	"	"	L.F.Hunt
1906	P.Foster	H.L.Strang	J.Davis	"
		(resigned-J.Davis)	(resigned-R.E.Cook)	
		(resigned-E.D.Huntley)		

1907	P.Foster	E.D.Huntley	R.E.Cook	L.F.Hunt
1908	"	S.H.Walker	"	"
1909	S.H.Walker	J.Duvall	"	"
1910	"	"	R.H.Walker	"
1911	"	"	"	"
1912	"	"	"	"
1913	"	"	"	"
(resigned-J.T.Meany)	(resigned-J.Brockway)			
1914	L.C.Williamson	J.T.Meany	R.J.Hall	S.Miller
		(resigned-F.R.Rynex)		
1915	"	"	"	"
1916	"	"	C.A.Loeffler	"
1917	"	"	F.R.Rynex	"
1918	"	"	J.Brockway	"
1919	"	"	F.L.L.Hiller	E.Swingle
1920	"	"	"	"
1921	"	"	"	"
1922	I.L.McCathran	M.DeLand	(Secy-Treas) F.L.L.Hiller	
			(resigned-H.G.Milans	
1923	"	"	"	
1924	E.Swingle	"	"	
1925	"	"	"	
1926	"	"	"	
1927	C.A.Loeffler	"	"	
1928	F.L.L.Hiller	"	R.E.Palmer	
1929	"	"	"	
1930	R.M.Milans	"	"	
1931	"	"	"	
			(resigned-F.L.L.Hiller)	
1932	"	H.B.Davis	"	
1933	"	"	"	
1934	"	"	"	
1935	"	M.Hynson	"	
1936	E.A.Cook	"	"	

(The Association was dissolved on May 30, 1937.)

APPENDIX II:
PRESCOTT OPINION

"Legal Opinion as to ability of the Association to collect delinquent assessments by civil action in the courts."

* * *

July 31, 1935

F.L.L.Hiller, Esq.,
Secy, Washington Grove Association
Washington Grove, Maryland.

Dear Mr. Hiller:

You have requested on behalf of the Board of Trustees of the Washington Grove Association an opinion As to whether it is possible for the Board of Trustees acting for the Washington Grove Association, to collect delinquent assessments by a civil suit in a Court of Equity.' In its broadest sense this would include every assessment made after the amendment to your Charter in 1886 authorizing them. Feeling that you do not desire the opinion to be that exhaustive I have approached it from the assessments of comparatively recent years and based a conclusion upon them.

I note that you mention I gave a verbal opinion sometime ago. That is entirely possible, but necessarily must have been given almost entirely from information furnished verbally and from some at least who were not entirely familiar with all of the legal ramifications of an extremely complicated situation.

The Washington Grove Association under the name of the Washington Grove Camp-Meeting Association of the District of Columbia and Maryland was incorporated by the act of 1874, Chapter 135, setting forth its objectives and powers which, for the purpose of this opinion, it is unnecessary to detail. By the Act of 1886, Chapter 90, Sections 2 and 6 of the Charter were amended and a new section added thereto. These amendments, among other things, authorized the Association to make 'Through the Board of Trustees, an annual uniform assessment upon the stockholders of the Association, OR upon the lots and improvements thereon, within the camp-ground limits, and enforce the collection of the same etc.'

As a result of this amendment, Section 25 of your By-Laws was adopted reading in part as follows. 'The trustees shall recommend such assessments as are authorized by the charter, or its amendments, the same to be levied as an annual uniform assessment, and shall be submitted to the stockholders at their annual meeting'.

It will be clearly seen from the above that the assessments in order to be legal must meet all of the following requirements:

(1) They must be annual

(2) They must be uniform

(3) They must be levied against the stockholders, *or* upon the lots and improvements within the campground limits.

Considering these requirements in the order above mentioned I do not interpret the meaning of the first that it would be necessary to levy an assessment each year, but that any assessment made would be for the term of one year. All of the assessments examined, in my opinion, comply with provision.

With the next requirement there seems to be more difficulty. The records disclose that apparently some are the owners of stock alone, some the owners of stock and land, and some the owners of land alone. I find several distinctly different forms of deeds recorded to the owners from the Association and in quite a number of them the Association covenants to hold and maintain the hotel. I am informed that this has been discontinued. I also find on page 5 of the Stockholders Meeting of May 30, 1932, the following-'Resolved: That the rate of assessments on stock for the ensuing year remain at the present rate of one dollar per share; and that the distinction in the rate of assessment between houses in the Camp Department and Cottage Department be abolished, and that all houses, irrespective of location or size, be assessed at the rate now prevailing in the Cottage Department, viz: $13.65 per year'. All the minutes of previous meetings have not been available to me, but the above clearly indicates that there was a distinction in previous assessments between houses located in the Cottage Department and those located in the Camp Department. It also indicates that there was an assessment against the stockholder, and also one against the lots and improvements.

Also on page two of the Stockholders Meeting of July 8, 1932, a resolution was passed that no Association taxes should be levied against certain Church property. While this is a very salutary resolution and the thought behind it to be highly commended, without authority in the Charter to make certain exemptions, can the assessments against other properties, with this exception, still be said to be uniform?

An examination of the amounts and character of the assessments disclosed a sincere attempt to be perfectly fair and to distribute the tax burden as equally as it is humanly possible to do so, but in view of the different manner of ownership, the different forms of deeds, the distinction between houses located in different departments, and the exemption of certain property, in my opinion, the assessments have not been uniform.

With reference to the third requirement, the record clearly discloses that there have been assessments against both the stockholders and the lots and improvements. The Charter distinctly states they shall be made against the stockholders or the lots and improvements. Repeating that the actions taken show every effort to make an impartial collection of the needed money, unfortunately the assessments have been made against both stockholders and lots and improvements and not against one or the other and in this respect is in conflict with the provisions of the Charter.

In view of the above, it is therefore my opinion, that the delinquent assessments made by the Washington Grove Association, limited as mentioned in the first paragraph hereof, can not be collected by civil suit either in a court of law or equity.

With kindest regards to you and all the members of the Association and being extremely sorry that this opinion could not be to the contrary, I am

Sincerely yours,

Stedman Prescott"

INDEX

192,267,340,343
McCathran, Roy
156,167,216,227,2540,2
63,267-9,271-3,281-
3,286,288,291-
2,296,298,300,304,307,
311,316-20,324-9,333-
6,360-5,3537,358
McCathran, S.J. 267
McCauley, James
28,148
McCauley Street 98-
9,124,166,168,213,215,
242,283,301,354
McKendree Church
13,19,178-9
Meany, J.T.
203,217,232-3,261,281
Men's associations
98,127,168,177,185,193
-4,197,211,227,252-
7,259,261-3,268,329
Metropolitan Church
39,59
Milans, Henry
226,289,312,334,343
Milans, Robert
289,300,306,320,326,33
4,343
Milburn, Page 27-
8,34,42,77,85,128,146,2
42,261,287-8,315
Mitchell, J.T.
28,33,40,81,83,106,109,

133
Morgan Park 166,257
Morgan, Thos. P.
87,109,125,149,166,253
,255
Moulton, H.B.
120,122,124,134,137,18
1,196,199
Myers, Charles
186,229,244,261,314
Myers, Mildred Couch
227-8
National Republican 73
Nugent, J.H. 127,299-
300
Oak Avenue/Street
87,99,122-24,181,184-
5,187,190,192,194,196,
200-1,224,237,239,245-
6,277-8
Oakmont
iii,29,116,161,254,277,3
38,367
Oddfellows
252,254,259-60,355
Osborn, A., 198,209-
10,229,259,261,268,271
,283,286-8,291-
2,294,296,300,329,336,
346,355
Osborn, Harold 363
Osborn, Sarah 268,307
Peck, M.D.
137,139,142-

NOTES

Made in the USA
Middletown, DE
18 December 2022

19330026R00239